J. PATRICK RICK

THE ABBEY & ME

RENEGADES, REDNECKS, REAL ESTATE & RELIGION

CounterfeitBill Publishing

ISBN-10: 1456491814

ISBN-13: 9781456491819

Library of Congress Control Number: 2011901999

CreateSpace, North Charleston, SC

Brother John Howard, CFA., is pictured on front cover

CONTENTS

PREFACE

This book evolved from a personal film project known as *The Novitiate*. Here is the nonfiction account of the invasion and seizure of a midwestern Catholic monastery. This narrative chronicles a certain 1975 American Indian act of civil disobedience. Thirty-four days of armed occupation in harsh winter conditions are detailed—wrapped in my memoir, I cannot leave untold.

Titled *The Abbey & Me*, this book is a contemporary, cavalry, Indian, and missionary story of hostages, vigilantes, renegades, and even Hollywood celebrity facing the National Guard. As a former cloistered, resident novice-monk, I recount and now tell the reader about this drama and a location of such great disappointment.

I was a student at the Alexian Brothers monastery in Wisconsin in the mid-1960s. Three decades later, I returned. The condition of my old home was appalling. During that unplanned stopover, I found nostalgia and ruins. I learned that it had been the site of an authentic "Indian uprising" in 1975. Long before, I had moved on to another phase of my life, just before the Catholic brothers discontinued that monastery as a site for religious formation.

This book describes insurgents from within nearby Menominee Indian people. With tribal status dissolved, young warriors attempt to reclaim something they imagined they had lost. Government-imposed harsh rules and regulations were believed infringing on their preferred traditional way of life. Ignited with a hostile takeover of the monastery, the hostile occupation brings out local law enforcement, the Wisconsin National Guard, ATF and the FBI. Personally familiar with the location, I describe a number of dangerous confrontations, one of which involved the late actor, Marlon Brando.

This chronicle is the story of this exceptional place in history. You will read of an edifice seemingly doomed never to realize its full potential. As a private residence, monastery, or even an historical site, the location could not get beyond labeled as an enigma. Contained is a sequence of events of that uprising, which in its own way, was every bit as significant as the more widely-known 1973 incident at Wounded Knee. However, the abbey did not garner as much press as Wounded Knee; there were no fatalities. The abbey at Gresham, Wisconsin was one of the last native American stands.

With an unfortunate stroke and bad timing, my unfinished book project had to be shelved—unlikely to be completed. That brain hemorrhage, Thanksgiving 2005, cost me the use of motor skills, loss of speech and the cognitive ability to finish this book. Today, you would not be able to detect my deficits. Thanks to many, including technology, the book is complete.

Finally in book form, *The Abbey & Me* is a follow-up to the short, award-winning documentary which enjoyed some acclaim and recognition on the film festival circuit. Viewers of the documentary have expressed desire to know more, see more, feel more—and this book provides them with what they want.

In addition, this written journey gives me the opportunity to share some cathartic memoir, with you via *The Abbey & Me*.

DEDICATION

To My Novice Class Brothers

Brothers Anton, Gordon (author) Nathan, Bennett,
Bonaventure, Ignatius, Mitchell, Kurt

ACKNOWLEDGEMENTS

I especially wish to thank Donna Carl Dahl. The abundant detail in this book could not have been included without her trust and cooperation. The Alexian Brothers' repository of history is fortunate to have Donna as its Director of Archives. Always helpful and quick to provide answers, Ms. Dahl's professionalism and opinions have helped guide me. A simple "thank you" is not enough.

Chris Sheridan, a Student Academy Award recipient, brought talent to the documentary, *The Novitiate*. Having spent many a day at Chris' elbow polishing that work, I came to appreciate his expertise in directing. Chris assisted in giving birth to *The Novitiate* and subsequently launching the writing of the book, *The Abbey & Me*.

There are many that have answered my questions and helped me with facts. There are others that have gone beyond with their contributions such as Reagan A Weber and Luke Holbach having helped me edit one of the chapters.

I

AULD LANG SYNE

The sound-absorbing quality of snow made it easier for the small band of intense, dark-complexioned men to approach their objective, a large house on the property of an estate located deep in the Wisconsin woods, near the town of Gresham. As they advanced through the dense forest on this, the last and arguably coldest night of 1974, they proceeded carefully, yet with grim purpose. Drifting snow driven by blizzard-force winds immediately covered any trace of boot prints on the white powder. Vacated nearly seven years before by the Alexian Brothers, a Catholic order of monks who had used the estate as a training site for candidates for their brotherhood, the complex consisted of an original residential mansion and a much larger institutional addition completed by the Brothers in 1955.

The group was comprised of members of a tribe that had been disenfranchised some years before when the United States Congress changed their status and dissolved their reservation. They saw the property as vital to their redemption and a key to their eventual reinstatement into full American Indian tribal status. They believed repossessing the estate would be in accord with the terms of treaties signed many decades earlier.

Stealth through the woods in any season of the year came naturally to the group's leaders, all of whom were Menominee Indians. They had been brought up with guns in their hands and were in their element; their native hunting skills serving them well this night. Others, less experienced and having grown up in cities, were unsure of themselves, along for the ride. Their presence was a calculated but necessary risk, as it created the illusion of strength in numbers. The leaders felt this posturing tactic would strengthen their position regardless of the outcome of the night's foray.

A few women tagged along, their movements tentative in the bitter-cold darkness. They were nervous about the potential for a violent reception. Staying behind would have made them lonesome for their husbands, braves, and lovers, but tradition did not welcome them on this raid. After all, the intention of this night was, in part, to return to the old ways, which would reverse the recent matriarchy that had become the societal norm within the tribe.

This was no time-honored hunt for deer, bear, or wild turkey. Righting past wrongs and a desire for vindication was the common thread shared among all the planners and many of the fighters. Few fully understood all the history, but they all knew they had reason to be angry. The motivations of these Native Americans to assemble in foul weather on New Year's Eve, a night when indoor celebration was customary, were as varied as their individual understandings of the real goal of the raid.

For those recently recruited from barstools of local taverns and from the many New Year's Eve parties in town and on the reservation, a different Wild Turkey was likely the motivation. For them, the current adventure was an impromptu nocturnal uprising, an opportunity to strike a blow for the "movement." For the more dedicated, there was no false warmth from bottled or canned holiday cheer. Adrenalin alone was enough to stoke the heat sufficient for executing their strategy.

The attackers crowded into blacked-out old cars and vans with floorboards rusted through by winter salt, duct taped windshields and broken heaters. They drove through the woods, south down Juniper Road to its dead end at Butternut, beyond the southwest boundary of Menominee County, Wisconsin's poorest and the former Menominee Indian Reservation. Within walking distance of their target, a short southerly trudge across the road brought them close enough to peer undetected through the ice-frosted windows of the residential building that was their initial objective.

Midnight passed without a mistletoe moment inside the house, and there were certainly no acts of intimacy in the darkness outside. One of the scouts sent to survey the objective returned to report at least two and perhaps as many as four people inside. An unfamiliar car on the property presented the first logistical wrinkle; it had not been there earlier in the day. The invaders had not anticipated visitors, but the leaders decided that once inside they would identify and deal with the car's driver and any others.

One of the leadership group, a solidly built, warmly dressed man they called Mike, was having trouble restraining some of his armed warriors. Despite the cold, they were pumped and jumpy, anxious for the action they knew would follow. And yes, some were just plain drunk.

This risky night had been a long time in coming. Months before, during a planning meeting held on a humid summer night at Legend Lake, Mike had asserted himself on some matter of importance, prompting a taunt from the back of the room, "Who made you General?" Partly out of a subtle Indian sense of humor, and partly as a function of the tribal pecking order, natural selection had inevitably elevated Mike Sturdevant to be "the General." From that moment forward, the warriors identified Mike as both the group's leader and the lightning rod in all situations of contention. His tongue-in-cheek title had bestowed awesome responsibilities that were to be tested on this dark winter night.

That summer gathering all those months earlier now contrasted in the extreme with these final freezing moments before the Indians' plan was to move toward its climax. Convincing himself once again that they were doing the right thing, Mike initiated the raiders' next move from his temporary snowdrift command post. Ignoring the NO TRESPASSING and KEEP OUT signs posted on the two gate pylons, he led the group forward. This petty but bold encroachment was the first in a string of felonies that were about to be committed.

Except for the flat, colorless voice of the law enforcement dispatcher managing sporadic complaints about countywide fireworks and celebration gunfire, radio traffic on the scanner the invaders were using to monitor the Shawano County Sheriff's Department was quiet. Mike led his warriors farther onto the monastery grounds and closer to the residential building situated alongside the estate's main mansion. At 12:10 a.m., the intrusive sound of a phone ringing inside the residence spooked Mike and the warriors, delaying their next move. Had someone tipped off those inside?

Known as Melvin (Buddy) Chevalier in 1975, Apesanahkwat was a tall, thin, very dark-skinned member of the Menominee Warrior Society. He stood with the fellow warriors he had helped round up earlier that night. Who would have bet then that this man would be tribal chairman and a Hollywood actor two decades later? In his on-camera interview with me twenty-five years after that night, he said, "Eddie Two Rivers was the first to knock on Joe Plonka's door." As with many of the details in his memory, this account did not jibe with the recollections of others or with official, written records. "Well," he rationalized, "cowboys wrote revised history, why can't we Indians do the same with our oral accounts?" Eddie, when he was finally located and interviewed, admitted to having been present that night but not to having played the active role others had attributed to him.

By then a noted Native American poet, rapper, and Chicago Red Path Theater playwright, Eddie was, after these many years, as curious about my interest in his history as I was in him. He was horrified that I had walked alone in the evening through a rough North Chicago neighborhood to his home on Kenmore Avenue to interview him. Nevertheless, even after sharing several beers, much talk unrelated to the subject at hand and frequent offers of various substances to smoke, Eddie sent me away. I had not learned much from him at all. Two Rivers insisted his son drive me back to my nearby motel, a baby-blue building whose usual clientele rented in fifteen-minute increments, a no-star accommodation where you sleep with one eye open. So went that investigative evening of 1999. It was to be one of my unimpressive but memorable efforts to track the story of that fateful winter night of 1975.

The New Year was less than fifteen minutes old, and the random midnight fireworks, attenuated by the blanket of snow and the thick forest, seemed to be winding down. John and Barbara Rogozinski, friends of Joe and Marlene Plonka, the occupants of the house, were sitting in the Plonkas' kitchen, quietly ringing in the New Year.

A few minutes after midnight, Joe, who was the monastery's caretaker, responded to a knock on the door. Cautiously, without opening the door, he asked, "Who is it?" A deep male voice responded that there was some sort of "car trouble" and that he "needed help." Relaxing just a bit, Plonka shouted for the man to "wait a minute," then turned and opened the door to the hall closet. Obscuring whatever views of him an outsider might have if looking through the glass panel of the front door, Joe slipped a tiny .22-caliber Derringer pistol into his right hip pocket. Ordinarily, while outside during the day, Plonka carried a larger handgun on his side. There were feral dogs and wolves about.

He knew to be careful out there in the darkness; trespassers occasionally harassed the family by driving onto the property at all hours of the day and night. A few weeks earlier, a pair of FBI agents investigating the knifing death of Father Marcellus Cabo, a Franciscan priest in the nearby logging town of Neopit, had dropped in on Joe. The murder alone would not have been a sufficient reason for an FBI investigation, but in the scheme of a general backlash toward Catholicism among Native Americans, it made sense.

The post-1973 Wounded Knee era was a time of mistrust and mutual suspicion, and for more than a half-decade of the American Indian Movement federal agents from various bureaus of the U.S. Department of Justice crawled all over Indian Country and were often viewed as "wolves in sheep's clothing." Failing to share with Plonka even the basics of an informant's tip that bigger things were to come, the agents took a tour of the property and monastery buildings, offering Plonka only understated warnings of "be careful" and "you could be next." Their veiled cautions replayed in Joe's head as he turned back toward the front door.

The Plonka family's modest home was, in effect, the caretaker's cottage for the property. It squatted in a stand of tall evergreens in an area near the U-shaped driveway that marked the western approach to the monastery.

During the 1950s and 60s, a small group of Norbertine priests who served as chaplains to the Alexian Brothers and their students had used the house as living quarters. Before that, the comfortable little house had been a livery facility, containing four garages and quarters for some of the staff who served the original owner of the mansion. Having been recruited from his hospital engineering duties in the Chicago suburbs, Joe and his wife Marlene had moved there some three years earlier. Thus, in the winter of 1975, Joe and his family were in temporary residence in the wilds of Wisconsin, keeping the institution in working order while it was offered for sale.

The single-story Cape Cod was quite drab, seeming almost to vanish into the deep snow, even in daylight. With white asbestos siding that had gone gray; a steeply pitched, weather-worn roof designed to deal with winter snows; and unremarkable trim, the place looked, and was, utilitarian. It was dwarfed next to the stone Georgian mansion that was the visual centerpiece of the estate. The architectural contrast between the two buildings made them odd companions indeed, as they shared a plot of sixteen residential acres near a corner of the 230-acre complex.

The rest of the property was farm, dairy pasture, and wooded river frontage with a few widely spaced agricultural structures—barns, corrals, haymows, and paddocks. While the cottage acted as a buffer between rural Butternut Road and the out-of-place mansion in the woods, its deferential appearance to the opulent manor house left it an unlikely candidate to stand guard.

There was, however, a genuinely symbiotic relationship between the two structures. Although detached above ground, they shared an umbilical link beneath the snow-covered earth. A conduit large enough for a man to crawl through delivered heat and other necessary utilities from the main house to the Plonka home.

Willing to be neighborly, but armed and wary, Joe approached the heavy front door with house guest John Rogozinski following behind. As Joe fumbled with the hook and eye latch, the warriors pulled the door from his hand. "Get back! Get back!" they ordered. The blast of frigid air and the barking of orders took Joe by surprise. He raised his hands above his head. As he stumbled backward, he was pushed aside by first one man, then another, and then a blur of even more men with guns—*Indians*.

Novitiate caretakers cottage.

Photo WI Dept. of Justice

John Waubanascum, his automatic rifle raised, was the first in, rushing Joe and driving him back into the hallway. At that moment, Waubanascum recalled how their raid seemed like child's play compared to his combat tour in Vietnam as a U.S. Marine. Perhaps enthralled by that memory, he fired an armor-piercing round in Joe's general direction, intentionally aiming high. The ordinarily intimidating caretaker dropped back into a fetal-crouching position as plaster and splinters flew helter-skelter from the wounded ceiling, showering a few of the entering invaders.

John Rogozinski and Joe, both large men, especially compared to some of the more diminutive Indian invaders, found themselves bouncing off each other in the narrow hallway. Overcome by manpower and unable to slow the invaders, Joe dropped to the floor and John retreated to the bathroom, locking himself inside.

The combined smell of freshly baked pizza and gun smoke greeted the next half-dozen warriors as they rushed forward and fanned out into the cottage behind their trigger-happy lead man. Marlene and Barbara had been in the kitchen when their husbands responded to the knock at the door. Fearing more gunfire, the women quickly shut and locked the hallway door. Holding hands, they moved to the farthest corner of the kitchen and huddled in terror. Even when assured that their men were not injured, they refused several demands to open the door. Finally, after hearing their husband's voices, the women relented and the raiders took over the kitchen.

John was ordered out of his hopeless toilet sanctuary, and Joe was told to stand up and hand over the Derringer that was protruding from his back pocket. When Plonka said, "You take it," John Perote moved to disarm him with Waubanascum sounding off in the background. "You mother-fucking bastard, I should have shot you!"

The Indian men escorted Joe and John into the kitchen, where they were quickly embraced by the women. Barbara began picking ceiling debris from her husband's hair and brushing dust off his shoulders. Suddenly the sound of small children crying came from the back room. Their captors seemed willing to ignore it until Marlene pleaded that she be allowed to attend to her two boys.

The Plonka family. Joe Jr., Philip, Marlene, Joseph Senior.
Photo by Curt Knoke

Mike Sturdevant allowed the women to retrieve Phillip, three, and one-year-old Joe Jr., who had been sleeping in a back bedroom. The presence of the children amid the pandemonium reminded the General of the gravity of his actions. The operation had reached the point of no return.

At age twenty-six, and standing well over six feet tall, John Waubanascum personified the aggressive nature of the evening's events.

"This is a takeover,...like Wounded Knee," he announced. "We are the Menominee Warrior Society."

His comments energized the others, who acknowledged his declaration with Indian war whoops. Their outburst may have marked the success of the operation's first phase, but it made Marlene Plonka's struggle to calm her two young boys even more difficult.

A moment later, Mike Sturdevant strolled into the kitchen unarmed and accompanied by a squad of Menominee warriors. Their leader's presence seemed to calm the Indians in the kitchen, who had been aiming all manner of weaponry at the six Polish-American faces. One enthusiastic young warrior even had a drawn bow and arrow trained first on one hostage, then on another. When the threatening language and gesturing with weapons ceased, the Rogozinskis and Plonkas sensed Mike's leadership and began to feel his arrival might restore a degree of sanity.

Unfortunately, their optimism was short-lived. After the General made a brief check on the situation, he exited the kitchen, leaving Waubanascum, the loose cannon, and his sidekick, John Perote, in charge. The tension resumed as Perote nervously loaded and unloaded his .38-caliber revolver and Waubanascum unsheathed a finely honed hunting knife with ugly serrations at the tip.

Their gesturing sent a vivid enough warning of the potential for brutality without any further need for ignition. And yet, it did not take long for the two guards to begin drinking the beer and other alcoholic beverages found in the cabinets and refrigerator. They were determined to restart the buzz they had worked up at the bar earlier and the adrenalin rush of the attack. To tease the captives, Waubanascum offered Plonka something stiff to drink. "You look like you need it, honkie."

Joe declined just as Mike returned and poured all the "fire water" he could find down the drain. As he left, he reminded them this was to be a sober campaign.

This ideal would prove to be difficult for the General to enforce. On his next pass through the kitchen just moments later he found the pair nursing coffee cups of whiskey. That too went down the drain.

"Who called here a few minutes ago?" asked Mike. John Rogozinski spoke up. "It was our baby sitter. We have twins and another child at home. She is expecting us back soon."

Interrupting the conversation, Waubanascum chimed in. "Yeah and you may never see them again if you don't cooperate."

The General's glare warned Waubanascum to be quiet. Mike knew where the man was useful and where he was not; negotiation skills and a tolerance for civil debate were not talents the decorated veteran possessed. As the almost macabre good-cop/bad-cop scenario played out, Joe Plonka played out in his mind what to him still appeared to be an elaborate robbery invasion. When were they going to be relieved of their purses, wallets, and money and then butchered? His wife, Marlene, spent her time remembering the recent visit from the FBI agents. A confessed young Menominee man sat in jail for crimes committed on Thanksgiving night, and she feared the same fate as that of the slain priest. Five weeks earlier on the reservation, Father Cabo had had his throat cut from ear to ear.

Sturdevant spoke more quietly to the two couples and the now silent, watchful boys, telling them they would be safe and that the warriors would release them as soon as initial negotiations had begun. His statements seemed to replace some of their fear with a small degree of hope; and yet, they did not have a clue as to what the negotiations would entail or how long they might take.

Mike made kind attempts at eye contact with the sleepy and startled boys. Joe Jr. hid his face and eyes in the folds of his mother's clothing. The sounds of thrashing and ransacking in other rooms drove Joe to intervene. He could hear the intruders emptying drawers and closets in the bedrooms and glass breaking in the garage. In his mind, their searching for valuables was idiocy. Hoping to give them what he thought they wanted, Joe yelled out to the looters. "Take it easy! Here, take my wallet and cash."

Waubanascum growled back. "Don't worry about material things, worry about your life."

One warrior, who had been ransacking the bedrooms, appeared and, looking pleased with his discovery, confronted Joe. He held up a recent copy of *Playboy* magazine in one hand and in his other waved a box of condoms with a flourish. He demanded that Joe explain why a good Catholic would have this depravity in his home on Church property. Joe saw through the attempt to goad him into a circular discussion on hypocrisy and responded with silence.

At this point, mixed signals became the order of the day. A steady parade of warriors wearing leather, feathers, berets, mirrored sunglasses, and variations of Vietnam-era military attire swarmed through the house barking commands at the six hostages. Other seemingly reluctant intruders stood by quietly, appearing to regret their participation. One would order the captives to stand and, moments later, another would force them to sit. Like cats with a nest of mice, the ever-present Perote and Waubanascum allowed the others come and play with their catch.

Robert, twenty-four, one of the four Chevalier warrior brothers, entered the kitchen with a Harrington & Richards .22-caliber snub-nosed revolver. Joe recognized it as having come from his gun cabinet, which also held other firearms and a quantity of gunpowder and ammunition. Several in the band were now wearing winter clothing belonging to the Plonkas. Clearly, the situation was not improving; their earlier optimism was not gone.

With the 2,600-square-foot residential building secured, it was time for the General to implement his next move. In polite and calm conversation, Sturdevant asked Joe to brief him regarding the management of the property. He wanted to know about the leadership of the Alexians and to whom Joe reported. Plonka had no choice but to cooperate. The caretaker told Mike he and his family had been there since 1972, that the Brothers had not used the institution since 1968, and that only a few Alexians had maintained a custodial presence until Joe relieved them as an employee and caretaker. Plonka explained that the entire package of acreage and physical plant was for sale. Sturdevant knew all of this beforehand, but he wanted verification before pushing forward with the plan.

Nine years earlier, in 1966, I found myself inching up on this very same cottage, but in broad daylight and with far less sinister intentions. Cloistered in the nearby monastery earlier that year, I was a postulant, a beginning student seeking membership in the Alexian Brothers order. Part of our formative routine and introduction to complete obedience included abstinence from newspapers, other periodicals, radio, and television. Distancing ourselves from the rest of the world was a centuries-old process. I would not be the first neophyte to have tried to quench my thirst for a little secular stimulation.

On that occasion, my outdoor duties had placed me within yards of the off-limits chaplain's residence. Father Damian Weiber, the Norbertine priest assigned to the Brothers, had his windows open on that beautiful summer day. The siren song of broadcast news and music wafting from the radio inside lured me closer. As I feigned concentrating on caring for the lawn, I listened to Percy Sledge sing "When a Man Loves a Woman," reveled in Nancy Sinatra's rendition of "These Boots Are Made for Walkin'"—tunes not conducive to a celibate life—and heard the bad news from Vietnam. All of it, beamed from the Green Bay radio station, poured from the rectory window.

In ironic contrast to my own fair-weather eavesdropping that day in 1966, junior Menominee warriors stood guard outside on January 1, 1975. They peered through those same windows, tightly closed against the cold, straining to hear the conversations between the hostages and fellow

Menominee Mike Sturdevant. The General queried Joe Plonka about the Alexian Brothers' hierarchy, the layout of the facility, access information, and the location of the keys to the monastery.

No more than forty-five minutes had passed since the intrusion, and yet it was time to launch the next phase of the plan. Following Mike's orders, John Perote held a gun to Joe's head as he escorted him to the telephone down the hall. Joe was told to dial the Alexian residence in Elk Grove Village, Illinois, to locate Brother Felix Bettendorf, chief executive officer of the Alexian Brothers suburban Chicago hospital, or Brother Florian Eberle, the Provincial and "main man" of the Alexian Brothers in the United States.

Minutes later, a sleepy Brother Louis Roncoli answered the telephone. It was 1:00 a.m. No sooner had Joe Plonka identified himself and begun to explain the situation than one of the warriors abruptly snatched the telephone from his hand and demanded to speak with one of the principal Alexians. When told none of the order's leaders were available, the Indian hung up, angry and frustrated.

As it turned out, neither Brother Felix nor Brother Florian were at the Illinois location; the former was gone on vacation, and the latter was recovering from cardiac surgery. Their absence in the context of this unusual call created confusion at the order's Chicago headquarters. When several Alexians were roused and discussed the mysterious call from Wisconsin, Brother Eugene Gizzi took it upon himself to be the point man. Within five minutes of the abrupt termination of the first call, Gizzi connected with Brother Gregory Isenhart, who was across town at the Province headquarters on Kenmore Avenue in Chicago. The two agreed that Brother Florian, still convalescing, was not to be awakened. Before making further efforts to find an Alexian superior with the seniority to become involved, Gizzi called the Plonka number. When Joe answered, Brother Eugene asked, "How are you?"

Hesitating, and in a calm, flat voice Joe answered. "Fine."

Brother Eugene expressed concern about the earlier call and asked Joe whether something was wrong or if someone was ill.

After Plonka said, "Just a minute," Brother Eugene heard a muted sound as if a hand was covering the mouthpiece of the phone. Then Joe's voice, still flat, continued. "I just called to wish you a Happy New Year. I have to go now." With that there was a hasty disconnect from the Plonka end. The warriors had found an extension phone and were monitoring both sides of the conversation. They, too, hung up at the same time. Joe had chosen to be brief while facing the business end of a weapon.

Brother Simeon Pytel had trained Joe Plonka a few years earlier on all the mechanical aspects of the novitiate before placing it in his care. Pytel, a quiet, unassuming monk, had a dry sense of humor just below his taciturn surface. During my days as a student at the monastery, he took me under his engineering wing and taught me the ropes. I recall being targeted for and routinely assigned the heavier, outdoor work. When the monastery converted from coal to oil, in an assignment I will never forget, I climbed into the boilers to prepare them for the retrofit. Brother Simeon directed that 1966 summer project, sending Jim Lehman, my fellow classmate from Midland, Texas, and me into the bowels of the boilers before they had fully cooled. We chipped away and removed the original brick inner lining, feeling as if we were experiencing a hell on earth. There and then, I surely reached my lifetime quota for asbestos inhalation. Our baptism by fire amused Brother Simeon. When I spoke to him years later, he still remembered the boiler assignment as well as my first blizzard at Gresham, when I broke decorum by hurling myself backward into a generous snowdrift to make "angels" in the snow.

The close mentoring Brother Simeon had given Joe before leaving him to operate the plant provided him ample time to become familiar with the new caretaker. When made aware of the details of the middle-of-the-night telephone call, Brother Simeon knew Joe Plonka's behavior was abnormal. When he shared his concerns with Brother Eugene Gizzi, the two men set off on a frantic search for a decision maker, preferably a member of the Alexian Provincial Senate. With so many brothers away, the search went from the Elk Grove Offices to the Boys Town infirmary in Nebraska to the Alexian hospital in Elizabeth, New Jersey. Finally, Brother Eugene located a good man to whom he could hand over the reins, Brother Maurice Wilson.

Gizzi briefed Brother Maurice, providing him with the little information he had and his feeling about the episode of ambiguous communication with the Gresham property. Just as the brothers were updating Brother Maurice in New Jersey, Plonka called Gizzi on another line. Without any supporting information or explanation, Plonka pleaded with Gizzi to send someone, anyone, to relieve him so he and his family could escape the cottage. There were prompting and directions coming from other voices in the background, and Joe's anxiety was clearly evident. But Gizzi had no idea that Plonka's insistence was being prompted at gunpoint.

When Brother Maurice Wilson phoned the Gresham property himself a few minutes later, the warriors did not welcome his call. Joe Plonka did not recognize the name and therefore could not explain why the warriors should speak with him. Amid the chaos inside the Plonka home, Joe tried to validate that Brother Maurice was someone with whom the Indians should engage. Repeatedly, though, the invaders forced Joe to hang up.

Concerned, and without an understanding of what was happening, Brother Maurice called the Shawano County Sheriff at 1:28 a.m. and reported what little he knew. Moments later, the police radio scanner crackled the alert the warriors were dreading. Sheriff Robert (Sandy) Montour's deputies now knew of, but were not dispatched to investigate, the Alexian Brothers' concerns about the monastery. With the sheriff's headquarters only ten miles southeast of the monastery, Mike Sturdevant turned up the heat. He demanded that Plonka reestablish contact with the last caller. Finally, after more confusion, telephone communication was re-established with Brother Maurice.

At 2:00 a.m. central time, 3:00 eastern time, the Indians' leader, Mike Sturdevant, and Alexian Brother Maurice Wilson were talking to one another. They spoke calmly and respectfully. Brother Maurice was no stranger to organized catastrophe. As a registered nurse for many years, he had responded to acute dilemmas at odd hours. Mike, a veteran of the Wounded Knee episode in 1973, was resolute in his mission and firm in his justification for being at the monastery.

Mike informed Brother Maurice that his people not only wanted the building and property, but that they believed it was rightfully theirs by treaty. Although not directly involved, Brother Maurice knew that the monastery was for sale, and he thought there were already some ongoing efforts with a Native American enterprise to buy or rent the novitiate for some worthy endeavor. Still, he listened without comment.

Mike went on to demand that Brother Florian Eberle, the senior leader of the Alexians in America, come to Gresham to negotiate the immediate transfer of ownership to the Menominee. When Maurice explained that the Provincial's post-surgical recuperation would make that impossible, Mike emphasized that the Plonka family would be held at least until negotiations were underway. At that point, Brother Maurice understood the gravity of the situation and committed to Sturdevant that he, as an authorized representative of the order, would travel to Wisconsin. Doing his best to buy time in which to assess the situation further, he reiterated the realities concerning the distance, travel time, and the necessary preparations he would need to make before departing. The Alexian also wisely stood his ground regarding the status of the six captives. He repeatedly insisted their detention was unacceptable and their immediate release, with confirmation, was mandatory.

Brother Maurice Wilson.

Photo by Curt Knoke

After a brief argument between two warrior factions concerning the wisdom of letting their hostages go, Mike agreed. However, he stipulated that Brother Maurice must call off the sheriff and insist that law enforcement take no action.

With a modicum of long-distance détente in place, the General breathed easier. He put Plonka on the phone with Brother Maurice, who told Joe that he, his family, and his guests would be freed and that Joe should call as soon as they were all safe and clear of the monastery.

The moment he concluded his conversation with the caretaker, Brother Maurice redialed the Shawano sheriff's department and laid out the Indians' stipulations. Since the hostages' departure was predicated on the absence of law enforcement, the sheriff's office agreed to forego any response for the time being.

The master set of keys for the facility, including the hibernating monastery, soon changed hands. But no one asked about the boiler room, and Joe Plonka saw no reason to delay their departure with a briefing on the critical care that important and sensitive area would need. With quiet satisfaction, he withheld his valuable knowledge. The warriors would have to learn later of their catastrophic error.

Flushed with their success to this point, the intruders eased their posturing. Mike urged the Rogozinskis and Plonkas to gather whatever belongings they wished to take and to get away. At this, the coldest point in the morning, with temperatures hovering just above zero degrees, the Plonkas and the Rogozinskis decided to take nothing and leave as quickly as possible. So, in the darkness of that early January morning, Marlene, Joe, Philip, Joe Jr., Barbara, and John rushed to the Rogozinski vehicle and prepared to drive off with only the clothing they were wearing. The car started with no problem, but in their haste to flee, John managed to become stuck in the snow. There they were with pajama-clad children in a cold car that was now snowbound. Joe thought, "Now what?"

Just then, they noticed a figure moving toward them in quickstep from the cottage. God, had their captors changed their minds? Was this a living nightmare where you are free but paralyzed and unable to run? The warrior banged on the car window, and Joe rolled it down.

Mike Sturdevant reached in to hand Joe his wallet, which had been left on the kitchen table along with a single dollar bill that another Menominee had given Joe earlier for cigarettes. In a Stockholm Syndrome fashion, where captives begin to identify with and rely upon their captors, Joe told Mike the car was stuck in the snow. In seconds, the General marshaled several able bodies to push the car and liberate the frazzled families.

A little red tractor and I became good friends during my time at the novitiate. Brother Cajetan Gavranich, who was certain this Texas boy belonged behind its steering wheel, first introduced me to it in the spring of 1966. Over the months that followed, I mowed the lawn, moved dirt, and leveled the soccer and baseball fields. The tractor and I often hauled debris and loads that most humans would be incapable of or unwilling to carry—including, from time to time, chicken droppings from the east farm area of the estate.

That all-purpose farm implement was my time machine. It represented a brief escape from the daily monastic routine. While my fellow students toiled at the end of a mop handle indoors, the tractor would take me beyond the confines of the monastery, not far away geographically, but away nonetheless. On those frequent homesick occasions when I was questioning my decision to be there, I believed I could actually drive that tractor the 1,350 miles back to Beaumont, Texas.

Winter, on the other hand, put different demands on the little vehicle, making it the means for a lifeline between the estate, recessed from the rural roads, and the rest of the world. My Southeast Texas vocabulary did not contain the word "snow" until my eighteenth year.

There, in Gresham, Wisconsin, Brother Cajetan strapped a plow on my machine and sent me out to move snow, lots of it. No doubt the released hostages and perhaps even the Indians could have used the plow and me on January 1, 1975. I was long gone but forever curious and somehow intent on going back.

At 2:25 a.m., Brother Eugene got a welcome call from Joe Plonka. "Thank God we're alive, and thank Brother Maurice for calling off the police." Joe was now venting, since there was no longer a revolver pressed to his head. The reality of the encounter, combined with the chill of the weather, forced Joe to speak in a quivering voice as he explained all were now safe and "...trying to find ourselves." Decompressing from two and a half hours of "fight or flight mode" and the reality that the caretaker and his family had walked away from all their possessions, both the Alexian and Joe Plonka understood that there was good reason to be upset.

The refugees, having driven directly to the Rogozinski home in Gresham, were planning their next move. It was still unsettling being only ten minutes west of the Alexian property. Brother Eugene urged Joe to create more distance between his family and the novitiate, encouraging them to come to Chicago immediately. The Plonka boys, chattering with the Rogozinski children in the background, were unaware that the gifts they had received, only a week before at Christmas, would probably be lost as casualties in a war they could neither understand nor control.

Borrowing clothes for their children and a car from their friends the Rogozinskis, the Plonkas drove to Shawano to make a 4:00 a.m. report and to brief the sheriff. Then, pointing themselves south, Joe and Marlene drove their children away from the novitiate, hoping never to return.

Reader, I must let you know that real trouble had only just begun in this out-of-the-way setting with a peaceful reputation.

2

FREEBORN FALLS

Sylvester Michael Killeen, O. Praem., the abbot of the Norbertine Abbey in De Pere, Wisconsin, loved the novitiate and was a frequent guest of the Alexian Brothers. On one of his visits, researching the characters surrounding the mansion and its property, he wrote:

> They were witnesses to the age of the "river pigs," these especially skilled lumberjacks who, equipped with hob-nail boots and pike poles, steered the logs on their course, and jumped from log to log at great risk to dislodge a laggard piece stuck in the bank at the bend of the river. These waters witnessed the jamming of logs on occasions. As one of the old residents in the area told me, "Sometimes the logjams would reach a height of 30 feet." The breaking of a logjam was dangerous. Only a few men knew just how to find the "key log" to break the jam. Sometimes men were seriously hurt or drowned in this line of duty. It is said that such an accident took place here. A man lost his life at this falls in the river. His name was Freeborn.[1]

---

1   All excerpts from the works of Sylvester Michael Killeen, O. Praem. Used with permission from Abbot Gary Neville, O. Praem. E-mail dated 13 December 2010.

Peters Hall, the mansion itself, stood on the north bank of the Red River, a hearty stream that flowed east-southeasterly toward the Wolf River near Shawano. Freeborn Falls was roughly a football field's length from the steps of the mansion. The Falls alternately hiss and purr constantly, but absolutely roar on occasions when the dam, a mile upstream at Gresham, is releasing. Typical of most Wisconsin towns, Gresham existed because the river was there. The middle of the nineteenth century saw a tremendous amount of logging in the area.

Gresham was just another one of those towns that grew out of the need to exploit the resources of moving water. Dams were constructed to manage the transport of logs. Usually, railroads hugged and paralleled the course of rivers like the Red. The Wisconsin Northern Railroad built Gresham's line of track, nicknamed "The Whiskey Northern," in 1907. Though it was used primarily to move freight and mail, there was also some passenger service. In the spring and summer, "special trains" provided Sunday excursion travel for the locals to see baseball games between the Indians in Neopit and the white folks in Shawano. The train tracks ran close to the south side of Freeborn Falls.

Trains no longer run there. As elsewhere in much of America today, a train no longer runs through Gresham or near the old Peters mansion. The rails have long since been torn out and recycled. The creosote ties that once supported the iron rails now border gardens and shore up leaning barns in the area. Nature was almost successful in completely erasing local railroad history, until the Wisconsin State Parks System intervened in 1994 under a federal program called Rails to Trails. One of the old rail routes through Gresham was included in the new Mountain Bay Trail running more than eighty miles from Wausau to Green Bay

All that remains is the right-of-way; the forest has practically reclaimed the track bed. The combination of thick stands of trees, the hissing, rolling falls, and the rapids below dampened the sounds of infrequent service when the Soo Railroad operated the line. On occasion, a rare whistle coming from a road crossing near the dam could be heard at the mansion. Today, bikers pedal over the pulverized granite trail, and in winter, it is the playground of snowmobiles; they are mostly oblivious to the history a short distance off the modern trail.

The abbot was not alone in his rapture concerning the falls and the property overlooking it. My first night there in 1966 introduced me to a very special tranquil constancy of sound generated by the waters. It may be traced back to this experience that, over the years, I have relied on "white noise" as an aid to getting to sleep. Thoughts of the setting and imagining an occasional return visit still soothe me today.

Abbot Killeen wrote extensively about the location during a two-year stay at the novitiate in the early 1970s as it was ramping down for closure and sale:

> Many times I have wandered along the river, or sat on the bank alone, or with some friends, and drank in the beauty of the river, its falls, and the wilderness around it. I found it the stuff of which dreams are made. I dreamed about the past and tried to capture a sense of the meaning of it all, and tried to live again the lives of the men and women who, from the beginning, had found both beauty and usefulness in the steadily reddish water. These waters flowed from the receding glaciers long ago, and carved deep crevices in the rock over which they passed for centuries. These waters perhaps saw the coming of the first human beings, and when the Indians' wigwams along its course gave way to the white man's axe, these waters solved the harvesting of the great pines and hemlocks a century ago.

Many in the area remember Abbot Killeen for his long hikes through the countryside, his hearty handshake, and his zest for life. On his walks, he gathered information for the series of articles he authored on the people and the place. "Smitten" might be a good description of how one would feel after encountering this beautiful location. No one immune to peacefulness and tranquility belongs there. Wealthy patricians, powerful bishops, indigenous warriors, religious hopefuls, Indian chiefs, American military heroes, poor farmers, even poorer native Americans, and even "A-list" movie stars—all have visited the novitiate, under a variety of circumstances; most have found it difficult to forget Freeborn Falls.

Prior to the fateful day upon which a certain young woman hiked onto this bit of heaven, the location had nothing to offer but scenery and serenity. Jane Peters was approaching middle age, but in many ways, she had always been cared for and treated as a child. Since her early teens, Jane had suffered from a chronic intestinal streptococcus infection that had not been cured—or even substantially ameliorated—by multiple and debilitating surgeries. Doctors had determined that there was probably no permanent cure for her condition. Due to her ill health, hopes of enjoying a husband and a family were out of the question. Born to wealth but never having had the luxury of behaving as though fully privileged, Jane had only her mother when the two "city ladies" discovered the idyllic property abutting the Red River; her father had died in 1922. Jennie Peters brought her daughter, Jane, to Gresham from Mount Kisco, New York, for a visit with Jane's former governess, Anna Schulte.

Lifelong Wisconsin resident Vicki Buettner, one of the more fascinated observers of the history only a few miles west of her home, published the following account of the visit to Gresham in the Wisconsin Historical Society's quarterly magazine, *Voyageur*:

In connection with a business trip to Chicago, Mrs. Peters and Jane made their first visit to the Schulte farm in Shawano County during the late 1920s. Anna took special care to prepare her home and garden for their visit. She knew Mrs. Peters would be especially eager to view the vegetable garden; she had an appreciation for homegrown flowers and vegetables. Although Mrs. Peters liked and respected Anna, this was a special reunion for Jane and Anna. If something happened to Mrs. Peters, there appeared to be an understanding that Anna would care for Jane; Anna was like a second mother to Jane. In 1932, the family chauffeur drove Jane from New York for a two-week visit at the farm. Although Jane had a colostomy during this time, she remained active. She even rode bareback on the Schulte pony.[2]

When the Peters family had first employed Anna, her last name was Fetzer, but she became Anna Schulte when she married Frank Schulte. Anna and Frank had met and become attracted to one another during their eight-day crossing on the *S.S. Vaterland*. They were both emigrating from Germany to escape the pre–World War I conditions in Europe. Otherwise, they would never have met. Anna had been born in Ebersheim, Germany, on January 22, 1886, while Frank had been born two years earlier at Odenwald, in Bavaria, many kilometers away.

Once they reached America's shores, they separated immediately. Frank's drafting skills took him to Saint Louis, where he found employment with an architectural firm, Barnett, Haynes, and Barnett, which had been commissioned to build the Cathedral of St. Louis. Anna remained behind in New York, seeking any employment she could find.

2   Vicki Buettner, "The House That Jennie Built," *Voyageur* 15, no. 2 (1999): 57.

They corresponded, but never were they able to visit one another. Nearly four years passed before Frank and Anna had independently saved enough money to make their next moves. Their pursuit of the American dream would bring them closer, but they would not yet be connected.

Frank was still struggling with the English language, and his heart was not in the city, nor was it with drafting. His native knowledge of the metric system conflicted with projects before him in feet and inches. Moving on briefly to another job, one that tethered him to a drawing board with a firm in O'Fallon, Missouri, he next found work in Indiana on a Quaker family farm. Frank was now in his environment of choice.

At about the same time, work and the lure of Frank brought Anna to St. Louis, a cherished destination for European immigrants, particularly Germans. Soon, an advertisement for a governess brought her to Chicago. There, she met Mr. and Mrs. Frank Peters and accepted their offer of employment to look after their only child, Jane Frances. The governess traveled internationally and extensively with the Peters family. Anna taught "Janey" German, and they bonded.

Not long after Anna was hired, the Peters family moved to Westchester County, New York. Anna, who had quickly become thought of as part of the family, found herself moving with them, and geography once again became a barrier between Anna and Frank. So thankful, though, were the two young immigrants to be removed from the outbreak of war in Germany and the rest of Europe, that Anna and Frank continued to assimilate in America.

One day, prompted by an advertisement in the *Chicago Tribune* offering farm property in Wisconsin, Frank boarded a train to investigate. The Gresham and Shawano areas had just emerged from a very successful lumbering phase. Recently cut wooded areas were for sale as farmland. Frank saw one particular parcel that sparked in him a comfortable memory of similar areas in his boyhood Bavaria. In very un-Germanic fashion, he acted on impulse and purchased a partially wooded farm perched on a hillside just north of the Red River. His vision now captured, a log house and barn waited for him to return and move in.

Frank Shulte, with his property backing the manicured timberland of the Menominee Indian Reservation, began his farming dream in 1915. Having finally created a foundation—and with something substantial to offer a wife—he proposed to Anna. In an emotional 1916 separation from sixteen-year-old Jane, Anna resigned from her position, joined Frank in Chicago, where they were married, then went with him to Gresham. The former governess' new life in dairy country was a far cry from the patrician existence she had become used to in Westchester, New York. Frank had a three-room log house waiting for her. Love helped her make the adjustment that October.

> Years later Mrs. Schulte told how her heart sank when first she saw her new home. The furs and nice dresses she had become accustomed to at Fernwood Farm in Mount Kisco seemed out of place in the log house that was to be her home, and in which she was to raise her family. (Killeen)

Anna Schulte was thrilled to host Jane and her mother in Wisconsin. Although Anna had not worked for them in many years, the bonds that had developed while she was caring for, traveling with, and raising Jane had remained unbroken. From these long years of tenuous connection evolved a major change that would alter both the geography and the history of Freeborn Falls, the Gresham area, and the lives of many people—living, dead, and yet unborn. Jane, an enthusiastic equestrienne and hiker, used any excuse to connect with horses, farmland and the outdoors, because this connection with nature always raised her spirits and helped to take her thoughts away from her illness. Moreover, because she was an accomplished rider and an enthusiastic walker, she was delighted to accept an invitation from Frank Schulte to take a stroll along some of the nearby country roads.

Their adventure took them both east and west along narrow Butternut Road where, on its north side, Frank Schulte's log farmhouse sat. Agitated pheasants noisily launched into the air from the side of the road, startling Jane and Frank as they explored. Next, they walked up another road, called Juniper, which led toward the Lamberies family farm. Jane was enthralled, drinking in all the peacefulness this wilderness area had to offer. As they were returning home, Frank encouraged Jane to follow him off the pavement, pushing the limits of her stamina. Carefully, they walked south down a logging path that led into the woods, soon dropping off in a gentle descent toward a swampy area. In a slight clearing, the two hikers heard the sound of moving water.

In his short memoir, *The Maiden of Freeborn Falls*, Abbot Killeen observed:

> It was during this visit with the Schultes that Jane discovered the falls. She was so captivated by it and its surroundings that she told her mother she would like to live there. While it seems strange for Jane to want to leave her native New York and take up residence on the Red River in a quiet farming community, we have to understand the kind of a person Jane Peters was. And we must also understand the mutual affection that existed between herself and her mother and the attachment each had for Mr. and Mrs. Frank Schulte, who lived nearby. Mrs. Peters immediately acquiesced to her daughter's wish.

Jennie Peters' decision was not entirely based on a whim. Jane's declining health had made it difficult—and in some cases, impossible—for her to participate in what was once the family routine. Annual travel to Europe, managing social engagements, horseback riding, jumping horses in competition, and social responsibilities were moving beyond her reach. Winning blue ribbons with her beloved dogs, West Highland Whites, would also soon end. Jennie believed that to bring Jane to this less-demanding setting would perhaps have a curative effect. Moreover, she hoped that reconnecting with Anna Fetzer Shulte might also help restore her daughter's well-being.

Another motivation for Jennie Peters to pick up and leave the East was her sensitivity to the political stirrings in Europe. Adolf Hitler was gaining influence at this time. Communication with her social and business connections overseas, along with input from Frank and Anna, brought her to fear the possibility of war on this continent. German-Americans were feeling the eye of suspicion in those years. Jennie reacted to the political climate, adopting a sort of "bunker mentality."

It was 1938, and, as if money were no object (as it was for so many others in these late years of the Great Depression), a dizzying pace of land purchases and site and structure planning ensued, and, shortly thereafter, construction began. Frank Schulte agreed to act as the liaison for this grand project. Anna was delighted that the mother and daughter were transplanting themselves to Gresham, just as she had herself done two decades earlier. Theirs, however, was to be in a style never before—or again—equaled in all of Northern Wisconsin and so close to the reservation.

When word got out that Frank was looking for prime real estate, agents beat a path to his door. Anxious to earn a scarce commission, and with sellers eager to turn their land holdings into needed cash, the Shawano County property market peddled its best. Shulte put up a valiant fight to keep the real buyer a secret. Savvy speculators soon realized that these choice locations were certainly out of the reach of a modest German immigrant farmer and his wife.

Early on, Frank was approached and shown land that is now a resort destination.

> An Appleton man, Frank Hyde, tried to sell Mrs. Peters property which included a small lake and several cabins, but it was located several miles north of the Schulte farm. He visited with Anna Schulte numerous times, hoping she would encourage Mrs. Peters to buy the property. The sale did not materialize; Mrs. Peters wanted a place closer to the Schulte farm. She purchased the Frank Traeger farm and personal property for $12,000 in September 1938; it was located less than a half mile from the Schulte farm. The following November, she purchased the parcel adjacent to the Red River for $6,000; Mrs. Peters decided to build a new home for Jane and herself on this land. (Buettner)

Not surprisingly, this was the same spot that Jane had explored with Frank on their walk more than a year earlier. The Wolf River Paper and Fiber Company, the most recent owner, had intended to tap the power of the falls for use at their mill. At about the same time that Shulte had shown interest on behalf of Jennie, the State intervened to protect the natural setting, killing the company's plans. This was perhaps the first—but certainly not the last—time the State of Wisconsin made a decision affecting this enchanted site. The timing could not have been more fortuitous for Jennie. Her six thousand dollars bought her fifty-seven choice acres and a slice of heaven for Jane.

With the help of talented friends back in Mt. Kisco and Chicago, Jane Peters took pencil in hand and sketched the vision she had of the home her mother was to build for them. Inspiration for this project came from a familiar property the mother and daughter had visited and admired often. Not far from Mt. Kisco, in White Plains, New York, was the home of Paul Thebaud. "Palatial mansion" is a more apt description. In the 1930s and 1940s, the Thebaud home had become a restaurant known as the Rosedale Corner House, a frequent destination and meeting place for mother, daughter, and those helping to plan their new life to the west.

Built in 1902 by wealthy importer Thebaud, *Hillair*, as it was known, was seized in 1944 by the city of White Plains for delinquent taxes and demolished two years later. Today, the prime location is the site of some of the most expensive homes in White Plains. It was the estate's majestic view of the Long Island Sound's waters that Jane and Jennie sought to replicate in the piney woods of Gresham. Although much more modest than the Sound, the Red River and its falls would have to do.

The process of planning and the prospect of completing the new estate and moving permanently to Wisconsin buoyed Jane's spirits. Alas, though, spirit was nearly all she had control over or working for her by then. As scheduling and construction activities were shifting into high gear, her physical health was plummeting. Even Jane knew that transporting Shamrock and Acorn, her prize horses, from New York to the newly acquired Traeger farm would be a race against the clock.

Abbot Killeen, researching this part of the story in the early 1970s, uncovered resources containing accurate facts, as did Vicki Buettner looking at the same period in the mid-1990s. This dual investigation, when composited, demonstrates that even time and the failing memory of the repositories of much of the oral history have not altered the story significantly; in fact, the two accounts parallel amazingly well. A family friend of both the Peters and Killeen sent the abbot a photo of Jane at her best and happiest, astride her dapple-gray, Shamrock. In his journal, Killeen remarked:

Her posture, her dark bobbed hair, her clean-cut profile, suggesting a strong will and an agile mind underneath a gentile demeanor, reminds this writer of an equestrienne statue of Joan of Arc that stands in the public square of Paris.

Even with my extraordinary access to the Alexian Brothers archives and the incredibly facile "finger-tip travel" afforded by the Internet, I have been unable to unearth the longer-term history of the Peters family, their New York life, and their connections with any immediate family outside of their Wisconsin experience. For people with such extensive holdings, influence, and social status, the elder and younger Peters women might as well have stepped onto the planet in Wisconsin. Before, during, and after the Gresham property development, there are virtually no fresh or reliable footprints to track their New York days. Even so, perhaps what we do know will be enough.

Overseeing the process from over a thousand miles away, Jennie Peters directed Frank Schulte in his newly acquired "project liaison" role. Frank, like many breadwinners of the time, certainly could have used the additional income Jennie paid him to handle the site acquisition and to oversee the planning, design, and construction activities.

Managing the beginnings of Wisconsin's slightly more modest legacy of the Westchester County landmark would awaken the drafting skills Frank Schulte thought he had laid to rest years before. Since he had become a friend of the family, and because he possessed a definite engineering talent, he could intelligently look over the shoulders of designers and builders. Frank Schulte was a perfect on-scene alter ego for Jennie Peters. The Hillair mansion of New York, admired and copied by the Peters mother and daughter, would soon have its counterpart, built in a more challenging and less sophisticated environment.

Skilled professional architectural talent for the substantial endeavor was scarce in the immediate area of Gresham and Shawano. To transform Jane's sketches and drawings into blueprints, Frank engaged the firm of Gordon Feldhausen and Gardner Coughlin of Green Bay. The site was truly wooded wilderness, and it was a bit swampy as it dropped off toward the riverbank and Freeborn Falls. Frank's first on-site duties were to engage laborers to clear the forest for the mansion and to create access to the main road so that construction vehicles could operate on the property.

This was logging country, so ample local help was available for stump and tree removal. Next, hundreds of loads of rock and earthen fill were delivered and graded, transforming the bog near the water's edge into a firm, gentle slope, which also then created an unobstructed and commanding view of the natural water features from the intended site. In 1939, once he had completed all the preliminaries, Frank began taking bids for the construction on the ten acres that had been painstakingly cleared and prepared.

Little time was wasted. Soon, Frank chose a general contractor from Green Bay—based on his low bid—to undertake the project, but the contractor's reach apparently exceeded his grasp. In a matter of just a few weeks, the apparently inexperienced low bidder withdrew from the project. A lawsuit ensued over the contractor's inability to manage such a large project and, in order to assure that the work would continue on schedule, the Baker Construction Company, a much larger Green Bay firm, was engaged to continue the work.

Frank Schulte is not remembered as a "warm" sort of gentleman. In fact, the rigid, no-nonsense manner he brought with him from Germany made him an ideal guardian of "The Mansion in the Wilderness," as the project became known in news outlets at the time. Schulte, the taskmaster, living just across the rural road within walking distance from the site, was ever-present. His regimented, precise routines and clockwork-like handling of the scheduling process kept the general contractor focused, and the Schulte attitude radiated down through the various crafts as they were brought in to finish and trim. By this time, Frank had overcome his initial lack of command of the English language, and so there were no barriers to effective communication.

Since she was continuing to manage most aspects of her late husband's business affairs, Jennie Peters made frequent business trips to Chicago. Often, she would bring Jane with her, and once finished with her business in the Windy City, mother and daughter would go on to Wisconsin to view the progress of the home's construction. One of those visits proved disastrous. During the summer of 1939, Jane had a relapse of her twenty-three-year-long chronic affliction while in the Midwest. She entered Chicago's Presbyterian Hospital, where she underwent her seventeenth bowel resection. Although she survived the surgery, so much of her bowel had been taken that there was essentially none remaining to be treated or removed in the future.

Anna Schulte traveled from the north woods to be—once again—at Jane's bedside. Jennie Peters paid for adjacent hospital rooms for herself and Anna. Unlike today's medical environment, with its in-and-out hospital stays, Jane's confinement lasted for months. Jennie arranged around-the-clock private nursing care to supplement an already attentive hospital staff. Still, the Wisconsin construction marched steadily on.

Frank Peters, Jennie, and Jane were bibliophiles and avid readers. Their collection of literature was, in every sense, a library. The space and detail incorporated into the plans for the library under construction at Gresham were on a scale never before seen in the region. A small sampling of Jane's collection had been shipped to Presbyterian Hospital during her recuperation. An open book of poetry was discovered in Jane's hospital room on Wednesday, December 13, 1939, just hours after she expired. Apparently, she had been reading the following passage, in which she must have found some comfort:

EARLY DEATH
by Hartley Coleridge (1796-1849)

SHE pass'd away like morning dew
Before the sun was high;
So brief her time, she scarcely knew
The meaning of a sigh.
As round the rose its soft perfume,
Sweet love around her floated;
Admired she grew—while mortal doom
Crept on, unfear'd, unnoted.
Love was her guardian Angel here,
But Love to Death resign'd her;
Tho' Love was kind, why should we fear
But holy Death is kinder?

Jennie took Jane's remains back to Westchester County in New York and buried her beside her father at Gate of Heaven Cemetery in Hawthorn, a small hamlet near White Plains. The Catholic resting place where she is buried is operated by the Archdiocese of New York and is also where Babe Ruth, James Cagney, Conde Nast, and Charles Schwab are buried. In fact, these famous names are only a few of the well-known people who share repose with Jane Peters, "The Maiden of Freeborn Falls."

Celia (Cele) M. Long of Chicago, a friend of Abbott Killeen, served for some time as the private secretary to Jennie Peters. In 1971, Cele Long wrote to the abbot in response to his request for assistance in reconstructing the legacy left by the Peters women and the missing pieces of the Freeborn Falls puzzle. Writing at great length for the

Alexian Brothers after his retirement, Killeen shared a letter in which Long provided details about the private persona of Jennie Peters and of her daughter, Jane.

An excerpt from that letter gives some insight into the events that followed:

> Mrs. Peters of course was a deeply religious woman and a convert which I believe must have occurred after Jane was baptized—the origin of which was the fact that Jane's father's father had been a Catholic. Jane's religion was a very private possession—she didn't talk about it but how many times I sat at Mass with them and know that this was physically arduous for her. Mrs. Peters really crumbled in her heart when Jane died, but carried on in her valiant way as she had done all through her life when she had to meet sorrow—and, of course, finished the Gresham House, which she had hoped to share with Jane in order that this change might prolong her life. She really loved the house and surroundings and stayed as long as she could.

How difficult it must have been for Jennie Peters to continue the project in Wisconsin! The primary reason for its origin no longer existed. Her anchors and social connections were in Mt. Kisco. Her immediate family, in effect, was there too. By late 1941, four years after Jane had roughly drafted the mansion's concept, the Gresham estate was complete. To all appearances, living out the commitment to her daughter had to be the motivation for Jennie Peters to follow through.

Throughout the property acquisition and construction of the Peters mansion, the Shultes and other confidants of Jennie Peters diligently kept her identity strictly confidential. Despite intense speculation about the ownership and purpose of the mansion, wealth had taught Jennie Peters to keep her business endeavors "close to the vest," and it was quite natural for her to swear her aides to confidentiality. A project of that magnitude, topping out at over $200,000 (in 1930s dollars) represented an enormous business transaction. The savvy New York businesswoman would not let herself be taken advantage of by contractors who might discover the strong emotional connection this home had for its owner.

Through its several years of development, owing partly to its sheer opulence inside and out, the evolving mansion created and supported a very lively local rumor mill. Now, at age sixty-six and recently bereft of her only daughter, Jennie clearly saw no reason to make an official announcement or offer any public explanation about the new residence. After all, she perceived the endeavor as simply someone constructing a home. Regardless, the grand and standout qualities of the property and its buildings fueled speculation about its purpose.

Somehow, a bit of information had leaked out regarding Jennie Peters's personal campaign to send supplies and care packages to friends and relatives in Germany. Trying to attach some sinister significance to that activity, some of the half-informed "sleuths" began to say that the new mansion was a project built and financed by the German-American *Volksbund*. Even though American involvement in World War II was yet months away, many Americans were a bit antsy about Germany and the possibility of a fifth column insidiously and clandestinely subverting American solidarity over war elsewhere.

This would not be the last time neighbors would disapprove of perceived or real activity in the mansion. The "not in my backyard" mentality that displayed itself in those years continues even today in the region, which, after all, is fertile breeding ground for militia groups. The Posse Comitatus is a very extremist and right wing organization with significant roots and, at one time, support in that part of Wisconsin. Very white, fiercely supportive of "the importance of local control," and extremely anti-government with racial overtones, these elements would surface years later with the mansion as the theater.

The *Volksbund* was a pro-Nazi organization that, pre–World War II, goose-stepped around supporting Hitler, mostly in Manhattan but with a strong presence in Chicago. The organization even established youth camps. Since the *Volksbund* was mostly composed of German immigrants who became U.S. citizens, along with others of German heritage, some suspected Mrs. Peters of creating a secret location for a headquarters in the forest. The term *Volksbund* acquired a tamer connotation over the years. It came to refer to a patriotic beneficent organization that maintains records and the memory of Germany's war dead abroad. Even today, youth still proudly march around, but typically they manicure the gravesites of their fallen, and none ever speak of (or even know of) having a connection to Jennie Peters and the Gresham property.

For the less suspicious (yet curious), the mansion was thought to be possibly an institutional sanatorium. Even that far back, people identified Jennie as being somehow connected with the Alexian Brothers' Oshkosh, Wisconsin, institution for the mentally ill. An area newspaper at the time went out on a limb and suggested that some elderly woman was building a secret rest castle near Gresham in Shawano County. Local rumor mills thrived on unsubstantiated conversations about the imposing project at the Freeborn Falls Mansion.

So, quietly and unassumingly, with no fanfare—and just a few days before the bombing of Pearl Harbor—Jennie Peters came to Wisconsin to stay. "Taking up residence" might better describe her relocation. Regular folks "move in," but Jennie arrived in a chauffeur-driven limousine—unpretentiously, but driven nonetheless. Jennie now had the dubious honor of being the closest thing to royalty living in Shawano County, Wisconsin. She now lived within a mile of the Menominee Indian Reservation, with its abject poverty, and her sumptuous quarters were nestled among simple country folk who lived off the land in a variety of ways. She came from Westchester County, where her station in life was well accepted and where wealth flourished. Now Jennie was a neighbor to men and women who had seldom, if ever, seen such advantage and creature comforts.

Shopping seems to be how women all over the world learn about their neighbors, gossip, and establish themselves in a new environment. As it turned out, Jennie was no exception. She was often seen alone, dressed in ordinary clothing, buying her own household needs and waiting in cashier lines, where she might find herself standing in front of the wife of a dairy farmer as well as behind an Indian lumberjack. There may have been a driver nearby to take her home in comfort, but she definitely made an effort to be a part of the community by getting to know the merchants and service providers in both the village of Gresham and the much larger town of Shawano, the county seat.

On Juniper Road, north of the mansion, Mr. and Mrs. Ed Lamberies lived on a farm. Juniper Road has its origin at the foot of the mansion property and runs straight north toward the western boundary of the Menominee Indian Reservation. The couple served Jennie Peters as both neighbors and servants. Ed looked after the landscaping and exterior, while his wife managed the household duties of the interior. They are both deceased now, but they are survived by their son, Willis. He remembers being a little water boy for thirsty laborers during the construction of the mansion so many years ago.

The Lamberies farm was a short, beautiful walk in the summer, but it could be a miserable trek on winter mornings—and it was worse, still, with the north wind in your face on the dark evening's trudge home. Ed's place was on the upslope from the river and looked down on the Peters estate. The barn, which was oriented east to west, stood between the south-facing farmhouse and the mansion, which lay hundreds of yards to the south. The strategic placement of the Lamberies home and its inhabitants would one day prove pivotal in an occupation of a very different nature than that of Jennie Peters.

Jennie, a fine cook, enjoyed time in her kitchen, a large and well-appointed room that was truly fit for a gourmet. She employed a local woman to manage the day-to-day kitchen activities. While entertaining, however, Jennie clearly wore the chef's hat. The wine cellar in the mansion dwarfed any other in the county—likely, it was the largest in the State of Wisconsin. Jennie kept the beverage cellar locked. No one on her staff had access. Soon after settling in, Jennie realized that the food stores and beverage pantry could not be kept up to her standards with local merchants' stock on hand, so she supplemented her inventory with regular special deliveries from New York City and elsewhere in the east and with special orders from Chicago.

Harvey, son of Frank and Anna Schulte, was called to war and could no longer manage, for Jennie, the old Traeger place just north of the mansion and directly across from the Lamberies. Vernon Schmidt, a local resident, recalls the day Jennie Peters hired him to replace the Shulte's son. With her connections, Jennie arranged for Vernon's draft deferment. He asked no questions and reported to an attorney in town, walking away from the specter of war. His responsibilities were basic farm hand chores. Vernon looked after a token collection of cows, pigs, and chickens for Jennie.

On one occasion, in the absence of the chauffer, Jennie asked Vernon to make a trip into Shawano to National Biscuit, an early food store chain. Vernon arrived in the estate's tarp covered pickup truck. On this very frigid day, he was encouraged by store management to stay in the truck cab, engine and heater running, with a warm cup of coffee. Store employees would load the purchases; Vernon was instructed only to drive and deliver.

But curiosity got the best of Vernon Schmidt. His job had always kept him up at the North Farm and at a distance from the main house.

Now was his chance to take a peek at how the other half lived. A little side road detour from the route back to Freeborn Falls gave him an opportunity to stop and investigate his secret cargo.

Vernon Schmidt-2003. On mansion staff in the 1940's
Photo by Curt Knoke

He had been suspicious about his exclusion from loading the truck, and upon throwing back the tarp, Vernon was amazed at the quantity of wartime-rationed items on board. Most striking to him was the enormous amount of expensive fresh meats. He would learn later that this meat was exclusively for the West Highland Whites. Their status in the mansion went beyond eating like royal pets. Built for them in the basement was a special room and their own semi-automated bathing and grooming facility. The show dogs were Jennie's last connection to Jane.

It may have been the winters, or it may have been the isolation and disconnect with friends back east, but sometime in 1948, Jennie Peters decided to put Gresham behind her. Any reasonable person could see that rattling around alone in that house, over-built for two anyway, had to be a lonely existence. Punctuating her rural and remote life of luxury with an occasional grand reception was not enough to satisfy her need for companionship.

Little is known about the relationship between Jennie Peters and Anna and Frank Schulte and its evolution during the Gresham years. Following Jane's death, Jennie's period of occupying the mansion lacked or lost the glue that had bonded the Peters and the Schultes in the past. For a variety of reasons, friends, family, and relations grow apart. Anna Schulte's responsibility of delivering and raising children in that log home was a far cry from her former employer, living across the way in splendor. Jennie was living well but was lonely.

Frank Peters, likely the source of all of Jennie's wealth, was regarded as brilliant. The attorney/inventor and recipient of sixty patents made a fortune in the cookie and cracker packaging business. He began his career with the National Biscuit Company (Nabisco). To this day, the most basic of foods are still packaged and owe their shelf life to the techniques developed by Frank Peters and the 105-year-old company he pioneered, Peters Machinery. A few who knew him speculated that Frank Peters might have suffered for his genius. After about two decades of success in the food industry, he abruptly moved the family to New York to take an executive position with American Radiator—a far cry from cookies, crackers, and cakes.

Some believe that, before the New York move, a nervous breakdown may have landed Peters in the mental health facility operated by the Alexian Brothers in Oshkosh, Wisconsin. It may have been here that Jennie developed affection for the Alexians. In any event, Jennie Peters had acquired, along the way, knowledge of the work of this order of Catholic men. It may have been the mutual German roots, their Chicago or St. Louis ties, or the mental institution in Oshkosh.

An interesting character founded the Alexian Brothers Hospital in Oshkosh. Sort of a pioneer and renegade monk, Paulus (Mathias) Pollig of Germany, purporting to be an Alexian Brother, persuaded the Bishop of Green Bay in 1879 to assist and financially support him in establishing a hospital in Oshkosh near Lake Winnebago. Pollig had, in fact, been a progressive Alexian in America. He was the Provincial Rector of the new American Province and led the effort to rebuild their hospital in Chicago following the Great Fire of 1871. This ambitious Alexian Brother, however, learned a lesson in humility when his superiors recalled him to Aachen, Germany, reminded him of his vow of obedience, and dismissed him from the order in 1877. Monastic politics caused him to lose the turf battle.

His transgressions, it seems, were his attempts to break away from German control and establish independent Alexian leadership in America. His modern ways and efforts in expansion did not fit the rigid monastic rule. Ironically, the twentieth century would eventually see the Alexians accept the wisdom and necessity in establishing governing figures in the United States. The determined former Alexian almost succeeded, until Bishop Krautbauer of Green Bay learned he was an imposter in bad standing—but with a good story. The Bishop withdrew his commitment to Pollig but not the effort the former Alexian had set into motion. He contacted the Alexians in Chicago and asked them to take over the hospital that Pollig had established. May of 1880 saw the first patient admitted to the hospital, which was converted from the home of the local monument maker, J. J. Moore.

For about a dozen years, the brothers operated Oshkosh as a general hospital until a Catholic order of nuns opened a newer facility. Then the Alexians fell back on doing what they had done well over centuries, caring for the unwanted, poor, alcoholic, and mentally ill. The institution became well known in U.S. Catholic hierarchy as a destination for substance-abusing priests. More frankly speaking, it was a treatment destination for Catholic clerics who abused their flocks, as well as the bottle.

Brother Julius was the Alexian Rector in Oshkosh during the time Jennie Peters was ending her chapter in Wisconsin. On October 6, 1948, he received a special delivery letter. The Reverend Francis X. Scott of St. Joseph's Catholic Church in Bronxville, New York, wrote Brother Julius with some surprising news. Mrs. Peters, a former parishioner of Father Scott, wished to bequeath all of her holdings in Gresham to the Alexians. His letter went on to say that Mrs. Peters was a very wealthy woman, an excellent Catholic, a widow, and had no one to leave the property to living in America. Father Scott described the gift she wished to convey to the brothers because of her admiration for their work. The method and approach Jennie used for this grand gesture is interesting and telling.

Follow-up correspondence from the New York priest to the brothers provided background information on Jennie, but it was basic with little detail. He said she had been born in the United States in 1876 to German immigrants. Scott described the ordeal with her daughter Jane, and the origins of the mansion. He told the brothers that Frank Peters was a Lutheran but had died receiving full Catholic last rites. Of interest was the fact that mother and daughter had converted to Catholicism in 1916.

Baffled yet intrigued, the Alexians were very interested in the bequest. Father Scott advised them that it was now appropriate to approach Jennie, and Brother Julius made his first contact by telephone with her on December 10, 1948. That call resulted in an invitation to the mansion scheduled for December 14. He described his impressions:

> Mrs. Peters was found to be a very refined and intelligent woman, of a retiring nature, very considerate of the poor, and at the time was engaged in sending numerous food packages to relatives in Germany following the war. (Killeen)

Brother Julius spent the day with Jennie discussing the options of accepting the property and the Alexians' best use of the gift. Jennie expressed her wish to see it somehow benefit the poor, but she put no restrictions on its use. The Alexians were free to utilize it as they saw fit. The way was made clear for a return visit the next month, January 1949.

Both the Superior General and the Brother Provincial of the Alexians paid a visit to Gresham to accept the property and express Alexian gratitude for the gift of two hundred acres of land, a farmhouse, barn, and the mansion. Jennie Peters shared with the brothers her plans to return to New York. She had kept her 127-acre property in Mt. Kisco, but the large home there had burned to the ground. She intended to rebuild with a modest one-story home.

Early in 1950, Jennie's newest home back east was ready. With that, she moved back to her comfort zone and away from the hollowness of the mansion. Properly putting to rest the memory of Jane, she handed the keys to the Alexians. She would return on only one occasion. Jennie Peters lived another thirteen years, and then the local newspaper announced her death.

Mrs. Peters greeted by Br Florian Eberle
at 1955 dedication of Gresham, WI novitiate.
Alexian Brothers Provincial Archives, Arlington Heights, Illinois.

At the age of eighty-six years and a brief illness of eleven weeks in the Mount Kisco hospital, Mount Kisco, New York, Mrs. Jennie Peters died August 12, 1963 of "general debilitation." She, too, was buried in the Gate of Heaven Cemetery, Westchester County, New York aside her husband and daughter.

Her last will and testament encountered a great ordeal in trying to locate any next of kin. Although she had specific arrangements made to distribute her wealth, none of it included any family. Indeed, there were none known, lending further credence to her loneliness. An exception was the daughter of an estranged brother, George J. Meyer, who had died a resident of Chicago prior to 1939. Charlotte, Jennie's niece, survived him. Therefore, Charlotte Meyer Skonberg of Falls Church, Virginia, the sole heir at law, was located, notified of Jennie's death and will, and served notice to avert a contesting of the will.

The legal process was now free to execute Jennie's wishes. That included the amount of $20,000 to her longtime maid and companion, Ana-Marie Jost; 740 shares of Peters Machinery stock valued at nearly $600,000 to her personal secretary, Celia M. Long; and finally, all her remaining real estate holdings and residual property to the Saint Frances of Assisi Catholic Church in Mt. Kisco.

Valued at almost two million dollars, this last and lion's share of her holdings went, again, to a Catholic institution. Astonishingly, her New York gift seems to have been forgotten among church members and clergy. Unlike the tribute paid to her stemming from the Alexian bequest, little evidence or record of Jennie Peters' final generosity could be found in Mt. Kisco.

3

GRAND SILENCE

As a grade-school youngster, I was one of the uniformed St. Anne Catholic School kids with spaghetti sauce smeared on our white shirts or khaki pants. This is how our mothers determined that day's cafeteria menu—we wore it home. At recess, we often stood looking longingly across Calder Avenue at a fifteen-acre estate. There, John Henry Phelan had built his mansion from oil money. Then, it was considered palatial, and it is still magnificent today.

Never will I forget the tree clearing and a hospital rising out of the adjacent private parkland within the manicured preserve. Phelan, the oil baron, bequeathed all of it to the Sisters of Charity of the Incarnate Word. That spectacular mansion in our oil town became a cloistered convent. For almost two years, during the construction, I felt a gravitational pull and attraction to that facility. I did not know then how closely the path I would take would be connected with benevolence and philanthropy. In 1962, the hospital sisters asked the eighth grade good boys and girls to participate in the new St. Elizabeth Hospital open house and ceremonies. I became hooked.

That hospital was built for me, I am certain. The medical library was my back door entrée. I volunteered my services in the library, looking like a junior physician. On one occasion, a local cardiologist asked me to be his guinea pig. "Oh, sure why not." It sounded great to me! The hospital had acquired the city's only defibrillator, and the cardiologist's task was to train the staff on its use. I became his model while he performed mock resuscitation procedures on me. Imagine that!

Today, cardiac defibrillators hang on the walls of public places like fire extinguishers. There they dangle, waiting for any amateur to snatch one and shock the dying back from the jaws of purgatory. Back in those days, I made every effort to get as close to patient care as allowed. Let me be honest. I was able to go behind closed doors where a kid, today, would never be allowed. Due to my volunteerism gone wild, my brother Michael teasingly branded me as "Dr. Gray Lad." I loved it.

In high school, I continued as an unpaid hospital volunteer. That work, in the medical library and elsewhere within the new hospital, was my introduction to the world of medicine. My connection grew into modest compensation as an orderly at another associated local hospital. Hotel Dieu Hospital had opened in 1898, and its useful architectural days were numbered.

Added to the old building and completed in 1949 was another wing named St. Martin de Porres Hospital. De Porres was a South American Catholic saint of "color," and perhaps not surprisingly for the time, this hospital was built for Beaumont, Texas, negroes (as they were called then). By the middle 1950s, St. Martin de Porres Hospital was taking on more politically correct services to the community. It became a destination for East Texas pediatric patients and white folks, like me.

In fact, when I was five, I was one of their unfortunate customers. It was there that I was forced to involuntarily donate my tonsils and adenoids. The surgery occurred just after I had started kindergarten. The episode prevented my return to preschool. I will always remember it as if it were yesterday. Then, anesthesia was administered by strapping the subject to the surgical table followed by the dreaded metal face mask containing cotton soaked with ether. Terrifying moments of claustrophobia and a hopeless struggle would mercifully give way to unconsciousness. If you were lucky, a talented anesthesiologist could keep you from prematurely awakening until the surgeon was nearly done.

Today, a medication called Midazolam is given to patients before such surgeries to reduce anxiety and prevent memory of the procedure. In my case, following what should have been a routine childhood surgery, it took a half-dozen units of whole blood and testing, after the fact, to discover I was a hemophiliac. Oops? This episode would firmly imprint upon my mind the fragile world of health care. I learned that having suffered pain and fear helps all of us to be compassionate with others when it's their turn.

Pediatric days well behind me, this lanky teenager doctor wannabe was the finest underpaid gopher that hospital ever had, I'm sure. I will forever remember the steep ramp I would have to negotiate between the two buildings to transport wheelchair and stretcher patients. A skinny but determined kid like me would have to get a running start, especially with a supersized patient. I never lost one, but nearly did so on a few occasions.

When the hospital was quiet, I learned to provide break-time coverage for the telephone switchboard operator. Located in the lobby, the board served as reception and information or direction for visitors. The old-fashioned beast was one of those classic switchboards with crisscrossing wires. Those were still the days an operator could listen in on conversations. Of course, I would never do a thing like that; well... maybe I did once!

If I was not dispatched emptying bedpans, I was babysitting the almost-never-visited and antiquated emergency department. Count me among the many thousands having received their childhood share of stitches in those ghastly, and probably ghostly, rooms. Regardless, they held an attraction for me. Ambulances had stopped routinely bringing patients, as most preferred the new and modern hospital to the west, where wealth lived. Occasionally, I would handle the odd off-the-street walk-in with a life-threatening splinter in their finger. The Catholic sisters kept the doors open for the needy within walking distance.

The approach to the emergency room was one of those classic circular driveways descending to the basement. The main entrance, with impressive three-story columns was just above. Grand steps, as if a monument, led to the hospital's imposing main foyer. This spared the public from daily arrivals of gruesome gore below. The ER served as an interim morgue on rare occasions, and on one unforgettable summer weekend day in that dubious part of town, I sat at my solitary duty station, the ER.

With tires screeching and frantic honking, a beat-up private car came to a halt at the subterranean ER entrance. I stepped out to greet an inebriated spectacle. It looked as if circus clowns were piling out of the overstuffed automobile. They were demanding that I assist them in unloading a bloody lifeless figure from the front passenger seat. After all, I was wearing white shoes, pants, and a smock two sizes too large yet smartly buttoned across one shoulder like Ben Casey and Dr. Kildare. Yes, I looked professional, but I was useless under these circumstances.

This victim had bled so much, it was running out the car door. Even this naive teenage orderly knew a dead man when he saw one. It was time for creative theatrics. I fetched a blood pressure cuff and stethoscope. With my reassuring nod, it took all the skill I could muster to get the living back into their car. I successfully pretended the DOA, stabbed through his left chest, might be much better off if his arguing "Good Samaritans" would just rush him to the newer hospital.

Pointed in the right direction, they lurched up and out the drive just as they had arrived. I continued fearing for my safety. I telephoned ahead to law-enforcement and the newer ER. I would learn later that the police ultimately caught up with that volatile domestic disturbance on wheels. The driver, I would read in the newspaper, was the murderer at a backyard picnic gone jealously bad. I can thank those drunks for providing my baptism into the real world of urgent medical care.

Houston, less than a hundred miles away, had become the global epicenter of cardiovascular surgery and other medical advances. I stumbled upon a copy of *Look* magazine and there it was! I wrote a congratulatory letter to Dr. Michael E. DeBakey. The article on his accomplishments was inspiring. My letter resulted in an invitation to visit Methodist Hospital and the Baylor College of Medicine.

One day in 1961, I boarded a 3:00 a.m. Greyhound bus from Beaumont to Houston, arriving just in time to be whisked away by DeBakey's secretary to the infamous Methodist Hospital. I was treated as if I were a visiting dignitary. Mesmerized, I was seated in the overhead surgical observation gallery and left alone to gaze for hours. This was not the final icing on the cake that day. Exciting as this visit was, the real prize was the cherished invitation to return that summer and work in the experimental dog surgical laboratory.

In retrospect, I now understand that grooming the young was important, and I had stumbled into that process. Momentum coming out of new talent, moving forward, would push the gifted to the top. I knew immediately I was out of my league. I found myself rubbing elbows with the crème de la crème of bright and talented high school students and sons of astronauts from Houston. As usual, there was the obligatory sparring with pompous snots in order to be noticed and heard. You can't be friends with all, I would be reminded. Employing a quick tongue and humor was, again, my survival method. Thank God my invitation to participate at Baylor had not been contingent upon good grades. Otherwise, I would have been pumping gas in Beaumont.

That summer, it was like being an exchange student hopping from country to country without even leaving Texas. It was muggy in Southeast Texas, but Houston was the world's "most air-conditioned" city. The daily chill of the operating room was always contrasted with the feeling of wearing an oppressively humid wet blanket outdoors. The Houston Medical Center had become a cherished destination for all manner of foreign physicians, scientists, nurses, and technologists wishing to be involved in groundbreaking heart surgery.

The value in encountering and dealing with different people, different languages, beliefs, methods, and goals would serve me well later in life. Even though I was operating on dogs and calves, just to have been present during those historic times was invaluable. The pursuits of a viable mechanical artificial heart, human transplants, or both made these heady times. Ironically, years later my mother's brother would find himself hospitalized there and the recipient of two separate heart transplants. Yes, I really once had an uncle with three hearts. Was all of that just coincidence or karma?

My brother Michael would find, independently, that same hospital and medical center. There, he furthered a respected career as a hospital administrator following his stint in Vietnam. Michael served his nine-month administrative residency in 1970 in the Baylor-Methodist system. Following, he was offered and accepted an administrative assistant position with Methodist hospital.

Our sibling rivalry yet mutual attraction to health care is a mystery. Perhaps it was that bonding kitty cadaver episode? I was not the first to turn our detached garage into a "procedure room." Michael preceded me by five years. At some point in Michael's Beaumont education, he acquired a properly embalmed cat. He brought it home to dissect for a college premed undertaking. Mother banished him and his feline to the garage. I wasn't welcome until I collaborated with my older brother. Our youngest brother, Kelley, was lured one day into the garage. It is possible that very day Kelley took the healing arts off his list of careers when Michael chased him, screaming, around the neighborhood with the cat's severed ear.

In defense of we three Rick brothers, I must insist on some clarity here. All of us grew up, lovingly, with a pet goat, dogs, cats, birds, lizards, frogs, and fireflies. We three would cry at their loss. Snakes did not fare so well. I admit to injustice in that department. If I remember correctly, a certain older brother constructed a miniature guillotine just for smaller nonpoisonous reptiles. The poisonous were executed from a distance. My mother was fond of commenting that the larger snakes, shot with our ineffective BB guns, did not succumb to the trauma. They died from "lead poisoning" she would say, laughing.

After ten years of lackluster school accomplishments, it finally sank in that I would never be a shining star of academia. My talent for practical hands-on skills would serve me instead. Nevertheless, I was finding my niche. The following year, I was proud to arrange a visit to return and observe surgery again with three of my classmates. If it was unlikely that the class clown would acquire respectable credentials, at least I would have exposed some of our class leaders to the best.

So Tom Peterson, Luke Petkovsek, John LeBlanc, and I launched our day trip. I was proud to show off. I told them what to expect and how to behave. My buddies were enthusiastic and anxious. Road conversations turned to the marvels of science. Because of all the petroleum refineries we passed en route to Houston, chemistry took center stage. We also conducted spontaneous mobile experiments with that always-risky gas, methane. Things never change with talented male youth: with the exception of the driver, we laughed all the way to Space City and back igniting farts.

We returned home charged up and dangerously sure of ourselves. We decided we would rock Beaumont with the most impressive science project ever attempted by high school geniuses. Without doubt, a Pulitzer Prize would soon be within our grasp.

We borrowed some old cardiovascular instruments, unfit for human use, from Beaumont's Dr. Milton M. Self, vascular surgeon. A respirator on its last leg from the Beaumont Fire Department and various surgical supplies from my hospital contacts completed our needs. My family's

detached garage became our third world-like surgical suite. Our team
found a patient volunteer who was surely in need of our newfound skills.
A local veterinarian donated one of his blood donor dogs, the volunteer,
to our cause. John LeBlanc chose not to collaborate. A wise kid, he must
have known better.

We were nervous and unpracticed but confident. We successfully
anesthetized and I intubated the poor trusting hound. Things seemed
good as we closed the entry to our Frankenstein-like laboratory. Donned
in sterile green gowns, caps, a mask, and gloves, we looked the part.
With reassuring glances, we picked up the scalpel and began. In spite
of respiration and a beating heart we dissected down to the descending
thoracic aorta, our destination. The team clamped off the large vessel and
we were bursting with pride. There was no turning back when we excised
the section of a perfectly good aorta.

With the assistance of Luke and Tom, I selected and cut a length
of the costly artificial artery material implant donated to us. Our patient
stirred just a little; that interruption was handled with a little more
anesthesia. The clock was ticking and we had a limited amount of time
to finish. Otherwise, our patient could survive but with permanent
paralysis in his hindquarters.

We were sewing feverishly and the dog started moving once again
making it difficult. Then an aggressive knock on the garage door came at
a bad time. We were certain our planned adventure in surgical prowess
had been kept secret from ghoulish mates. Who could be bothering us at
such a vital time? A quizzical glance among ourselves at the same time
the garage door was opening was coupled with our patient now trying to
come off the table. "Hey, what the hell are you guys doing in there?" In
that *oh shit* moment, we were discovered at the worst of time.

Albert Fumuso could not believe the macabre scene before him.
There we three stood in our surgical attire and desperate faces partially
hidden by our masks. We could not have appeared any guiltier if we had

been discovered on Main Street naked next to a bloody dying dog at dinnertime. Inadequate anesthesia, uncontrollable bleeding, and more questions from Albert, our visitor-turned-consultant, forced us to decide. While losing our concentration, we watched our plan domino into dog-death disappointment. We had no choice but to put our patient down.

Mr. Dog was laid to rest in the wooded area next door. Our cardio-vascular wannabe team learned a lesson that day. We appreciated why there are so many years of medical school, internship, residency, fellowships and only began to understand why the career is called a "practice." The word would spread throughout Kelly High School that we were dog killers. We tried. We failed.

Tom Peterson would go on to become our senior class president and an attorney in Beaumont. Luke Petkovsek, predictably, earned a B.S. in biology/chemistry and his M.Ed. in exercise physiology. Albert Fumuso, a.k.a. "Conrad," was unstoppable on the football field, but we would learn that Albert's undiscovered talents included the theater. The play *Bye-Bye Birdie* would never be the same after he was cast as the Elvis-esque title character, Conrad Birdie. Fumuso is still keeping his community glued together with his masonry engineering skills in the petroleum refining industry. John Leblanc owes no apology to our hometown canine descendants. John's dental patients can rest easy because he became a real respected Beaumont doctor of dental surgery. Me? I would never finish college.

These four friends, unsurprisingly, were jocks to whom we looked up to. I wasn't able to play sports because of my hemophilia, but I found ways to be a contributing team member. I taped ankles, applied ice and butterfly Band-Aids, and poured cruel crimson stinging substances into raw abrasions. There, I learned why wounded warriors need a clubhouse to whimper, moan, and cry where fans cannot hear or observe. It was never easy restricting unforgiving fathers from barging in at half-time to yell at and humiliate their sons. Soon after graduation, I left for

Wisconsin and the religious life, yet I continued to search for something, something medical. Here lay the ingredients, motivation, and reasons behind how I found myself eventually joining the Alexian Brothers.

We began to gather in Chicago on Saturday, July 16, 1966, and within twenty-four hours all of our class of fourteen had arrived. Some came by plane, others by train, and still more by automobile, delivered by tearful families perhaps unable to afford the cost of a round-trip flight. Some, I am sure, simply wanted to extend any final remaining hours with their sons before we were to be locked away.

One thing we all had in common was that among our personal possessions we each carried a one-way airplane ticket from Green Bay (GRB) to "back home" (in my case, HOU), prepaid and open-ended. The order required us to obtain the ticket in advance. Decades of young men, homesick or for other reasons, predictably would jump ship, parachute out, or be shown the door. The return ticket was a safety net on reserve. It saved the Alexians big money; air travel was expensive.

My parents had driven me from Beaumont to Houston's Hobby Airport, about a ninety-minute trip on Interstate Highway 10. We traveled alternately through piney woods and flooded rice fields, punctuated by an occasional refinery belching out something obnoxious. July is hot and muggy in Southeast Texas. I was anxious to see what Illinois and Wisconsin had to offer. We spoke little to each other during the short road trip. Leo, my Catholic father, and Marian, my Presbyterian mother, both with an unspoken "He'll be back" demeanor, wished me well. They saw me off to my new life on a Braniff Airways nonstop flight bound for Chicago's O'Hare Airport.

We parted without drama or a sense of finality as Mother and Dad watched me board an ugly, pastel-painted Boeing 727. As if I was simply departing on a school trip and would return later that day, we turned from each other, emotionless, and I strolled down the jet bridge, boarded the aircraft, and took my window seat. My parents seemed to acknowledge no permanency in my departure; there was no sense of an absolute or final "goodbye." Perhaps, although I have never asked them, they may have stood in the gate area to watch the plane push back and taxi, choosing to reserve any emotion until I was gone.

My "so long" was not so warm either. I left as we had lived—distant and reluctant to show emotion—shying away from physical affection. The whole "stiff upper lip" discipline is part of our family. I cannot even recall if, as I left, I received a hug from Mom or a handshake from Dad. I do know that to be demonstrative, even when I am very fond of someone, has always been very difficult for me. However, part and parcel of all our household coolness and reserve was the unwritten rule about no yelling, screaming, or slamming of doors—behaviors I often encountered as I observed my friends in their "close" families. Ours was always closer to *businesslike*, with all the advantages and disadvantages that come with that dynamic.

My journey that day was not my first flight. It was, however, my first time on a jet airplane. I am just old enough to have had an earlier experience in a Douglas DC-3 tail-dragger, a twin-engine, propeller-driven workhorse that evolved from its original military use into basic civilian transport. Passengers entered aft, near the tail, and climbed up the steep cabin incline toward the cockpit until they reached their assigned seats. My older brother, Michael, had once—several years earlier, but never forgotten—treated me to a ticket for a half-hour flight from our local airport in Beaumont to Houston and back. After that, I was totally hooked on flying. Later in life, I would get my pilot's license and use it to make a living. Later, my father would chuckle when he told others I decided join the Alexian Brothers for no other reason than that reaching them involved air travel.

Many years later, a window seat for me would become intolerable, but not that day. This was a completely new adventure. It was exciting, yet unsettling. With my nose pressed to the scratched, inner plastic window and peering through smudged airplane glass with dead bugs in between, I watched 1,200 miles of Texas, Oklahoma, Arkansas, Missouri, and Illinois pass distortedly underneath me. At one point during those three hours of reflection that I have learned is virtually unique to air travel, the gravity of my decision began to overwhelm me. Two hours into the trip, how could I be having homesickness on the first day? Today, psychologists would call it separation anxiety.

Then, though, it was all about the forward momentum of the plane itself, thoughts about my modest belongings, thoughts about the future, all merged with an inevitable realization that—right now—I had moved beyond the point of no return. I would not be coming home between semesters, during the holidays, or at spring break. My big permanent decision was at altitude and on cruise control. I needed release; I cried, mostly inside but a little outside, too. But in the dryness of the pressurized cabin, those few tears dried quickly. No one saw.

The novelty of airline food, along with one of those free miniature packs of Marlborough cigarettes that the airlines provided in those days, added to my adventure. Not a serious inhaler at the time, I lit up and fouled the cabin, as selfish smokers were allowed to do then. For a few moments, it helped to make me feel grown up and allowed me to get past my doubts and fear of monastic failure—for the moment.

My mind drifted back five or so years earlier. A neighbor kid came over with smuggled cigarettes and we snuck away to the wooded area next door. We lit up. "Pat?" My father shouted from the open distant kitchen window. "If you want to smoke, come inside." In a flash, I had been caught. I will always remember Dad's effective choice of words. He couldn't say don't; because he did. He rolled his own cigarettes and smoked like a furnace. But he was an adult with the power of dissuasion, and I didn't.

Brother Cletus met me at the arrival gate at Chicago's O'Hare Airport. Known more recently as Brother John Howard (having been given the opportunity to return to his birth name as the order "modernized"), Brother Cletus was a recruiter for the Alexian Brothers. I had corresponded with him as I investigated the various Catholic orders of men engaged in the vocation of health care, a career path I had decided upon during my senior year of Catholic high school.

With an intense interest in medicine and my years of experience doing volunteer work at local hospitals, I felt this was a good fit for me. Desperate to be, somehow, a medical professional, but lacking the money or the smarts for medical school, I weighed my skills and options.

As a part of the application process, Brother Cletus came to Beaumont to visit with me and my family. On that crisp, fall day, several months before my 1966 spring graduation, the very soft-spoken yet gregarious Alexian arrived. I was impressed with the black clerical suit he was wearing and the collar that was priest-like, yet different. I imagined myself proudly dressed as an Alexian Brother someday as he painted an idyllic picture of their monastery in Gresham, Wisconsin. This was where Alexian postulants and novices lived, worked, and studied.

Br John Howard–2005. Recruited the author for the Alexians in 1966
Photo by Curt Knoke

By way of definition and contrast: a brother is a man who is a member of a religious congregation or order and usually lives in community with other brothers. He is not ordained but does take vows of poverty, chastity, and obedience. Priests are ordained in the Church and celebrate or administer the sacraments such as Mass and Confession. A priest may or may not be a member of an order and live in community; he may serve in a diocese under a bishop and usually, in that situation, works and lives in a parish. I had no interest serving in the priesthood.

Since there were two nuns and a priest in our family at the time, I concluded, quite logically, that I was destined to combine my medical hopes with a religious calling. As we sat on our couch listening to Brother Cletus ask probing questions about my intent, scholastics, family life, and Catholic background, we also explored my German heritage. I must have passed inspection; shortly thereafter, I received a letter inviting me to join the Alexian Brothers. No one was excited but me. "Well, if that's what you want to do…" was the typical reaction I got from friends and family when I announced my future.

Already shipped to Wisconsin ahead of me, in a cheap but new Sears and Roebuck footlocker, was all I would need to begin the monastic life. As I recall, the list of items we were to provide for our arrival included the following:

- One pair of black dress shoes
- One pair of tennis or athletic shoes
- 1 week's supply of plain white t-shirts
- A swimsuit
- A jock strap
- A bathrobe
- Several pairs of white athletic socks
- Several pairs of black dress socks
- One black tie
- A few white, long-sleeved dress shirts
- One pair of black, cuffed dress pants
- A week's worth of white boxer shorts
- Winter outerwear
- A few pairs of jeans
- A few long- and short-sleeved casual shirts
- The most basic of toiletries and deodorants OK, fragrances NOT OK.

After I retrieved my one checked bag, Brother Cletus went out of his way to show me the city. He drove toward the Loop, where the Eisenhower Expressway was built so that it went right through the main post office structure. Chicago, with its high-rise buildings and bustling sidewalks and streets, was simply jaw dropping for a boy from the swamps. I savored the tour, knowing that my classmates and I would soon be transplanted from this fascinating "den of iniquity." I took a hard and long look.

The building at 1200 West Belden Avenue was home to Alexian Brothers Hospital. When we arrived, a brother showed me to a room in the school of nursing. The place buzzed with men in crisp white male nursing uniforms, coming and going with large medical textbooks. I had worn a similar uniform of white pants and a "Dr. Ben Casey" button-over loose-fitting smock while I volunteered at our little hospital in Beaumont.

I was encouraged—but not ordered—to stick close to my room. Since I was a relative stranger to obedience—at home I ran free but not lawless, more or less—I was not enthusiastic about beginning a cloistered existence so soon. Slowly and carefully, somewhat guiltily, on the lookout for "men in black," I ventured through the halls, looking for fellow Alexian recruits. Of course, I would not have known one if I had seen him. We did, eventually, gather for awkward introductions and to eat dinner later that evening. What a mixed bag of young men we were! Fat and skinny boys, tall and short boys, brown, white, and pale white boys—different, yet so much the same—that was our postulant class that summer.

For most of the next day, we took written psychological exams. The Alexians needed to know just how crazy (or not) each individual was in this odd group of mostly eighteen-year-old men with raging hormones—young beings about to launch into a life of poverty, chastity, and obedience. I never doubted that my scores and performance would doom me to one day use my return flight ticket. The following day we started early with Mass. After breakfast, we gathered our belongings and the brothers took us to Chicago's Union Station, where, together as a class and completely without Alexian supervision, we boarded a Chicago and Northwestern train to Wisconsin. George Martinez, from Kansas, was the oldest and was consequently placed in charge of keeping us with the group. He was also responsible for our safe arrival at our destination: Gresham, Wisconsin.

The train crept out of the terminal and passed slowly through the section of town known as the Loop. The C&NW crawled only a little bit faster in the northern suburbs, with their closely spaced road crossings, whistle blaring incessantly. Some of us agreed that walking to Wisconsin might be more efficient than riding the train.

Just when it looked like we had escaped the dense population of Chicago and Cook County, the train came to a full stop. We were somewhere in Lake County, Illinois. We sat and waited. And waited some more. Then the train began to move again, but in reverse. Finally, with no explanation from the conductor and perhaps twenty minutes of backtracking, the train ground to a halt, we waited some more, and then (as it turned out) we were on our way.

Suburbia gave way to rural, and rural gave way to farmland. With our snail's pace start behind us and a little wind beneath our wings, we finally began to feel that we would actually make it to the monastery. Many of us made attempts at conversation with the guy next to us or the fellow across the aisle.

My train seatmate, Jim Lehman, and I talked for some time, feeling a kinship of sorts because we were both from Texas. He was from Midland, in West Texas, and he was an Eagle Scout. We bonded immediately and soon decided that we would present a united front to the world in the future. His mature demeanor and adult height suggested additional leadership qualities, and such qualities did, indeed, surface during the following months and his Alexian years.

Next stop was the Great Lakes Naval station, where a few sailors left the train for their basic training post. Soon the train rolled into Kenosha and deposited many passengers who appeared to be Chicago daily commuters. In this, the first major Wisconsin city beyond the Illinois border, our northbound train took on only a handful of additional travelers. The load was already light. Then, as we repeated the arrival and departure process in Milwaukee, I remember being almost obsessively fascinated with the Miller Beer motto, which appeared on billboard after billboard: "The beer that made Milwaukee famous." Thereafter, from time to time, Lake Michigan itself would come into view until the track veered toward the northwest.

For most of us, I discovered, this was the first time out of our own state or climate. For me, this was an eyes-wide-open adventure. I was taking in views, sounds, even smells I had never experienced before. Seeing cities that had infrastructures different from my Texas home was something of an education in itself. A brewery, grain silos, and rail service for people; all of this was foreign to me. As the scenery gliding by the window began to change from rolling farmland to the more wooded northeastern Wisconsin forests, I delightedly soaked in the contrast. Sticking my nose out between the coaches at each stop, I noted that the air was increasingly dryer and crisper, smelling distinctly of evergreen—mixed, of course, with the odor of diesel fuel.

The entire class both anxiously and eagerly anticipated our arrival at our final destination. Someone in the know spread the word that we were soon to pull into our stop, Shawano, which for a short time ratcheted up our group's enthusiasm, further increasing the volume of our conversations. At about that time, the off-the-wall thought crossed my mind that we had been traveling back in a "time machine" on rails. We had started the day in the modern hub of the Midwest and had made our way through cities and towns of lesser sophistication, places exhibiting fewer signs of having embraced the latter half of the twentieth century. All at once I noticed that the hum of conversation had faded and that many, if not most, of the young men accompanying me had fallen silent, entertaining deeply personal thoughts not meant to be shared. Apparently, our own pace was symbolically slowing, too, as the train came to a grinding halt.

Next to the classic, wooden depot with its high-pitched roof and sign that read SHAWANO stood three men of the cloth; clearly distinguished by the black clerical garb they always wore in public. Two were dressed as I remembered Brother Cletus when he visited our family. The other wore the distinctive collar of a Roman Catholic priest. Our reception committee proved to be warm and welcoming, and, with little delay, they whisked us away in the three cars they had driven to the station.

Green! I was struck with the rich greenness of the town's lawns and the somewhat darker green shade of the sturdy trees protecting strong-looking two-story homes set back from the streets, with concrete or brick sidewalks. Shawano looked like an illustrated book. For me, it was a Tom Sawyer sort of place. The houses appeared to be well maintained, yards painstakingly manicured—all in all, real estate that was ready for the winter elements. Soon we reached the edge of town, and we knew that we were now inevitably on our way to our new home in Gresham.

Our small westbound caravan left a main highway after crossing one of the Wolf River bridges and began to zigzag west-northwest through farmland. These, mostly straight roads were narrow and required courtesy with opposing traffic. Unlike the train, this time we were up close and could see men tending to cattle and tractors. Homes with beautiful gardens, barns, and large acreage had professionally painted signs in their front yards proclaiming their affiliation with some large dairy company. Dogs barked warning-welcomes at our passing.

We rolled on silently, taking in the pastoral countryside and sparse neighborhood, to our destination. This was the late afternoon, and there were chores being performed in barns and out of view from the roads. Cows were being milked and other animals getting their feed. Our brother-driver announced during another left turn that we were on Butternut Road and we would soon see the monastery just ahead on the left. He pointed out farm-land and the chicken coop to his even more quiet and subdued passengers.

Next was a clearing, a field obviously for sport or recreation with soccer goals, unheard of in Southeast Texas. We had slowed to make another turn after a block-long buffer of forest. Immediately after that was a drive ahead with an elaborate stone entrance and another one just like it one hundred yards farther west.

It was not until our procession had passed that natural stand of trees that we could see the novitiate. There, in the middle of beauti-ful northern Wisconsin, stood our new home, school, and family. The length of the modern stone institution stood two hundred yards back from but parallel to the road. My first impression was that it looked like a university. Forest framed it on three sides, and choice trees spared at the time of construction decorated the groomed and huge freshly cut front lawn in the foreground.

Passing the first entrance, the cars filed, one by one, into the last drive. It was lined by tall, thin evergreens and paved with a salmon-colored stone pulverized to a pea size. The driveway passed by a residen-tial building with four attached garages. It looked like it did not belong but had obviously preceded the construction of the monastery.

A gasoline pump for fueling vehicles stood nearby. The path in allowed you to take the *U*-shaped driveway paralleling the long mon-astery and back out to the main road. Another option was the rounded driveway serving another striking and less institutional-looking attached wing. Our drivers took the circular approach with a full stop in front of an impressive wooden shuttered building covered in ivy.

Alexian Brothers Novitiate circa 1975
Photo provided by Jake Hendzel

As if welcoming a motorcade of emissaries for a state visit, there emerged several young men in black. Their white collars looked familiar, but they were dressed in the traditional habit of the Alexian Brothers. All wore a black ankle-length tunic buttoned from the neck to a wide black leather belt cinching the garment at the waist. Other greeters also wore a black chest-wide scapular that slipped over their head, resting on their shoulders around the neck and falling both front and back to the feet. They lined the columned portico of the magnificent structure that we could not fully appreciate until making the circular turn to face it.

Weary from the cramped cars and all-day train travel, we tumbled out of the cars to eager handshakes from our new brothers. Undoubtedly, the receiving line had studied our names and hometowns. In the uneasy moments of trying to remember "Brother This" and "Brother That," who all looked identical except for their faces, we surveyed our new circumstances. As if someone had whispered in my ear to do so, it was then that I had the delight of glancing over my shoulder to catch my first glimpse of the river and falls.

This was Peters Hall, we were told as we stepped one at a time through great leaded glass double doors into its foyer. Wood was everywhere. Finely polished wooden floors reflected back the image of more monastic men standing just inside to receive us. They descended wooden stairs that had multiple landings. They came from richly paneled rooms off the main entrance and invited us into an elaborate library rivaling any I had ever seen. That wood flooring was everywhere, and in this larger room, I could see that natural pegs, rather than nails, had been used to construct it. Coffee and light refreshments awaited us.

I do not believe any of us knew what to expect upon our arrival. I certainly had not anticipated the grandeur into which we were received. Fine touches I had only seen in film, books, and on rare occasions in public buildings surrounded us. Missing was plush and ornate furniture. There were no art objects of great value. No vases, and few expensively framed paintings or assorted treasures were in view. The structure and fixed adornments were extraordinary, but the furnishings were tastefully institutional and modest. The mansion, stripped of opulence, competed within a dichotomy of sterility.

It seemed that every direction you looked, a wide and deep fireplace with a finely crafted mantel looked back, promising warmth on another day. Rearing back in one of the chairs, unable to hide my involuntary yawn earned from the long day, the ceiling revealed impressive artisan detail in plaster and crown molding throughout. An inviting sunroom opened off the library and transitioned to a more informal tile surface and feeling. This crescent-shaped indoor/outdoor room with a wall of windows looked south onto the back monastery grounds that sloped down to the water's edge. As intended, this sunroom would prove to be transitional and a part of the mansion in the winter yet an extension of the out-of-doors when warm.

A few of us gravitated to this solarium. Its crank-out casement windows were open to catch a breeze and to hear Freeborn Falls. Most of the falls and the river were already shaded from the setting sun, except for some shafts of the "magic light" associated with that afternoon hour. The constant resonance of the falls helped to wind down our day. I breathed in dry summer air unavailable at my Texas home during a muggy July.

The brothers announced that we would soon have dinner in the library after an introduction to our living quarters. We returned to the foyer and climbed the wide grand stairs from the entry. The white painted banister and steps took us to a landing and a 180-degree turn up another flight to the second floor. The same detail of fine finish below was seen here, but with far less natural woodwork. Large ornate doors with polished brass hardware led to what I was sure would be our rooms.

But I was mistaken. Our trail of big-eyed recruits snaked behind Brother Pius. Thin and slightly hunched over, as tall men often are, Pius led us up another two flights, terminating at the third floor. The feeling here was quite different. Somehow, instinctively, our chatter had ceased. This level in no way had the same presentation as the first or second floors. While not quite attic-like, it was clearly spartan.

In the dark and with subdued lighting, we learned this was to be our home for six months. We had already learned in the library that Brother Pius was our Postulant Director and that he was the individual to whom we should go for our needs and direction in this first stage of our formation to become an Alexian. Pius explained that our living level was one of the cloistered areas and strict silence was to be observed here. Exemptions to this rule were mentioned. His tour explanation for us was one of the exceptions. Fire was another.

On the south side of this third and uppermost floor, the architectural plan and layout had been remodeled from the days it had served as storage and quarters for the staff. The Alexians had reconfigured the top floor and created cubicles measuring about eight by eleven feet. The walls did not extend to the ceiling and stood about eight feet high, leaving a feeling of additional spaciousness yet maintaining privacy. No insulation or spacing existed between the thin divides separating the sixteen or so rooms.

Each area assigned to a particular postulant was numbered and had a door with no lock. Inside, it contained a single iron bed frame, covered by a military surplus woolen blanket. An additional blanket lay folded on the narrow bed. Our cubicles had no individual plumbing. One item decorated the walls—a crucifix. A mirror was mounted at face level for grooming. The only other furniture was a dresser with drawers, a metal desk, and a wooden chair. Greeting us at the foot of each bed were the footlockers we had all shipped from home. We, at the bottom of the pecking order, lived at the top and most austere. Our level could be described as a garret for a grand hotel.

Brother Pius gave us half an hour to freshen ourselves and use the community bathroom facilities before we were to come back down. The facilities were never intended to accommodate a group of our size, so we took shifts, struggling with our new handicap of monastic silence. This would be the first of many exercises in brotherly compromise. I spent most of this time surveying the contents of my footlocker and hanging a few clothes. Lured to my half of a shared window bisected by the divider wall, I peered out at the falls once again in the fading light. I sensed my unseen neighbor quietly doing the same only inches away.

Never late for anything, I made an early return to the library to find it transformed. Banners with welcome signs hung and music was now playing. Greeting my fellow postulants and me were even more Alexians in the black habit with younger faces. Some wore a crisp white kitchen apron and stood behind a buffet line, offering to learn our names and serve us food from a spectacular bounty that seemed out of nowhere.

Hot dogs, hamburgers, chili, beans, buns, and m Relish, condiments, ice cream, and other deserts invited us to return. At the end of the serving line was an assortment of cold drinks. Alongside them was a worn heavy cardboard box with twenty-four divided sections containing two dozen beers of three different varieties. Several of us indulged, thinking it might be our last. So far, the poverty angle wasn't looking so bad.

Brother Michael, an aged, Nordic-looking giant of a man with a full head of white hair, made his way around the room. His significant limp did not slow down his gregarious nature. Dressed in a chef's white smock and pants and sporting the appropriate tall pleated kitchen hat, he thrust his big German hand out to each new postulant to learn their name.

Brother Michael was the magic behind all of the edible spread we were consuming, particularly the baked items. It was clear that he delighted in seeing everyone push away from a table full from his creations. I do not know why, but Brother Michael's "need to feed" reminded me of an elderly nun at a hospital in Beaumont. She was fixated on filling stomachs. *Sister Cholesterol*, whose real name I've forgotten over the years, was known to walk around the two-hundred-bed hospital with fried eggs stashed away in the folds and pockets of her white habit. I never accepted her generosity but was amused by her eccentricity.

It made sense that routine had been broken at the monastery to accommodate our welcome and arrival. The overwhelming reception and eagerness seemed genuinely enthusiastic, particularly coming from the younger brothers. Our new postulant class, totaling fourteen, learned only days before that several had just made the transition from postulant to novice. As in any fraternity, I am sure there was some relief among

GRAND SILENCE

n that here was a new group, poised to endure the lower rank they once occupied.

Without being asked, most of us pitched in to clear away the tables and restore order to the library with the efficiency of an elaborate magic act. The entire community then gathered in the chapel, located in the middle of the monastery, for evening prayers. In the back and on both sides of the marbled chapel sat the older brothers wearing the scapulars. In front of them and on the left side sat the novices. Opposite was our class of postulants, unsure of when to sit, stand, or kneel, and fumbling with unfamiliar hymnals and prayer books.

The solemnity of this exercise, known as Vespers, was in stark contrast to the festive atmosphere we had just left. We were being eased into the monastic routine: a process that had been honed over the ages since the Black Plague and Alexian origins. Following Vespers, we joined the novices in their recreation time. On the eastern end of the long monastery, opposite the mansion, was a three-story wing called the administration building. The entire third floor was dedicated as the recreation room. In daylight, it had a commanding view of the countryside to the north, east, and south.

That night while ascending the stairs for the first time with the novices, my fellow postulant and cubical neighbor, Tom Scholler, attempted to engage Brother Andrew, a new novice, in conversation. Firing back, Brother Andrew abruptly informed Tom that the stairwell was a part of the cloistered area and we were not allowed to speak there. Tom never forgot the verbal exchange. Today he fondly remembers the moment six months later, as a novice himself, when he, too, lectured a new postulant about the rules of silence. That new recruit, a down to earth Alabama country boy, snapped back, "Kiss my ass." Times were a-changing.

Thomas Scholler Jr.-2004. Classmate with author in 1966-67
Photo by Curt Knoke

All manner of art supplies, hobby projects, and board games were available to us in the recreation area. Playing cards, musical instruments, and a record player with no current recordings stood ready. The same assortment of beer and soda was waiting for us. We were informed the beverages were routine. This was an order originating in Germany. Beer was traditional and no big deal. Some things were looking up.

Noticeably absent were the middle-aged and older brothers we had met earlier. Their day unwound far away in Peters Hall on the second floor, where there was radio, television, newspapers, and tobacco. Brother Pius, however, joined us this first evening and explained that for the first few days the postulants would be on an amended schedule. We would be allowed to sleep until 7:00 a.m. We would be spared the 4:50 a.m. bell until we became acclimated. More than one glance was exchanged upon that questionable news. Yes, ten minutes until five sounded more civil.

Like roaches scurry when lights are turned on, the same thing happened when ours went off. At 9:00 p.m., an unknown person cycled the room lighting off and on, snuffing out any conversation in mid sentence. Grand Silence had begun.

Robotically and in a hushed discipline, the recreation room was restored to order and novices began to disappear. Their rooms were one floor below in the same wing. Brother Pius motioned for us to follow him for the long hike back to Peters Hall and our third-floor cubicles. Quietly, we put ourselves to bed, alone now in our cells. The running water of the river falls provided a lullaby for our new reality.

Our introduction to the schedule was rather swift. Soon, the annoying school-like bell was ringing for us at 4:50 every morning, summoning us to prayer at 5:00. The Alexians had an institution to run, and it ran like German clockwork. Every six months, new postulants would arrive, immediately following the previous class that had become novices. Those new novices would remain an additional twenty-four months. And so it went, with young men staying there two and a half years before moving on to further training in areas suitable to them and the order of brothers.

In a low-key ceremony in the chapel on July 21, our class of fourteen was invested in the habit worn by postulants. Each of us was presented with a dismal gray cassock with a round non-rigid collar. The garment had a cloth belt and buttoned across one shoulder. I do not recall one of us having a garb that fit properly. If yours was right around the waist, it was either too long or too short, and vice versa. Many were getting threadbare from years of recycling. This may have been our first lesson in humility. Whether in religion or the military, a uniform has a way of siphoning off individuality. We were now all ugly duckling postulant monks.

A division of labor was absolutely necessary to make a place like that run well. I am not sure how it was decided who would do what. Perhaps the psychological testing in Chicago was forwarded and the results used to pigeonhole us.

Brother Pius, we learned, was another Texan from Amarillo. I hoped the Texan fellowship would buy favors. It seemed to work out, at least in my situation. Jim Lehman, the other Texan, and I were earmarked for the boiler room and outdoor labor. Perhaps they concluded that we must be rugged if we were from Texas. Jim and I used our tough and rugged mantle to every advantage. Surely, they decided, we would do well on a tractor and understand the function of both ends of a cow.

Other postulants found their way to the kitchen under the tutelage of Brother Michael, peeling potatoes or stirring the huge institutional stainless steel soup kettles. We were to learn the myriad of ways boiler generated steam was harnessed as a tool in the kitchen.

There was sewing and tremendous amounts of laundry to be done. The basement was outfitted with giant industrial washing, drying, and folding equipment. Both novices and postulants worked side by side in that duty as well as in all the other routine chores that existed to make the place work. While we were low on the totem pole, we were not exclusively given the dirty work. Undesirable tasks were rotated among all.

I was delighted with my lot in the work life there. The day Brother Cajetan hitched a trailer to the pickup truck and drove Jim and me down to the chicken coop was an exception. The very quiet and shy man left us there with two shovels and instructions to transfer a decade of chicken droppings from the roosts to the trailer. Cajetan came back at midday to return our load and us to the monastery in time for lunch. We were unfit to join our brethren at the table.

Wearing our habit was required at all times while in the monastery, but there were exceptions. When working outside or involved in a dirty project, we wore ordinary work clothes. It was a challenge to make the change back into the habit and adhere to the strict schedules of prayer, meals, and formation instruction. On exceptionally warm days, the extra layer of clothing was an additional burden to those who had come in from working outside.

Duties inside the cloister usually meant wearing the black habit of the Alexians or the gray of the postulants. Aprons for cooking and other tasks kept us compliant. Then there was Brother Michael. He was a master at baking and other delights, and his enthusiastic style of cooking created a cloud of flour that made him look a bit like a sanitized Pigpen from *Charlie Brown*. If he did not wear white, he would have been wearing white by the end of the day. His chef's attire was one of the habit exceptions. Assistants gave him wide berth in his kitchen to avoid the dusting from his delicious crafts.

With the dress requirements, a little extra sweat and grime was a small price to pay to be out of the confining walls. Chores on the farm, with an opportunity to drive some of the vehicles and a large variety of projects, were liberating. I enjoyed the sense of achievement. Accomplished in nothing, I had always enjoyed mechanical endeavors. Building, repairing, and operating tools suited me. Brothers Cajetan and Simeon either sensed that, or we discovered it together.

When I was five years old, my parents learned that I had Hemophilia A. The diagnosis did complicate my growing up years—my mother could not help warning other supervising adults that I could spontaneously bleed to death at any moment within a few seconds. This, of course, was not true. I knew it and she knew it. The Alexians were perhaps the first environment in which I found myself doing dangerous things and surviving without concern. I enjoyed playing a role in keeping that physical plant up and running. I did not hemorrhage; I thrived with a sense of accomplishment.

Jim Lehman had a practical and can-do side to himself as well. We were usually tapped as a team and given the heavy work. Together we endured an unforgettable project. The boiler room was a scary place, with all the pipes and valves knocking and hissing. Pumps to draw water from the river and a well intermittently buzzed with regulators clicking and clacking, opening and closing. The heavy equipment was intimidating. It looked and sounded threatening, and it was.

The enormous below-ground room contained two huge coal-fired boilers. One was larger than the other, and they were used alternately according to the season. The constant need to feed and care for them fell on the shoulders of Brother Simeon Pytel. Brother Simeon seemed to be a very wise man of few words. He knew the bowels of the monastery and what made it tick. He had no fear of the fire-breathing boilers and tamed them into submission as they growled.

Soon after we arrived, a decision had been made to convert the plant from coal to oil. New equipment was ordered and the giant, dusty, awful, underground coal bin was not replenished. A new era and technology had arrived at the novitiate. No expert came to install it until Simeon took on the project and the initial dirty work of preparation.

A twelve-thousand-gallon fuel oil tank was ordered and installed to feed the two monsters. The larger boiler was taken offline and allowed to cool for several days. Simeon announced one day that Jim and I would be helping. "Helping," we learned, would consist of Jim and me climbing into the fire chamber of the behemoth. With chisel and hammer in hand, we were to remove the brick and asbestos lining from the cramped interior. Now maybe a good time for the reader to familiarize oneself with the story of *Jonah & the whale*.

The monster had not fully cooled, we learned after cautiously entering it. We would wait an extra day. The next attempt was only a little less like hell. Brick and mortar dust clogged our breathing while we chipped away. Asbestos insulation was a part of the material we were removing. I am not fond of confined spaces and don't mind admitting to some claustrophobia.

Amid the heat, debris, dehydration, and two men squatting to work, I kept an eye on the heavy metal door. We feared pranksters, in silence, might think it funny to briefly lock us in. Brother Simeon was amused at our resemblance to coal miners when we emerged. We watched with pride when Brother Simeon ignited the new fuel supply and a hot jet of fiery oil shot in, resuscitating the beast. It was one down and one to go. The twin boilers and their vital role would later prove to be calamitous in inexperienced hands.

The religious life attracts very different people. Some of the traits less suited to the outside world are a better fit in a monastic setting. I found Brother Cajetan to be very patient and tolerant when showing me how to do something new. Practicing silence extended, to a lesser degree, during our workday. The only dialogue allowed was that which was necessary to complete a task.

So it was with an extreme economy of words that Cajetan managed us in our chores. Profoundly shy and unable to look me or others in the eye through his Coke-bottle eyeglasses, Brother Cajetan was perfectly suited for the monastic life. I will always wonder if his manner with the older brothers was different, without novices and postulants present. After his recent death, I learned of his heroics as a medic in World War II. I never saw it, but his ability to pick up a saxophone and belt out a tune then retreat to his quiet demeanor was legendary among the senior brothers. In his later years at the beautiful Signal Mountain, Tennessee, retirement home, he was known to swing a mean tennis racket, which is what he was doing when he passed away.

Cajetan introduced me to two tractors. Why me, I will never know. Perhaps my high school "permanent record" had revealed that I was experienced in driving the school tractor to level the football field and manicure the baseball diamond. You see, high school had prepared me for something. Somehow, I just fit the part. This monastery was a self-sufficient institution in the middle of nowhere. Someone had to do it. Compared to others in our community, I was rugged enough to be up to the challenge. My duties allowed me to exercise the free spirit lone wolf within me.

My fellow brothers were content in their more genteel assignments. Less of a team player and more of a maverick, I was energized by my more harsh duties. When the work schedule rotated and all in training were shuffled around, my chores never changed. I drew the conclusion that I was either good outside or unwanted inside. I was relegated to needed labor beyond the confines of the monastery.

If I was not mowing the lawn with the little John Deere, I was plowing snow or hauling some load with the larger and more menacing tractor. My connection with the religious and cloistered duties was limited. However rewarding it was, my work was coarse and not of the contemplative nature experienced within the walls. The degree of ceremonial and spiritual exposure others were experiencing escaped me. I did not feel I was ready for the pomp and ritual. The Alexians may have sensed that too.

I think I had let it be known that I was experienced in mixing automotive paint at my father's auto parts store. While my classmates were perhaps preparing the chapel altar for some High Holy Mass, I was up at the North Farm masking and spray-painting the surplus school bus owned by the brothers.

Brother Cajetan could not have found paint in an uglier baby blue color if he had tried. Likely, it had been given to us, as the brothers were loved at the time by most of their neighbors. Again, I was proud of the job, and no one complained about the hue when we piled onboard for a field trip to let off a little steam. That old beat-up blue bus was just large enough to accommodate the full census of novices and postulants in 1966 at the Alexian Brothers Gresham, Wisconsin, monastery. The numbers were dwindling. We did not know we were a sign of the changing times.

Like clockwork, and exactly six months to the day, our time arrived to be recognized as an Alexian Brother. Our original fourteen had fallen to only eight survivors. We anticipated the sense of accomplishment we would be allowed to display to our visiting relatives. We had not been allowed to speak with family except for an occasional handwritten letter.

On that crisp clear January day in 1967, my mother, father, and two brothers arrived, but our class had been sequestered away from our families. We were eight men who were soon to take on individual new names. The atmosphere was palpable. The postulant director and the novice master were skilled in the art of building anticipation. The novitiate had acquired a fresh deep shroud of snow; it had taken on the appearance of a Christmas card. In our ragtag postulant gray garb, we, as a class, moved toward the chapel. Weeks before, we had been given the opportunity to submit three names in order of preference, from which one would be selected. From this day forward, we would forever be known by that new name.

I will confess the ceremony known as investiture was a blur. I experienced the broad spectrum of emotions, from pride that goes along with reaching a goal to fear that I was making such a public and permanent commitment. Throughout the Alexian ritual, I still had no confirmation that my family was actually there. I had yet to lay eyes on them.

One by one and according to age, we gladly gave up the candidacy status of a postulant. The black habit and white collar of the novice was fitted around us, and we were given our religious name. "Gordon." What? Who? No one ever discussed the name Gordon with me! Whatever happened to Ian, Luke, or Zeno? Perhaps there had been a mistake, because it certainly was not one of the names I had chosen and submitted. I came to the realization that I was the only new novice who had not been given one of his three choices. Now, I know Zeno may have sounded a little odd, but in fact it was my grandfather's middle name. My humility and obedience were immediately tested. We left the chapel proud and anxious to connect with family. A stolen side-glance proved mine had arrived. I beamed with accomplishment.

I had developed rapture for the Wisconsin outdoor winter. I wanted to share this with my family during our painfully short visit. It may have been genetic. As a young man, my father had spent some of his early teenage years in Denver, Colorado. There, he learned to ice skate; he was delighted to strap on monastic skates after so many decades. My family was not dressed to fit the frigid occasion. Nonetheless, we marched out to a pond and watched my father perform his solo version of the Ice Capades.

In the early 1950s, my dad had had the vision to acquire a Kodak 8mm movie camera and projector. Leo brought the camera with him to Gresham. Mom and Dad are no longer living, but they have been memorialized with silent film at the monastery. My dad went 'round and 'round on the frozen cesspool as if competing in the Winter Olympics.

It came time for them to leave. My brother, Kelley, was anxious for the train ride back to Chicago. Michael, my older brother, had documented the events with his still camera skills and was soon to be deployed to Vietnam. My thin mother, Marian, was looking forward to extracting her open-toed high-heeled shoes from the snow.

Our resident monastic dog's name was Alpine. He was a St. Bernard and dumb as a rock. He looked like he had come from central casting; the only thing missing was the little barrel of brandy around his neck. Alpine was convinced that it was his job to be in the middle of everybody and everything. Alpine did his best to perform as a canine cleric. He anointed everything within his reach with slobber and copious amounts of drool. He sensed the Rick family was fond of dogs—he was right—and adopted us by helping me hug, shake hands, and wave goodbye to my folks.

Saddened, I returned to the warm novitiate inside. I found my fellow classmates dealing with the same down from our high. As for Alpine, he was not welcome inside and this was to be one of the last times I would see him. The St. Bernard had a propensity for crossing the river and the waterfall to reach the nearby train tracks. Neighbors would tell us he enjoyed sitting between the two rails as if to defy approaching locomotives. He miscalculated one day.

It was one clear cold February night near my birth date. I don't recall who or why the first brother stepped outside on the fire escape. A few more stepped out. Whatever the attraction was, their exclamations, as if awed by a fireworks display, made me curious. We were being treated to a celestial display known as the aurora borealis or northern lights. Some never left their chair to get up and come take a look. Others, like myself, chose to start "grand silence" early that evening. The phenomena had made us contemplative and speechless, anyway. It was one of my never forget and breathtaking life experiences.

A daily routine in the winter included inspecting our method for managing our sewer waste. When Jennie Peters built the mansion, a septic tank was sufficient for that one structure. In 1955 when the novitiate was completed, the existing solution was inadequate. A cesspool measuring about 150 feet by 100 feet was dug a few hundred yards east of the monastery and adjacent to the Red River.

The process was simple. Our waste was piped to the end of the cesspool nearest the monastery. The organic solids floated to the top and the inorganic fell to the bottom. The natural occurring bacteria in the pool broke the organic material into liquid. Ordinarily, the resulting clear liquid was supposed to flow out the far side into the surrounding earth. Ours, however allowed the discharge to reach a certain level and then overflowed through a pipe into the river. To this day, I am not sure if that complied with state or county regulations at the time. Most assuredly, the effluent would not be allowed to discharge into the river today.

It was necessary to check the overflow daily in the winter. Since the pond would freeze over by several inches, a simple but ingenious apparatus with a high intensity light bulb was concentrated at the point of release. I would make the slog through the snow and wooded trail to verify that the light was on and melting the surrounding ice to maintain the runoff. Ignoring this duty would be the undoing of life as we knew it.

We made the most of waste. In the spirit of humility, our cesspool, with its gray green ice, served as a downsized hockey rink when frozen (in fact, this was the very "pond" where my father demonstrated his prowess on figure skates). Brother Jeffrey Callander of Winnipeg was a tough little Canadian and swung a brutal hockey stick. I was among those who had never worn ice skates. Our athletic equipment storage had enough pairs for those who wanted to brave Jeffrey's challenge. We were cautious not to venture too close to the thinner ice near the bright light.

I had the opportunity to catch up with Brother Jeffrey while writing this book. He is the only novice during my time there who remained an Alexian Brother four decades later. I had been searching through the Alexian archives when Brother Jeffrey was making an annual visit to the Chicago headquarters from his missionary post in the Philippines. I recall Jeffrey as the most saint-like man in the monastery. Never an unkind comment came from his French Canadian face bearing a constant gregarious grin and a permanent five o'clock shadow.

Jeffrey had spent a few weeks roaming Chicago in search of leftover medical supplies and equipment. He had become an accomplished beggar. In the spirit of the order in the late middle ages, Brother Jeffrey pleaded, and some gave to his wish list for the rural Philippines. He had single-handedly amassed an almost fully loaded seagoing container before his return to the mission.

Skillfully, he cajoled me into helping him. Actually, *shanghaied* might be a better description of his technique. We spent a day loading heavy medical hardware and supplies until the huge metal bin could take no more. That day gave us the bonding opportunity to renew a friendship and recall the monastery experience. I picked his brain about the details lost over time and my duration there. We ended with a few beers and conversation reminiscent of the novitiate.

I was saddened when he revealed that he had suffered a recent heart attack and doctors had told him to cool it. We said goodbye while a brother grumbled to him about the mess he'd made in the hallway. The charity goods he had worked so hard to acquire—but had no room to take—lined the walls. Shrugging with a grin, he ignored the complaint.

In comparison to so many others, I was a relative short timer at the Gresham monastery. Explaining why today I have such an attachment to the history, have spent so much time, money, and effort writing and documenting people, places, and events surrounding it, is unclear. Perhaps my career and the business travel it entailed facilitated the personal revival. I have tracked down and spoken to so many who left, or had been asked to leave, under a variety of circumstances. Some fabricated their recall to avoid a little embarrassment. The simple daily monastic journal entries offered no explanation when one of us would disappear. Succinctly terse, the record did indicate in code if it was voluntary or involuntary. "Novice So and So *left* today" or "Postulant John Doe *was sent away* today." Without a trace, a face would be missing from the breakfast table. Poker-faced senior brothers ignored silent questioning glances from younger postulants and novices.

The routine when one jumped ship or was thrown overboard was quite efficient. The misfit would attend Mass while Grand Silence was in effect and vanish during the brief period allowed for personal hygiene before the morning meal. There were absolutely no goodbyes. Usually, the Norbertine priest and resident chaplain to the brothers would drive the man out of the way past Lambeau Field to the Green Bay Airport. Although Chaplain dined apart from the Alexians, his absence offered a clue. Word spread quickly in our muted world.

Regardless of how well-liked he was or how long his tenure, the departed always left a partial vacuum. Their work duties were easily absorbed, but in one way or another they were missed. The vacancies seemed to come in waves of two and three. First one, then days later another would vanish. Looking back, the timing sometimes suggested some unacceptable connection between the two. Departure seemed to be triggered by an approaching transition or recent change in status. The cycle of becoming a postulant or the shift into the novitiate never failed to create uncertainty in the mind of those remaining. For hundreds of years, Alexians, as well as other religious hopefuls, have doubted they should enter, hesitated about staying, and questioned their own parting for a myriad of personal reasons.

There is no hiding the fact that religious communities of both men and women have always been an intentional destination for some seeking company with the same gender. The circumstances and atmosphere are ripe for others to stumble into it. If it was not present upon arrival, the awakening, for a few, might surface after settling in. Looking back today I can see the tremendous amount of emotional immaturity among us that snuck past the battery of psychological testing intended to identify misfits. The emotional maturity and capacity for commitment of a seventeen-year-old in 1966, I believe, was far greater then than now, more than four decades later. Religious communities want to see much more mileage on their new recruits these days.

Some of us were only seventeen years old, with little or no intimate experience whatsoever with anyone. Our peers back home were packing their bags to go off to college and raise hell, get naked, and experience drunken conquests. Instead, we found ourselves sequestered under one roof with the strictest of instruction to avoid comradeship with any one person or group. Our set of rules stated:

> Be careful about cultivating particular friendships or the formation of cliques. This can be accomplished by watchfulness over yourself at recreation and on outings, so that you do not associate with the same confrere constantly. Apart from the incidental touchings unavoidably associated with sports, you are not allowed to touch, pinch, pat or hold on to anyone. The first sentence is a requirement for fraternal charity; the latter is necessary for religious modesty and decorum.[3]

I know of no one then who did not struggle with the natural needs for human contact and creating wholesome friendships at the novitiate. Amid the ever-present paranoia of being labeled, we fought the innate tendency to bond with some more than others. It would have taken the qualities of a saint to befriend everyone equally. We all know that is an almost impossible ideal for anyone to achieve, but it was put before us as a goal.

I had come from a family that was not demonstrative. My schooling had exposed me to mates that were the product of huge Italian families. Our proximity to Louisiana and the French Cajun influence only allowed me to be on the outside looking in. I was oblivious to the tight family connections shared by so many during grade and high school. Frankly, I believe it was easy for me to assimilate at the monastery due to my disconnection at home.

---

3   Alexian Brothers, "Rules and Regulations of the Novitiate, 1954," TMs (photocopy), p. 3, Alexian Brothers Provincial Archives, Arlington Heights, Illinois.

In spite of all the twenty-first century revelations of abuse in the church, I did not see any of that type of behavior at Gresham. Over the years, there were novices and postulants that had paired off and eventually left. No evidence or mention of older or senior Alexians preying on younger students came my way then or now.

The Alexian Brothers seem to have been especially vigilant in dealing with the inappropriate behavior so many other communities ignored for years. Looking back at sexual abuse through the microscope today, it appears that communities that were less liberal, more rigid and conservative, with a reduced social secular connection, seem to have fared better. The Alexians are among these, in my opinion.

Our routine was strict but evolving in the wake of the Catholic Church's Second Vatican Council. I am sure every monastery had its spoken history. We heard that not so long before us the monks were required to tuck their shirttails in with a stick to avoid touching themselves. Another tale was the voluntary practice of denial by placing mustard as a topping on the rare occasions the brothers were given ice cream. Other silly things were handed down that were likely fabricated lore, but nonetheless amusing.

There were times when I could clearly see that I was a part of some very interesting men who had seen a little bit of everything. The subject of Chicago, organized crime, fire, FBI, and hoodlums captured our attention. Then, there were many brothers still living who told vivid stories of the lawless days in a big-city hospital emergency room.

We wanted to hear about the cops and robbers. The most notable story was of John Dillinger, the bank robber. J. Edgar Hoover of the FBI was determined to get his man. Led by agent Melvin Purvis, Dillinger was shot dead after being betrayed by the "lady in red" on the evening of July 22, 1934. Brother Vincent Geist proudly reported:

Dillinger was the FBI's #1 criminal, and he was shot by FBI agents as he came out of the movie on North Clark St., and they killed him on the spot....The police took him past three hospitals to get to the brothers.... When they had a dead person they took it to the brothers and had an intern pronounce him dead before taking him to the county morgue. The *Tribune* had a picture of him on a stretcher. Caption was "this picture was taken along of the hospital because the brothers refused to admit him." The police held him up to get a photo for the reporter. We never admitted the dead person....We had to leave a policeman at the hospital door for hours after as people tried to see inside and the streets around the hospital had traffic jams.[4]

With no radio, television, newspapers, or magazines available for the novices, we were desperate for information, even if the news was almost thirty-four years old. The spoken history was rich. The Alexians are one of those congregations that place value on recording and documenting their past. Their internal archives thrive, I would learn years later.

Religious instruction and Alexian history was a part of our training. An amazing peek into the Alexian archives was sparked one day in our classroom by the casual mention of the "St. Louis Exorcism." Well, this sounded interesting, and we pressed for details. An evening at recreation was set aside to give the verbal account of an extraordinary narrative.

---

4   Brother Vincent Geist, "The Alexian Brothers, Givers of Life to Man's Soul and Body, 1982," TMs (photocopy), p. 7-8, Alexian Brothers Provincial Archives, Arlington Heights, Illinois.

In 1973, William Peter Blatty would write the book and a film would be made, entitled *The Exorcist*. Blatty's fictional story of a possessed young girl in Washington, D.C., has, as its basis, the true story of a fourteen-year-old boy treated for demonic possession. In 1949, this documented case played out in the old Alexian Brothers Hospital in St Louis, Missouri.

Today, a federal law known as the Health Insurance Portability and Accountability Act (HIPAA) even further protects the privacy of this individual. The Alexian Brothers are often approached to reveal the details of the case by the press, Hollywood, and the relentless. As long as the subject of this famous exorcism case is living, however, the brothers are sworn not to reveal details.

Kept secret by the brothers and the Jesuit priests for almost a quarter of a century, a diary was found in the old hospital before it was demolished. Locked away in a desk, in the very room where the exorcism took place, was the detailed account. For medical and legal reasons, the Alexians have never made public the revealing facts about that patient, as they would not about any other patient. That included us, the novices and postulants.

It was in the Washington, D.C., area that a young man began to display odd behavior, and demonic phenomena seemed to surround him increasingly. A psychiatric consult did not indicate that the boy was ill, but his torment began to include super strength, unexplained noises, and inanimate objects moving on their own in his presence. The family summoned the Lutheran clergy when medical aid offered no relief. The minister felt that there was some connection with the boy and a deceased aunt and their prior experimentation with Ouija boards. When the boy's symptoms began to manifest themselves as writing on his body, the Lutheran minister advised the family to seek a Catholic priest.

The Catholic Church, after careful examination, permitted the first official exorcism in one hundred years. The boy was admitted to

Georgetown University Hospital in Washington for observation and evaluation. He became a threat to staff and injured a priest. They decided to move him to St. Louis, and the Jesuits there at the university would oversee the ritual of exorcism.

Including the university campus, other secluded locations were tried to manage the task. The violence and restraint needed to handle the boy required institutional skills. The Alexian Brothers had a great deal of experience in housing and treating mental illness and other substance abuse maladies involving difficult to control patients. The psychiatric wing of the old hospital was the ideal location for the bizarre events that were reported by the observing and assisting brothers.

We listened with our eyes bugging out about the supernatural happenings in that room, the exhausting efforts of Father Bowden, the Jesuit in command, and the diary he kept and placed in the room that remained unused following the successful rite. Years later, I would watch the movie in a crowded Dallas theater with goose bumps altogether different from the rest of the audience. We were a little high strung that evening after being exposed to the Alexian secret and horror story. The 9:00 p.m. signal of flicking the lights off and on took on an eerie significance that night.

Grand Silence went into effect, severing the discussion of revealed history. We shuffled off to the mansion and to our rooms, pushing the envelope of the rule of silence by making scary noises in the long dark cloister walk to rattle each other. Spooking the other guy lessened one's own nerves. But what demons were watching us from the blackness beyond the frosted glass windows?

Not to be outdone, and a little devil myself, I devised a plan that Tom Scholler, my cubicle wall neighbor, and I shall never forget. The postulants, in usual quiet routine, prepared for bed, replaying in our heads the satanic saga we had just heard over beer at recreation. I rolled up my extra wool blanket into a tight snakelike shape. When the final lights out darkened our third floor, the silence was deafening. I waited about five or more minutes, then stood on my single bed. Estimating where Tom would be reclining on his side of the partition, I launched that heavy curled blanket over our common partial wall. My trajectory must have been perfect. I scored a direct hit, resulting in a scream from Scholler similar to the utterance of one possessed. Others giggled and someone gasped, "Oh my God!"

You had to know Tom to appreciate the prank. His home was Pittsburgh, Pennsylvania, and he had intended to fly to Chicago, as I had. His airline's union was on strike, so at the last moment, Tom was put on a Greyhound bus and rode all night in his business suit and tie. During the duration, a fat lady slept on his shoulder. Anyway, he turned out to be the "best-dressed-on-arrival" in our class.

Tom was skinny as a rail and one of the most proper. He was the right kind of man to oversee any event. He dotted every *i* and crossed every *t*. He had an acid tongue and seldom did anyone get the best of him. Tom took everything seriously and was gung-ho about always doing the right thing. Nicknames were not acceptable, an infraction of our monastic rules. Scholler inherited the name "Iceberg" anyway, because of his inflexibility.

One day in the kitchen, Tom's insistence on some insignificant detail pushed one of the novices over the edge. Without a word, the other novice, armed with a slice of pie, launched the chocolate and meringue into Iceberg's face. Had Tom been ordered to take the vow of poverty to another level, he would have removed the loose change from his penny loafers. I lived to torment him and keep him off balance, and we formed a friendship then that lay dormant for thirty-four years. We reconnected during my research.

With more than seven hundred years of history, there were plenty of Alexians who joined the order, served, and died. At our evening meal, we would remember them. A lectern stood in the northeast corner of our refectory, the dining hall. Each day an assigned novice or postulant read spiritual messages to a silent audience slurping soup. Included in that was the daily remembrance of brothers who had passed on through the ages on that particular day in history. After several centuries, hardly a day went by without reciting the name of some brother who had died on that day in the past.

The European Germanic origins of the Alexian Brothers resulted in some real tongue twister–sounding names. Cunibert Schmitz comes to mind. Many names just sounded funny to American boys incapable of resisting infectious laughter. It required extraordinary restraint on the part of the reader and listeners to maintain decorum and suppress snickering, or worse, laughing out loud. The stern faces on the senior brothers dared us to crack.

I always enjoyed my time at the podium delivering the day's inspirational message. I had developed a talent for crossing only one eye at will, and would occasionally flash my goofy gaze on an unsuspecting brother who might look up from his plate at the wrong time. Choking back food and amusement, he would struggle to regain composure as I would innocently read on in deadpan fashion.

Not long after our class of postulants settled in, our director, Brother Pius, introduced us to a book on table manners by Emily Post. Over the ages, the brothers learned very well the necessity of putting their best foot forward in a public dining setting. It was unclear which path lay before us as individuals.

Pius would expose us all to the value of etiquette dictating which knife, fork, or spoon—and when. Any one of us could have been the most likely to succeed as an Alexian toastmaster. On the other hand, fate could have pegged any one of us as the most erudite hospital administrator. In that case, we would need to be capable of entertaining or managing medical professionals and skilled at finding funding from benefactors.

We were fed well, and beer was available at the noon and evening meals. On arrival, my five-foot-nine frame was not too skinny, but it was certainly not filled out. The work and the three great regular meals a day plus collation (a mid-afternoon snack of coffee, milk, or tea and pastries) rounded off my bony parts.

Rhubarb was one of the few regular dishes I would avoid, and the taste of lamb did not suit my palate, either. I preferred the little creatures at the petting zoo. We stored our food in the basement of the novitiate. Needed supplies were sent to the first floor kitchen via the dumb waiter or the freight elevator.

Installed in the basement below the chapel was another food processing area and a walk-in locker-cooler. Many empty meat hooks traversed its ceiling. By the time we arrived in 1966, cattle were no longer being raised and slaughtered by the Alexians. On occasion, a lamb or side of beef that needed some butcher work would be stored in the locker. Once, I had the duty of cutting up mutton for stew. In the waste to be discarded, I could count only one testicle. I now had another reason to pass on lamb.

Between the mansion and the river falls stood a small orchard of apple trees. We would pick several bushels a few times a year and process them into applesauce in the basement. What Brother Michael could do with our homegrown apples and other pie ingredients was legendary. He could be seen alone on occasion, plucking the smaller variety from the trees. It was not unusual, either, to see Michael seated near Freeborn Falls on a rock with a tackle box and fishing pole. The catch was never large enough to feed all of us. He would clean and freeze any yield from the river for a special visiting guest.

The falls and the river played a big part in our routine, more than most knew. A large pipe inserted in the natural pool below the dam took in non-potable water from the Red River. That resource fed the boilers, watered the lawn, and washed our clothes—giving a slight red hue to our whites. A separate well provided water for cooking and drinking.

The falls themselves formed a widening in the Red River at the base of the hill where the mansion was perched. It was our swimming hole and the launching point for our tubing excursions. A large supply of inner tubes was stored in our sport locker. Brother Simeon had an air compressor we used to inflate the tubes on summer recreation days.

Those of us who could swim would make the float trip downstream to the east where the Red emptied into the Wolf. The city boys and non-swimmers stayed behind. Especially after hearing about the often-sighted nonpoisonous water snakes, they would move even farther from the water's edge.

Navigating mostly gentle waters and a few aggressive rapids, depending on the dam in Gresham, we steered leisurely past the finest scenery Wisconsin had to offer. Our biggest challenge was about twenty minutes into the outing. Carefully we would to steer our way past "The Rock." This was an outcropping of huge boulders near our east farm that bordered the river. This tricky part of the river required some control and paddling to pilot through safely.

There was always someone needing to be righted or rescued. It made sense to put the experienced and stronger swimmers in the lead. This was always a fine day, with a picnic at the end. Brother Cajetan, accompanied by the laggards, would drive the blue bus the ten miles downriver to retrieve us along with our tubes.

That ugly bus with its inadequate heater took us other places, too. We sang at retirement homes, visited orphaned Menominee children on the nearby reservation, and made a memorable trip to the Wisconsin State Reformatory, now known as the Green Bay Correctional Institution. It must have been some attempt at instilling in us the corporal works of mercy: Feed the hungry/Give drink to the thirsty/Clothe the naked/Shelter the homeless/Visit the sick/Visit the imprisoned/Bury the dead.

I never did understand the point of that trip. We stood in the prison common area, surrounded by youthful offenders locked behind bars. It was more like a day at the zoo. We were struck by the high percentage of Native American faces staring back, almost certainly thinking to themselves, "What are you looking at?" They sensed our naïveté. Our visit did nothing to comfort or relieve their plight, but we took away an appreciation of our own self-imposed form of confinement. It is possible that a few of those angry faces may have found their way inside our very monastery a decade later.

One particular day's excursion ended with a visit to St. Norbert Abbey, located along the banks of the Fox River in De Pere, almost within walking distance from the prison. There we would meet Sylvester Michael Killeen, a very beloved Abbot to the Norbertine priests and brothers. Abbot Killeen was a frequent guest in our monastery; as our guest he could briefly escape his overwhelming duties.

The Norbertines are a Catholic order of both brothers and priests. At this Wisconsin location, they own and operate the nearby St. Norbert College. While they shared a meal with us that day, we had the opportunity to compare our secluded monastic existence to theirs. The scholastic endeavors of the Norbertine order were quite apart from our simpler pursuits. This mingling of those in different aspects of religious life was a new trend. The Second Vatican Council, in a way, mandated this cross-pollination. It would prove to be a bit unraveling when, a few years later, men and women would grow weary of their flag, leave, and then join another order where the grass seemed greener.

Once, the Franciscans came to visit us on our turf. Perhaps an hour or more to the east of our monastery, the Franciscan order maintained a school to train their version of men destined for their brotherhood. We invited those men from Pulaski, Wisconsin, to join us and enjoy a meal. I could not help but notice their sandals over bare feet. When the average person thinks of monks and friars, it is the Franciscan look most conjure up—brown with the hood collapsed around the neck and shoulders and a white rope cinched around the waist. Below zero temperatures combined with barefoot sandals convinced me I had joined the right team.

Still, the day finally dawned when I decided it was time to knock on the novice master's door. Many a young man had done so before me, and their motivations were many. More often than not, the meeting was at the request of the novice master.

That office was a conduit to the outside world and a release valve. On both sides of the Atlantic Ocean, dating back to the Black Plague and the Alexians' earliest form of organization and leadership, either the master or the novice was there to receive or deliver good or bad news. The novice, with trepidation, was usually unaware of why he had been summoned.

I knew why—indeed, it was my idea to meet face to face. I was rehearsed and resolute in my decision. My plan was to call the shots, drop the bomb, and depart. The Master was unflappable. I blurted out that I had "decided to leave." His response was slow in coming and practiced more often than my immature attempt to burn bridges and simply walk away. This was not the first time a novice would broach the subject of leaving with that stoic face on the other side of the desk.

In a way, I was relieved that Brother Florian had snuffed out the rapidly burning fuse I had ignited. The ordinarily rigid man allowed his softer side to be seen in this private meeting. His demeanor converted from authoritarian to parental. This was a classic encounter of youthful immaturity and senior experience and skill. Using few words, he did not allow me to complete my mission that day. Instead, I was dismissed and encouraged to rethink it.

Even though the wind had been taken from my sails, a win-win space had been created if my departure would inevitably come about. I would learn years later how increasingly difficult this meeting and others like it were becoming for senior brothers like Florian. I was unaware that I was part of a tremendous exodus of religious hopefuls, like rats fleeing a burning ship.

I closed the door behind me and started the long trek down the doglegged cloister walk. Only a handful of novices were about their duties, exchanging silent inquisitive glances. Even with the practiced discipline of silence, we could speak volumes using no words. Either I was feeling vulnerable or the monastic grapevine had exposed me as the most recent occupant of the hot seat. They watched me as puppies anticipating something positive or special. I had some thinking to do.

As usual, that evening during recreation, we gathered as a community of novices to relax. The usual suspects, fearing they might be left as the last man standing, approached me. There were always those who kept their ear to the ground. Dismissing the importance and shrugging off the significance, I denied my real purpose of the meeting with Brother Florian with the same skill they possessed to read faces. Luckily, the bell rang, heralding Grand Silence and buying me almost another twenty-four hours to get my act together.

Instead, days passed, and I continued to withdraw. Simply put, the vision I had created for myself as an Alexian Brother was retreating. I began to explore the needed balance in being both a man of medicine and a man of religion. It was becoming clear that the elements of zeal, piety, and obedience were not native within me in sufficient quantity. I was not feeling any worse about myself—it just started to dawn on me that I was not a fit in this very structured community. In retrospect, not a lot had changed since Brother Florian and I had met weeks before. I was no longer straddling the fence; I was a deserter.

When I spoke with him again, Brother Florian Eberle made no effort to change my mind. This time, he too had probably come to the conclusion that this was not the right place for me. Now, the Master would set into motion the swift process that would remove me with the least amount of disruption. He explained that my one-way round trip ticket would be used to return me to Houston the next morning. He asked that I be considerate and not create a disturbance. The brothers would forward my footlocker home.

There was no way I was going quietly, nor would I consider a silent goodbye appropriate for close friends. I sought out four classmates and one other older novice that evening at recreation. I told them I was "not leaving mad, just leaving." The inertia created that evening was a complete reversal to the emotions that played a part in creating the enthusiasm and excitement when I joined the Alexians. I felt guilty sending friends to their cells in silence.

Five peers at the next morning's Mass now knew. If there was ever a time Grand Silence was a friend, this day was it. Morning monastic prayers and daily Mass were performed in painful slow motion. I looked neither left nor right. We scattered back to our rooms for personal time prior to breakfast. By the time others would notice and calculate who was missing, I would have slipped out the side door of the kitchen.

Father Weber sat in his car with the engine running and warmed up. Both of us unspeaking, we drove away. We passed the property of Frank and Anna Schulte, the German immigrant lovers closely connected to the Peter's mother and daughter. I mentally said goodbye to their nearby hill, where we had sledded, tobogganed, and employed other manners of pine tree dodging through the snow.

This was our chaplain's routine. He drove to Green Bay every morning to teach mathematics at St. Norbert College in the suburb of De Pere. It was convenient for him to drop the occasional losers off at the airport. I was not feeling good about my decision and method of execution that morning. I started to imagine alternate courses—perhaps we would accidentally hit a crossing deer and have to return to the monastery. That was unlikely to happen, and I knew it.

Father Weber broke the silence a few miles down the snowy road. "You are a jerk," came out of his mouth. We were the only two in the car; he must have been speaking to me. This was one of those rude awakenings that drove a point home. We are all human, including priests, nuns, and brothers. Just when I thought a man of God might be taking me to the airport, I had to bite my tongue. Realizing Father Weber was behaving no more charitably than I was that frigid morning, I chose to exercise the modicum of humility learned at the monastery that was now no longer in the rearview mirror.

The next hour of drive time had bled off just enough built-up steam between us. The chaplain had his say. I was in no position to argue. Remaining quiet, I felt wounded by the same man who routinely heard our confessions: doling out penances and the forgiveness yesterday and insulting me today. "What a dichotomy," I thought to myself.

Quiet anger built up inside of me. This was not the first time nor would it be the last that I dealt with some perceived hostile authority figure. I realized that the closer we got to Green Bay, the closer we came to the point when one of us would need to speak. But what was there to say?

It was Wisconsin, winter, and nothing new: cold. Discussing the weather was out of the question. Father Weber fell back on the local icebreaker always sure to stimulate instant bonding. "There is the Green Bay Packers stadium and field," he said. That was not enough to raise a response from me. "The team has a mechanism under the field turf preventing the sod and soil from freezing," he said. He was trying. I grunted acknowledgment and nodded my head, feigning interest. How appropriate that we were discussing the technology of thawing.

We had found a way to establish gentlemanly détente between two men who would likely never see each other again. I found myself stepping out of the car with a handshake. It was over and there was no longer a connection between myself and to all that religious life. The option to turn back was long gone. Though still unsure of leaving, I felt guilty for having left friends so abruptly. Pretending indifference and callousness was my coping mechanism. How selfish I was: perhaps I was really was a jerk! I walked to my gate and plane unescorted to fly away and back south.

4

NO DEED NO DEATH

In 1968, the Alexian Brothers stepped away from the facility in Gresham, Wisconsin. The number of men wishing to be accepted and trained dwindled. That facility was planned for large classes of novices and postulants. In the late 1940s, following World War II, Catholic vocations were at a peak. As a matter of fact, this Gresham facility was originally intended to have been built in an upscale suburban area west of St. Louis known as Clayton, Missouri.

Instead, with minor design changes, the monastery was built and attached to the Wisconsin mansion gift. The wisdom of that strategic move was hotly debated within the Alexians and not universally promoted by brothers believing it to too remote. With a "FOR SALE" sign posted, some brothers rolled their eyes silently speaking "I told you so."

This religious complex was never an "abbey," but that word rolled more easily off unfamiliar tongues and into foreign ears than the word *novitiate.* As a result, the misnomer *abbey* sticks, even today. The nickname may have originated from the microphone of a law enforcement radio dispatcher, a Menominee warrior, or a cub reporter for some backwoods newspaper searching for a description of that troubled churchlike place. At sunrise on the first day of 1975, with the takeover just beginning, the monastery became known as the abbey, though it never had been and never would be connected with an abbess or abbot!

Nearly vacant of furniture, the sterile facility offered no resistance to the Menominee Warrior takeover. The warriors entered before their captives had given their snow-bound cars time to properly warm up. The main building was protected by an even temperature, kept sufficiently above freezing. Unfortunately, the number of disciplined dissidents could be counted on one hand. Some looked for food that had been stored away. Some simply wandered about, puffed-up and impressed with what they had conquered. Few appreciated the need to fully understand and operate the impressive physical plant.

Not unexpectedly, many set their sights on securing and claiming the best of sixty-six sleeping rooms as their own. The warrior leadership had sent out a search party posing as legitimate buyers many weeks before this night. That advance team had been given the grand tour by the real estate agent, allowing them to "case the joint." Now, they saw it as their very own prize.

The property was most assuredly an alluring place. Having once been a location where young men came to launch their intentions to serve, now other young men were there for different reasons, and with questionable methods. The warriors now inhabited a dormant facility that served no purpose and was simply for sale. Although opulent in appearance from the outside, the mansion with the attached monastery was sparsely furnished.

The Alexian Brothers were originally called Beghards. In the late thirteenth century, these layman informally banded together to live out Christ's commands to feed the hungry, care for the sick, and bury the dead. By the mid-fourteenth century, they were fighting the scourges of the "Black Death." If they were unable to save the bubonic plague victims, they buried the dead, risking their own lives to the contagion. Begging for food and living in small cell-like rooms, these men came to be known as Cellites.

Later, the Cellites evolved into the Alexian Brothers. Eventually recognized by the Catholic Church, these men, already living in a monastic environment, chose as their patron the saint known as Alexius. Alexius was a member of a wealthy family and native of Rome. History tells us he died in or near the year 417 as a pious "man of God" after having lived an ascetic life caring for the ill in the city of Edessa in the Syrian Orient. Only after my formal separation from the Brothers, and during the writing of this book, did I uncover the intriguing history of the Alexian Brothers that dates back to the Late Middle Ages. There are several literary efforts that probe the more than seven hundred years of Alexian history. The work of Christopher J. Kauffman, entitled *Tamers of Death: The History of the Alexian Brothers from 1300 to 1789*, is the most thorough.

Always on alert for those willing to have a conversation about the Menominee, I got very lucky. David R. M. Beck, Ph.D. was in the process of writing *The Struggle for Self-Determination: History of the Menominee Indians since 1854*. At the time, Beck was an associate professor of Native American studies at the University of Montana. Eventually he became a professor and chair of the department. I met him one day while on the reservation gathering data from the tribe. Both he and I were attending an annual spring sturgeon fish festival in the city of Neopit on the Menominee reservation.

Beck was enjoying an enthusiastic and festive crowd that was delighted to share the oral history of the tribe with him. The professor already had a proven trusted relationship with the Menominee. David Beck had previously written *Siege and Survival: History of the Menominee Indians, 1634–1856*. His new book was to take up where the first publication left off. On the other hand, I was known to be a former Alexian Brother. I'm sure I was regarded as a suspect fly in the ointment by some. The middle aged men, in particular, had no interest in resurrecting those uncomfortable days when the tribe was divided. I encountered cordial but tight lips, having little or no success finding anyone to admit to having been a warrior in 1975.

Stan LaTender, a proudly admitted Menominee warrior, was there with his family. Weeks before, Stan and I had already sat together for an interview. Although a Menominee, he was an employee of the Oneida Tribe near Green Bay then. His younger brother, John Mark LaTender, became a person of interest for me. Stan pointed John out to me at the celebration. John had paid his debt to society and was a free man. But on Thursday, November 28, 1974, Thanksgiving Day, John had presented himself to the Menominee County Sheriff's Department claiming, "I killed Father Marcellus."

In fact, John had stabbed the Franciscan priest to death during a struggle while burglarizing the church residence. He threw the knife into the nearby river by the dam before turning himself in almost immediately. Nearly three decades later, LaTender found me sliding over empty seats to sit next to him. We were in the Neopit school gymnasium on bleachers watching the Menominee Nation traditionally celebrate the return of the sturgeon with a feast and celebration powwow.

Not wishing to be cruel, I believe I ruined John's day of celebration. With no eye contact between us, I introduced myself in my unabashed style. Caught off guard and showing shame, he answered only a few of my questions about the murder. His head hung low and he appeared beaten down. Proud, he was not. His responses were hushed single words.

It is a small world. It is even smaller within two adjacent Wisconsin counties. Was it, perhaps, coincidental that the Franciscan missionary to the Menominee was killed four weeks prior to Mike Sturdevant and company making their stand? I was hearing stories of sexual abuse and the using of young Menominee in other unsavory ways by Father Marcellus M. Cabo. The unpleasant incident, at a minimum, was a harbinger to the takeover crisis. The priest killing may or may not have been connected to the month-long story I began telling in chapter one. Here's the rest of the story.

It was perhaps bad timing that a large and beautiful yet empty monastery neighbored an Indian reservation at a time in history—the

1970s—when Native Americans were overtaking empty facilities and claiming them as their own. But what to do?

I constructed a factual timeline to tell the following month-long story. I gathered Wisconsin law enforcement radio dispatches, the print media, and FBI documents acquired via the Freedom of Information Act (FOIA). Also, based on my memory, participant's journals and a decade of personal research, these elements are woven together to tell the following complicated, yet true, story.

Day 1—Wednesday, January 1

The FBI described, in detail, the dizzying string of midnight phone calls launched by Joe Plonka. Joe was the custodian of the monastery in Gresham, Wisconsin, and his employers were the Chicago-based Alexian Brothers. Brother Eugene Gizzi had already made desperate calls to Alexian facilities throughout the United States to locate the next man in the chain of command. As it happened, it fell upon Brother Maurice Wilson at the Brothers' hospital in Elizabeth, New Jersey.

Brother Maurice immediately phoned the Novitiate to introduce himself. He was rewarded with the words, "I want to talk to Brother Florian or else," followed by an abrupt hang-up. Brother Maurice repeated the call and met with the same demand followed by another disconnect. He knew of nothing else to do except call the law enforcement—a potential mistake.

12:30 a.m.: A band of armed Indians enters the Alexian Brothers novitiate and holds Mr. Joe Plonka, his wife, two children, and two friends at gunpoint. One warning shot is fired into the ceiling. About 3 a.m., the entire group is released. The abbey is located in the Town of Richmond, Shawano County, about nine miles northwest of the city of Shawano.

1:30 a.m.: Officer Fischer of Shawano County, Wisconsin sheriff's department receives an alarming call from Brother Maurice Wilson notifying law enforcement.

Determined to speak with Alexian leadership in Chicago, the warriors forced Plonka to call again. Sturdevant finally accepted the fact that the fiercely protected Brother Florian was ill and unable to handle such a grave issue. He agreed to deal with Brother Maurice. Chicago called back to New Jersey and asked Wilson to try the call once again.

Brother Maurice made another attempt. Joe answered, explaining that Brother's earlier call to the police was a "bad" decision that had endangered the captives. Joe was beginning to see freedom fading. The warriors were envisioning complications if the police were to arrive so early in their plans. Likely, with prompting only an earshot away, Joe found a cooperative and calm Brother on the line with. Brother Maurice agreed to call the sheriff back to encourage downgrading the police response.

2:00 a.m.: Brother Maurice calls the sheriff back. Chief Deputy Chester Dahl claims to "hold off."

As agreed earlier, Brother Maurice called right back, speaking again with Joe Plonka. The warriors saw value in allowing the captive to plead his own case. Joe revealed more. He painted a picture the Alexians did not know in detail. Joe said that the Indians had guns and their threats were convincing and believable. Joe went on to explain that the warriors intended to hold them hostage. The telephone was then handed over to Mike Sturdevant. Mike introduced himself as the leader of a young faction of the Menominee Reservation. It was now 2:45 a.m.

Sturdevant went on to explain that he wished to meet with representatives of the Alexian Brothers. He further insisted that there would be no release of Joe Plonka without a commitment by Brother Maurice to travel to Gresham. Joe had been allowed to monitor the conversation on the cottage extension phone.

The tide was changing, for the better, for Joe and his family and friends. Joe assured Brother Maurice that Sturdevant could be relied upon to keep his part of the deal. Sturdevant agreed no harm would come to the captives. In response to the warrior commitments, the Alexian reciprocated with his pledge to immediately travel to Gresham.

3:10 a.m.: Deputy Dahl receives an additional call from Brother Maurice briefing him on the agreement reached with the Menominee warriors. Dahl reassures the brother that law enforcement will continue to withhold action.

The chief deputy expressed concern that the captives were really freed. Dahl needed some certainty that six innocent captives were no longer in harm's way. Another telephone exchange took place, with Wilson calling the Novitiate back. The voice on the other end of the phone assured him that Plonka and company had left minutes earlier. Wilson called Dahl to tell him the news, which was welcome but needed confirmation.

Brother Maurice Wilson was finishing his New Jersey preparations to depart for Chicago. Brother Eugene Gizzi in Elk Grove Village, Illinois, made another call to Brother Maurice. Plonka had just phoned the Chicago hospital to announce that he and his group were safe and provided a telephone number for verification. They were at the house of their friends, John and Barbara Rogozinski.

Frightened but relieved, Joe Plonka answered another phone call from Brother Maurice. Joe was reassured that the Alexians would take care of him and his family. Joe was instructed to bundle up his family and immediately exit Shawano County via the Sheriff's office. Before hanging up, Plonka thought it important that it be known there were probably as many as ten women and children in the group participating in the takeover. Having spent the last few hours at the business end of weaponry, he stressed the arrival and handguns aplenty. Also, not that he'd had any choice, but Joe had just walked away from several of his own vehicles at the monastery. The Rogozinskis loaned a car to Marlene and Joe. Now Barbara and John felt vulnerable. It would be almost another four hours before full sunrise.

3:20 a.m.: Brother Maurice makes a final call to the Shawano sheriff's office and Dahl, confirming the safety of the hostages and telling him to anticipate their arrival on their way out of town to Chicago by car.

Now, the situation was in the hands of Mike Sturdevant and Brother Maurice Wilson. Wilson had been catapulted into a crash course called *Negotiation 101,* and Sturdevant flirted with felony kidnapping and more. The brothers were skilled at handling life, death, and contained tragedy within the confines of their own hospitals. These circumstances fit nothing they had ever experienced. No game or rulebook book existed for either side. This was a disaster never before rehearsed; it was confusion and potential mayhem.

4:30 a.m.: While outbound to Chicago, Joe Plonka and family make a police report at the Shawano sheriff's office.

Throughout the United States, there was no Alexian Brother awake and at ease over the disconcerting news coming out of Wisconsin and Chicago. The San Jose, California, brothers had not yet learned of the predicament. Not since war in Europe had the brothers been faced with such a circumstance, rendering them helplessly blindsided.

Nervous members of the Menominee Warriors Society waited, eyeing the caretaker's telephone. The warriors thought that they had successfully aborted the sheriff's earlier response. Then, the warriors overheard the radio dispatch crackle over the stolen mobile walkie-talkie. It sounded to Mike like the cavalry was on its way. The Indians scrambled to their posts. Mike Sturdevant, still insistent on using Brother Maurice as a telephone go-between, waited.

The sheriff, in fact, had launched surveillance, but unknown to the Indians and Brother Maurice, the one-man marked cruiser with a solo deputy had been taken out of service after hitting a deer, a common winter occurrence. Elroy Stroming, a Wisconsin state trooper, is dispatched to assist. Trooper Stroming, more than a year later, would find himself involved in some life and death political intrigue on the reservation.

There was another incoming and confirming call to the caretaker cottage. The Alexian brother had promised he would come if the hostages were released. That done, Brother Maurice jetted west to Chicago to keep his side of the bargain. Mike Sturdevant had no way of confirming that the brother was on his way, so he continued to allow plans to unfold. At first light, armed silhouettes could be seen patrolling on the fourth-story roof. A trickle of weapons, ammunition, and human support began to emerge from the woods out of the north.

8:30 a.m.: Judge Myse is contacted by local authorities and permission is given for phone surveillance of the abbey. Twenty minutes later the phone tap is in.

Beginning in 1972, Judge Gordon Myse served in the Tenth Judicial Circuit, initially appointed by Governor Patrick Lucey. He would later run and win the office. Myse lived in the city of Appleton and covered the counties of Outagamie, Menominee, Langdale, and Shawano. He drove up that day to Shawano to hear the motion for the wiretap. Law enforcement wished desperately to listen in on Menominee Warrior telephone conversations from inside what everyone was already calling "the abbey."

When the judge arrived at the Shawano County Courthouse to hear the motion, however, he became aware of a much more serious issue:

an imminent frontal assault on the monastery under heated discussion by locals at a huge conference table. The judge was taken aback by what he perceived to be a dangerous rush to action. Judge Myse suggested a novel idea. He recommended picking up the telephone and speaking with those that had taken over the Novitiate. So they did just that. When the Indians were reached by phone, the judge reported that they said in a calm and resolute tone, "This is our land. It is part of our reservation. We are reclaiming it."

That conversation released some of the built-up steam in the courthouse. Judge Myse said that the telephone contact had, at least, suggested this was not "…a murderous band of masked murders running around." Unsure what to do next, the judge made this suggestion: "Why don't we offer them amnesty if they leave now and no serious crimes are later discovered?" The Indians could simply walk away, and no prosecutions would occur. There was plenty of local resistance to that proposed offer, but the FBI supported the idea. Judge Gordon Myse was the only individual who had the capacity to deliver and make the offer of amnesty. Myse volunteered to make that bid in person.

Judge Gordon Myse-2003. Negotiated with Warriors 1975
Photo by Curt Knoke

10:15 a.m.: Participation by members of the Wisconsin state patrol begins when the county sheriff asks District 4 to cover accidents due to the takeover. Trooper Richard Gussert is sent to the Shawano area.

11:00 a.m.: Sheriff Sandy Montour asks that state patrol answer all routine local law calls until further notice. The sheriff dispatches his few deputies to man roadblocks.

"The sheriff's people were very angry and regarded this [the takeover] as a real confrontation to their authority," said the judge. Since Judge

Myse knew Governor Lucey very well, he placed a call to Madison, the capital, and told him, "You've got to get the National Guard in here or there will be blood. Governor, people are going to die here unless you get us the National Guard." Lucey did not blanch; his response to Judge Myse was, "Okay."

11:00 a.m. to 3:00 p.m.: Mike Spencer and Colonel Simonson arrive. The local authorities decide they will try to bargain with the Indians. A group comprised of Circuit Judge Gordon Myse, Indian affairs attorney Murtagh, and Wausau attorney Linehan go to the abbey. This is agreeable to the Indians, and the three enter the abbey and stay for twenty hours. The sheriff makes a request that we fly a team in from Oshkosh from the Alexian Brothers' main office. This is cleared through Captain Walsingham, and Brother Maurice Wilson and Neil Bennett are flown in by Trooper Grover.

3:00 p.m.: Mike Spencer and Sheriff Montour approach Sergeant Mauel with the request for twenty-five troopers to assist with roadblock duty. Major Sterba and Captain Walsingham are advised; Walsingham immediately starts for Shawano.

Never had an Alexian Brother been so abruptly catapulted out of a monastic environment and into the jaws of celebrity as Brother Maurice Wilson on this first day of a new year. Awakened from sleep in New Jersey, traveling by jet to Chicago, hearing his name repeatedly paged on arrival at O'Hare, whisked away by Wisconsin law enforcement aircraft and squad car, he was then finally dropped on the doorstep of Sheriff Montour. Brother Maurice's day had only begun.

Having joined the brother at O'Hare, Chicago-based Neil Bennett was a business executive vice president of the Alexian Brothers. Already, "who's on first" confusion had begun. Neil Bennett was not an Alexian Brother; he was an employed layperson with hospital administrator experience, skills, and credentials. It was Bennett's responsibility to guide the Alexians through the growing modern maze of secular health care. Bennett was there to assist and advise Brother Maurice.

The Alexians owned five U.S. health care institutions at the time. The monastery in Gresham belonged to the Alexians, but it was a completely different animal with an entirely different set of financial and administrative matters. There were no other twentieth century United States Catholic institutions that had been overtaken by Indian uprisings from which to lift guidance and experience.

Bennett and Wilson were between a classic rock and a hard place. Brother Maurice Wilson found himself the man of the hour. Externally, he appeared composed. Later, he would admit to feeling like a deer in the headlights, unaware of what was in store.

6:00 p.m.: Approval is given for the twenty-five men. Briefing and accommodations are set up. A state command post is arranged in the north wing of the sheriff's building. The repeater system is set up. Repeater radios from districts no. 1, 2, and 3 are sent. At this point the plan is to hold all positions. No one is to leave and no one is allowed into the abbey. The original plan was that the state patrol would provide men every day from 4:00 a.m. to 2:00 p.m. There are a lot of mutual aid officers arriving, and a guess will put the number at 100 to 150.

The Alexian Brothers had already been in extensive conversations and negotiations with Adam Webster. Webster, a member of the Oneida Indian Nation located in Green Bay, was making plans and securing federal funds to purchase or lease the Novitiate as an alcoholic rehabilitation facility.

The monastery and the Oneida tribal offices were about fifty miles apart. It was important for the Alexians to understand what had gone wrong.

They could not understand why there were hostile Native Americans with guns in their monastery, while at the same time there were ongoing reasonable businesslike transactions in place to create a facility on behalf of all Indians with the Oneida. In his Shawano, Wisconsin, hotel room, Brother Maurice met with Adam Webster that evening only to learn of his surprise and astonishment, too, over the new predicament. This first obvious wrinkle would prove this was no clear-cut disagreement between White and Red faces.

Empty of warriors and hostages and left in disarray from pilfering, the cottage lay fallen. Not all, but many, picked through and took some of the Plonka family possessions while moving into the monastery. A handful of young innocent Indian children played with the Plonka boys' Christmas toys in the cloister.

Anyone familiar with the action of hundreds of dominoes sequentially falling against the next in countless directions and speed can appreciate what had now been launched. That first irreversible domino was triggered by warrior John Waubanascum. It was approaching the twenty-four hour mark after he had fired a rifle round over captive heads.

A widespread response was being mounted by neighboring law enforcement. Sheriff Montour reached out everywhere. The sheriff had already activated the assistance of the Wisconsin state police. Usually, the troopers handled issues only on the open roads beyond municipalities. The need to activate an ad hoc mutual aid deployment was coming alive. Adjacent counties were being called upon to come give support to Shawano County. Emergency responders in the form of sworn law enforcement personnel, with support, were most needed.

Day 2—Thursday, January 2

Milwaukee Sentinel—"Takeover Not First Militant Act," by Ron Marose.

"The seizing of a religious estate near Gresham by a band of Menominee Indians Sunday is another example of militancy exhibited by some Wisconsin tribes in recent years....Militant Indian leaders, including members of the American Indian Movement (AIM), always have exhibited a willingness to negotiate in conflicts....But they are also willing to risk standoffs and armed defiance when words fail to resolve issues with the white man."

Milwaukee Sentinel—"Armed Indians Take Over Estate in Shawano County."

"A group of armed Menominee Indians seized the Alexian Brothers estate near here about midnight Tuesday and sent out the message that the band would hold out until death unless the estate is given back to the Indians....The group took over the estate's three buildings and held the caretaker, Joe Plonka, his wife and two children as hostages....The group identified itself as the Menominee Warrior Society."

Milwaukee Sentinel—"Indians Say They'll Die Before Giving Up Land," by Rick Janka.

"'We die for what we believe in....We have done this because the building and the land is needed for the poor people of this area....We are in need of food. We have everything else but food,' (Menominee Warrior)....The group is planning to use the structure for a hospital or school for Indians, the spokesman said."

4:00 a.m.: Troopers are assigned to five roadblock points. In all cases a Shawano area police officer is with them. The instructions from the sheriff and district attorney remain the same—no long action only until the three bargaining people come out.

7:30 a.m.: Captain Walsingham en route from Mosinee with Mr. Artley Skenandore who was called in by police emergency services to help mediate the action.

Effectively carrying an invisible white flag of truce, with loaded weapons pointed at his back, Circuit Judge Gordon Myse emerged from the monastery property. He and his team were exhausted after marathon negotiations and conversations with the warriors. Their efforts lasted all night long and then some.

The Indians limited his access and did not allow the Myse party to enter the novitiate proper, with the exception of the large dining hall. Known as the refectory, it was where my brothers and fellow novices had eaten our silent meals years before. This was the closest Myse had come to observing warrior preparations. It was clear that the warriors had some sort of unseen tactical plan and were not allowing the judge to observe their preparations.

Myse reported they had spent almost the entire time closely guarded by armed Indians in the caretaker's cottage. "Until I got out there, I didn't feel personally in danger. I couldn't believe they were going to kill a guy who came out to offer them amnesty," said the judge. Always looming nearby and verbally threatening, that giant of a man, warrior John Waubanascum, reminded Myse by saying under his breath, "I want to waste you." Waubanascum indicated he would be happy to kill the party if it wasn't for intervention by the general, Mike Sturdevant.

Almost everyone, that day and a half, was a familiar white face looking back at another familiar, yet masked, face. The judge was trusted, liked, loved, and hated by some, but by and large, he was considered fair in his rulings. For years, he had seen so many of these native faces in his courtroom across from his bench; some guilty and some innocent. Gordon Myse was walking away from the Alexian property carrying with him warrior hopes and his personal ominous concerns whether there could be any common ground. Sturdevant had shot down the offer of amnesty.

10:30 a.m.: Command group meeting—District Attorney-elect Rick Stadelman, outgoing district attorney and new assemblyman Earl Schmidt; Captain Walsingham; Sergeant Mauel; Sheriff Montour; Neil Bennett; Brother Maurice; Circuit Judge Gordon Myse; Mr. Langhan, Wausau attorney; and Mr. Skenandore. Judge Myse relates that during his overnight stay at the abbey he was treated well. They shared their food with him and all parties did a great deal of talking. The Judge feels that the situation is a powder keg and he believes that some are willing to die there. The Indians don't seem to have a firm or attainable goal. They do want the abbey turned over to them but don't really know now what to do with it if it is taken. They want to talk to Brother Maurice inside the abbey. Neither the sheriff nor the district attorney will allow it. The following observations are made by the judge: 1. There are about thirty-five to forty people that he saw and counted. Included are four children and six women. 2. He saw a 30.06 and at least two handguns. Mr. Skenandore will attempt to set up negotiations with them.

It is important to note that the lone Alexian Brother, assisted by a lay hospital administrator, had unknowingly stepped into a hornet's nest. On the surface, over the last twenty-four hours, a reasonable person would assume Brother Maurice was there to negotiate the proper use of a monastery in the woods with a "FOR SALE" sign in the front yard.

It was not that simple, however. Every time he turned around to answer his hotel room telephone, Brother Maurice was meeting, or soon to speak with, someone new. That new person would have—or believe they have—good reason to become involved in this multifaceted racial, social, political, religious, and gender dilemma.

3:10 p.m.: Indians are seen in yard of the abbey. Six troopers and eight to ten county officers go in to assist the observation point. No further action is taken; however, this is the first open incident involving weapons.

In the spirit and practice of "mutual aid," nineteen men from communities to the south arrived in Shawano. This manpower was made up of five city of Oshkosh police officers and fourteen deputies from their own Winnebago County. A school bus, rented locally, dropped them at the already swamped office-headquarters of Sheriff Sandy Montour. The men in from Oshkosh were briefed. They were assigned to work together as a team.

Shawano County officials recognized this group to be the best choice to manage, the most forward position, Checkpoint 6. Lt. Edward Misch saw this as an opportunity to exercise some desperately needed professionalism. Already on site at that checkpoint were law enforcement officers from the nearby city of Neenah. Neenah is located on the north shore of Lake Winnebago. Neenah city officers gladly turned over command this late afternoon. They were already outnumbered and exchanging casual gunfire with the Indians having more powerful hunting rifles with scopes.

5:11 p.m.: All troopers off post are replaced. It is decided that a roving vehicle patrol in Menominee County on Highway VV is needed. The Shawano district attorney feels there is a legal question about mutual aid doing it, so he requests state help. Two two-man cars are assigned to start at midnight and work through the night.

Checkpoint 6 was coming to be known as the most significant location and flashpoint. Unofficially, it became tagged as "Broken Feather" by the half dozen agencies providing mutual aid. Outagamie sheriff, Oshkosh police, Winnebago sheriff, Little Chute P.D., Green Lake County, Florence County, and Vilas County were to serve Checkpoint 6. These seven agencies held down their fort while facing the more invincible stone and steel monastery roughly nine hundred yards away.

The checkpoint was located north of the monastery on a slight rise overlooking the novitiate. On the other hand, the monastery was a large three-story fortress topped by a lighted bell tower and gold-plated dome with a cross affixed above. Even though Checkpoint 6 was on higher ground, the warriors had a commanding view of the north and east, a partial view to the west, and a southern view across the river and beyond Cherry Road.

Mr. and Mrs. Willis Lamberies had evacuated and allowed law enforcement to commandeer their home and farm. Due west and just across Juniper Road was another farm owned by the Alexians. Combined, these two properties, with two separate barns and miscellaneous structures, made up Checkpoint number 6. Depending on opinion, it was questionable whose side was better off. To the north, the law was pinned down, and to the south, warriors were pinned in. In western movie style, both sides began to swap lead bullets.

Bernice & Willis Lamberies–2010. Farm-home was checkpoint 6
during takeover
Photo by Curt Knoke

In the early evening darkness, Lt. Mitch assumed command from and relieved officers representing the town of Neenah. With a few more men to spare, the lieutenant was able to place manpower and a guard detail in both barns under the cover of darkness. Established and dug in, these men from the Winnebago area accomplished the second most important mission, coffee and sandwiches of cheese and cold cuts. They shared their food and warm coffee with Checkpoint number 5, located nearly a mile farther back and to the north.

The day was exhausting for all. This was the first attempt to negotiate a suitable and mutual use of that facility. Authorities would not allow a face-to-face meeting with Brother Maurice Wilson and the warriors. The sheriff feared another hostage circumstance if they were to allow Brother Maurice to enter the monastery. The disappointing result was an unproductive day of negotiation by proxy. The gravity of the situation was made quite clear to the Alexians when they learned that the barn to the north was full of cops.

Day 3—Friday, January 3

Green Bay Press Gazette—"Talks with Indians Expected,"
by Dale Gross.
"Talks broke off twice Thursday between the 40 or so Menominee Indians and the order, at the former Alexian Brothers Novitiate....A spokesperson for the Indians said the group holding the estate wanted complete control but said the order balked at giving up control at a loss estimated at $1 million."

1:46 a.m.: Troopers Hair and Zuhlsdorf report that they spotted a couple of people jump out of a car and run into the woods. The information is sent to Menominee County. About two hours later the Menominee officers flush four men from the woods and capture them. Troopers Hair, Zuhlsdorf, Schroeder, and Perry assist Menominee with search and handcuffing. Food items and ammunition of various calibers found.

Willis Lamberies was summoned back to his farm to make water available to the Winnebago lawmen—besides, he needed to feed his cows at four o'clock in the morning. At the same time, Outagamie County arrived to relieve Winnebago before sunrise. A pattern of inconvenience upsetting agribusiness was beginning to develop.

Scheduling and arranging round-the-clock duty for a dynamic and dangerous situation is what the police do for a living. That was not so for a certain dairy farmer, his wife, and his animals. Willis Lamberies had a fixed farm routine, and he was only forty-eight hours into an experience that was becoming more than awkward. He had neighbors who were also beginning to feel the squeeze.

Brother Maurice, on behalf of the Alexian Brothers, was involved in marathon meetings, one right after another. Everyone seemed to be scrambling and reaching out to find suitable arrangements that would make everyone happy. There was discussion about folding Menominee healthcare needs into alcohol rehabilitation efforts to present to the warriors.

Either the warriors detected naïveté on the part of the Alexian Brothers, or the Indians were genuinely impressed with the credibility Brother Maurice brought to the table. No one knew which for certain, yet. This day, the new district attorney continued to write and fine-tune a document offering immunity to some or all of the dissidents. This was contingent upon their peacefully vacating the property.

It was agreed that four individuals from each side would gather inside a Winnebago-type recreational vehicle situated halfway between that barn full of cops and the monastery full of warriors. Alexian representation was finally to meet warriors and anticipated a productive face-to-face meeting. The warriors performed traditional ceremonies within the abbey before making their way up to Juniper Road and the no-man's-land Winnebago.

1:30 p.m.: Troopers Jeschke and Kujawa transport a sick child from Checkpoint number 5 to Shawano Hospital—child is from the abbey.

One contingent wore their stern and uncompromising face. The other side hoped for some solution to empty the novitiate of warriors at all costs. It was not a friendly encounter. One of the warriors remembers, "We went out to negotiate out in the trailer, and they had liquor in the trailer, and we made them dump it out because we figured, this old trick again, get the Indians drunk, and get them to sign."

With darkness nearing, the warriors were not impressed with the Alexian proposal. Simply put, Mike Sturdevant and his people wanted the property lock, stock, and barrel. The warriors pointed out a federal law they believed supported their insistence that it belonged to the Menominee. The warriors claimed ownership reverted back to the Menominee when the Alexians discontinued living and working at the location. A 7:30 p.m. deadline to accept the Alexian compromise came and went. The warrior position became their motto: "Deed or Death."

4:00 p.m.: It becomes apparent that better communications are necessary. Sergeant Mauel asks the local officers if arrangements can be made to have power installed to the top of the water tower in Gresham. Our repeater radios are not getting out to the remote posts. This is completed and the repeater moves to Gresham. The move did not help us at the command post, but it did give communications to the field posts.

Today, it would be text messaging from nervous thumbs, e-mail, or some other form of social networking. Originally, it was surely smoke signals. The well-practiced grapevine was up and running. That first week of 1975, accomplices often used federally tapped telephone lines that spread the takeover news far and wide.

Chicago photographer Al Bergstein told his girlfriend he was waiting for an important call from Owen Luck, another more experienced photographer. Owen had a "First Nation" heritage and Al had no reason to disbelieve the man claiming to be a patriotic Green Beret medic in Vietnam. It was not important that Luck prove he was partial or full blooded. Owen Luck would be Al's front row ticket to something big.

When I contacted Owen Luck twenty-five years later by phone, he was unwilling to speak with me further regarding the Gresham details. When I interviewed Al Bergstein in person, I asked him to describe Luck. He said "Owen was not a member of AIM, he was simply a photojournalist. He claimed to have been very patriotic prior to Vietnam. Like many of us, there were many reasons to stand aside of patriotism in the early 70s. It was, as you know, a very different world to the one we currently live in." Luck's photo-press credentials were essential to access the abbey—he had been at the Pine Ridge Indian Reservation during the Wounded Knee incident and would be recognized in Gresham, Wisconsin, as trustworthy. Al Bergstein was a twenty-two-year-old confronted with an adventure.

The telephone rang for Al that New Year's night. He and Owen Luck came up from Chicago. The two men initially touched base at the drop-in center on the reservation. They then found their way into the abbey on the second night, when the weather bureau recorded a low of -7°.

The perimeter set up by law enforcement around the monastery was full of unsecured holes. It wasn't pleasant crossing the river from the south with temperatures in the single digits. Up to their chests, they waded across with film, supplies, and cameras held high risking severe "shrinkage." I can testify that the Red River water can be cold even on the Fourth of July. I can't even imagine it in January. Owen and Al didn't have to be invited to strip down and thaw out next to the large subterranean fireplaces in the mansion basement.

When I located him for this book, Al was a Seattle-based Microsoft marketing executive. Although businesslike and straightforward with his answers, I suspected he had not outgrown the call of adventure. Out of nowhere, I asked him if he was Jewish. Al fired back, "I'm an ethnic Jew, why do you ask?" Admittedly, my question had been a bit blunt, but I can be frank to a fault on occasion. I told him that while researching, I ask many what their religion and sometimes their political leanings are, and besides, "It was interesting to me that a twenty-two-year-old Jewish man, born too late to pursue photojournalism during the Vietnam conflict, riots in Chicago, racial unrest, and Wounded Knee would find himself freezing in a Wisconsin river to gain access to a Catholic monastery so he could get naked in an Indian sweat lodge while being shot at." Conversational ice now broken, we laughed.

Al corrected me. "I didn't miss the riots in Chicago. I was there on the streets as a thirteen-year-old photojournalist the weekend after MLK was killed, and a massive peace march to the plaza across from city hall ended up in a prelude to the Chicago Convention. Police closed down all entry points into the plaza and began beating people senseless. I witnessed a *Chicago Tribune* photographer who was sporting a crew cut, suit, and press badges get beaten to the ground by police clubs. It ended any pleasant thoughts I had about law and justice in Chicago." In Al Bergstein, I had found someone to provide an insider view of the frozen monastery during the takeover who was not a warrior.

Now in the abbey, which was an achievement, Bergstein had to run the gauntlet expected of strangers. No one trusted anyone except the best of Menominee friends from Neopit or Keshena. Even they were questionable. Early on, Al was approached by in-house goons and unwillingly forced inside the monastery chapel. A pistol was pressed to his head; threats of scrambling his brains followed. Al got the message from very tough guys that a government operative was not welcome, in case he was one. He stuck to his story, reminding the Indians he was as white and as out of place as one could possibly be. It took a while to earn his full acceptance.

Warriors removed chapel pews and installed basketball goal

Photo WI Dept. of Justice

I detected that Al had sympathy for the big picture but was certainly capable of sifting through the various causes and characters. He had a unique perspective that afforded him more neutrality than anyone else inside. I believed he was providing me information as best he could recall. His recollection and observations seemed to be in sync with mine and others I have since collected. Al and Owen were recording a campaign that was becoming multifaceted. Every time someone would emerge from the woods wishing to be a part of the occupation, he or she brought their own modified agenda. Very few were unified. But many wanted hundreds of years of hurt healed.

Both Bergstein and Owen Luck agreed they would stay for the duration and made commitments to the takeover leadership. They were assigned the more exposed rooms on the novitiate's second floor. By the process of first come-first served, but more so by pecking order, the warriors and their companions had commandeered primarily the stately sleeping facilities in the mansion. This afforded the leadership a hasty retreat to the most secure subterranean level of the mansion.

I often wonder who inherited my room, with its corner, second floor, semi-secure southwest view of the river and falls. With fading details, Bergstein recalled that his room left a lot to be desired in terms of safe exposure and protection. The two photographers went about their business of documenting "hours of boredom punctuated by moments of stark terror," as test pilots would describe their own profession. One of these adventurers would hold out for the duration of the takeover.

9:00 p.m.: Law enforcement radio repeater moved and is operational.

Day 4—Saturday, January 4

Shawano Evening Leader—"Tribe Members Reject Offer."
"Talks between a militant band of Indians that took over a monastery and the religious order which owns it broke down Friday night after the Indians rejected an offer which would have ended the occupation....The Alexians apparently offered to make a "concentrated effort" to set up a medical facility for Indians in the building....The offer also provided the Indians would not be jailed for the takeover if they would lay down their arms and leave peacefully."
"Gianoli Directing Some Operations at Novitiate."
"Sheriff Louis Gianoli (Wausau, WI, Marathon County) has been directing some of the operations at the stand-off between the Indians and law officers near Gresham....Officers, however, said they know Indians are breaking through the cordon at night to bring food and other supplies to the embattled Indians....The surrounded Indians have a radio on the same wavelength and they break in once in a while."
"Lawmen Cut Off Indians' Telephone Link to Outside."
"Armed Indians occupying a north woods religious estate lost a telephone link to the outside world Friday night in an apparent attempt by authorities to speed negotiations....Little progress was reported, meanwhile, in talks between the religious order which owns the estate and the Indians involved in the takeover....They rejected an offer to convert the mansion to a health facility under the supervision of an agency in which the Indians would share supervision with the order."

4:00 a.m.: Shots fired both sides—numerous random reports of gunfire heard. None fired by state patrol.

Brother Maurice attended 7:00 a.m. local Catholic Mass. This was the only activity even remotely resembling the structured monastic routine he was used to. In contrast, the warriors constructed a sweat lodge. The lodge shared an adjacent area of the woods where the Alexians had constructed a rough portrayal of the Way of the Cross. The fourteen stations, depicting the passion and death of Christ, were anchored to sturdy trees.

There, just inside the wooded area to the west beyond the mansion front door, the Indians practiced their spiritual and traditional ceremonial beliefs. At one time or another, humans feel the need to connect with nature. The men felt that this location was appropriate and good. This was looking more and more like an awkward standoff as the principals continued to literally and figuratively dig in.

9:00 a.m.: At 5:41 a.m., the sheriff asks that an announcement be made that no one is to fire unless fired upon.

Checkpoint 6, by now, had already seen duty shifts change several times. Brown County relieved Outagamie County and had been on duty for five hours that Saturday morning. Outagamie reported one of their cars attempting to drive from the east barn to the west barn and drawing fire from the nearby woods rather than the monastery. The officers safely made it out of view from the abbey. While attempting to unload their vehicle, they drew fire once again. They realized it was coming from their eastern flanking woods, just south of the Lamberies farm. For another three hours the men of this checkpoint stayed low, then the rounds resumed from the monastery itself.

It was more important for the checkpoint to determine where the shooters were located as opposed to blindly returning and exchanging fire. Their observations and surveillance resulted in this report: "One or two men did the shooting from the bell tower with scope-equipped rifles. They accounted for about 20 percent of its shooting. The rest was a mixture of shotgun and rifle fire from the mansion tower. We were able to observe four males and one female at this position. Some of these shots were directed north and south. Rounds hit the Lamberies silo and also the west farm."

While researching this saga, I came to learn that at least one other man had occupied that bell tower during a different time and under different circumstances. Before the novitiate was ramped down and its purpose and training moved to Chicago, a classmate of mine had found his way to that same bell tower. Tom Scholler, a.k.a. Brother Bonaventure, sought the solace and escape provided by that solitary location.

Tom confessed to loneliness, and I suspect that he also suffered from significant depression at the time. I thought I knew every nook and cranny the monastery had to offer, but it seems that I didn't after all. While I had the luxury of work responsibilities outside and away, Tom would find his own private place to disappear and decompress on occasion. What better place for Tom than the belfry?

The bell tower was Tom's crow's nest, hideaway, and escape. The tower could only be reached by going to the third floor recreation area, crossing over to the adjacent attic, and ascending the steel ladder to that grand perch. I wish I had found that "King of the Hill" location first. I would have used it as therapy on my personal days of doubt and homesickness.

During the takeover, it was now the precarious hideout of warrior snipers. There was ample room to stand and shoot, but limited space was available to crouch and fire from a more stable position. The tower was fitted with cream-colored opaque glass on all four sides, capable of being opened slightly to accommodate a gun barrel. At night, light from inside would illuminate the tower as a beacon in the woods.

The tower stood above tall pine trees on nearby hills. On a few instances, the interior lighting came on briefly until the warriors extinguished it. Otherwise, tempting warrior silhouettes made good targets when the Shawano sheriff deputies returned fire. The tower was the most frigid and wind-whistling post and was only made tolerable with a few bales of hay. With the exception of the gold-plated dome, fifteen feet above, there was nothing more strategically aloft for several miles than this commanding 360-degree view.

An unknown warrior on lookout and guard duty on the mansion roof
Photo by Al Bergstein

9:27 a.m.: 10-33 call that "They are coming out shooting." Numerous state and local units respond. Observers find it was actually only about three or four people and all positions are held. No injuries. No shooting by patrol troopers.

9:40 a.m.: Sergeant Lovas is instructed to go to Checkpoint 5 to pick up two civilians (Mr. Lamberies and his son). They own the farm at Point 6 and were involved in being shot at. Trooper Kujawa and Sergeant Lovas go to Checkpoint 5 and wait. They are told to hold position and the people will be brought out. While parked, the sergeant is being shot at from the abbey. No fire was returned. At 10:20 a.m. Sergeant Lovas is instructed to pull out as the civilians are pinned down.

10:45 a.m.: Sergeant Lovas gets information that several hundred people are going to demonstrate and march on Point 5. Sergeant Lampa and Sheriff Montour decide to create Checkpoints 16 and 17 which would provide a buffer area. Manpower assigned with Sergeant Lampa in charge and Sergeant Nickerson as backup.

A tipping point was nearing. It must be remembered that Menominee was a county at the time. Paddo Fish was their police chief. He managed with an iron fist. Until this point, Fish and his officers had been able to manage restlessness on the former reservation. The "law" was very comfortable with knocking heads, there, when needed. Now, the various native factions began to act out, march, threaten, and demonstrate their own "saber" rattling. For obvious political and practical reasons, Menominee County was not participating in the mutual aid.

The Menominee feared their own sheriff more than all the imported mutual aid white faces wearing badges. Ironically, one of the warriors within the abbey was Ken Fish, Sheriff Fish's nephew. Unofficially, this bright young man was serving on the command staff of Mike Sturdevant. Under the conditions, Ken was among the clearer-thinking dissidents pushing for "Deed or Death."

11:30 p.m.: Sheriff Montour is advised that another demonstration is going to be held in Red River (Township of Richmond) at 12:00 noon. This one is a rally in support of the sheriff. Sheriff Montour is afraid they will march on the abbey and asks Sergeant Mauel, who knows the people, to go there and convince them to go home. No problem develops. Sergeant Mauel convinces them to meet the next day in Gresham off the road.

On this fourth day of the occupation, Sheriff Montour realized the cowboy and Indian gunmanship was unproductive. Early on, it was recognized that Lt. Misch of the Winnebago County sheriff's department brought needed professionalism to the front line. Richard J. Stadelman had only been the new and young district attorney for Shawano since New Year's Day. Stadelman had to hit the ground running, and his first significant duty was to inform Lt. Misch that the sheriff was placing him in charge of Checkpoint 6.

1:00 p.m.: At Point 16, about three hundred marchers approach. Sergeant Lampa is in charge. He has eight troopers and ten full-time locals. He sets up a line without shotguns and backs them with three men with shotguns. Instructions are to not let them through on the road but also to not chase them into the woods. Mr. John Teller is the spokesman of the Indians. He is a local Menominee. Sergeant Lampa and Mr. Teller discuss whether Sheriff Montour will come out and talk. Radio confirms that Sheriff Montour will talk to him on the phone or at Shawano. The group peacefully leaves and heads toward the Shawano jail.

Misch returned to checkpoint duty alone. He approached the Lamberies farm and barn by way of Checkpoint 5 well to the north. The last knoll on Juniper Road provided protection from the sporadic fire coming from the monastery. This was no romp in the woods, though. I fondly remember my novitiate days, when we assaulted and charged up those same hills with toboggans, sleds, and inflated inner tubes. I remember exhausting, uphill struggles, wading through thigh or waist-high snow. All that just to ride down twenty or thirty seconds while dodging pine trees. Of course there was one crucial difference: we were not being shot at!

Stepping off the road and east into the woods allowed Misch to continue downhill and south. He used the cover from the Lamberies farmhouse and barn, where he joined those on duty. Misch announced that he was now in charge. A discussion followed sparked by typical professional jealousy. His appointment was supported with a phone call from Sheriff Sandy Montour. Lt. Misch was now in command at the front line.

2:00 p.m.: The earlier dispersed group marches on the jail—still peaceful. Sheriff Montour meets with them and hears their complaints. No action taken; no injuries.

3:25 p.m.: Message from sheriff announced by District Attorney Rick Stadelman, "If fired upon, use reasonable force to protect yourself." This goes to all cars.

The men from Winnebago County joined Misch, following his tracks over the hill and through the woods. They relieved Outagamie County. A new discipline was now in place at this checkpoint hotspot. Lt. Misch wrote in his report, "At this time, we did not have a communications man; however all officers were advised that only the officer appointed to return fire would do so. The order was to shoot near the person firing from the abbey, but not to hit him. All rounds shot by Checkpoint 6 were to have a report for every round expended."

5:06 p.m.: Troopers Brown and Voss stop on Cherry Lane to observe the abbey tower. Two shots are fired at them. Trooper Brown fires two shots back to clear the tower area. No injuries known. Shots fired with a .35 Remington.

A shooting log was implemented. The men discovered that some of the gunfire was coming from locations that didn't make sense. Their ears and eyes were telling them that their various checkpoints and the Indians themselves were not responsible for all of the gunfire. The men at Checkpoint 6 were recording the shots as best they could, while at the same time they were returning target shots in a tit-for-tat fashion. What was clear was that the mystery firing was not intended for law enforcement. Somebody else was shooting at the monastery from random locations.

5:30 p.m.: Troopers Kujawa and Zimdars report that they were asked to transport an injured woman to the hospital. At 5:40 p.m., Trooper Kujawa advises he is en route to the hospital. Says she isn't injured but complaining of a sore stomach. 6:05 p.m. at hospital.

6:00 p.m. to 12:00 Midnight: No special action. All our post cars are off to duty. Radio technicians install a special high gain antenna which improves our communications. The repeater system is being used beyond what it was intended for. Base patrol radio is perfect. We have excellent cooperation from communication section and technicians.

When the Shawano sheriff's department, Wisconsin troopers, local neighbors, and other agencies providing mutual aid put two and two together, it became clear. Someone unknown to them had introduced another, more unwanted, element into the mix: brazen vigilantism! Authorities at the checkpoints began to compare notes. Either small groups or single individuals were approaching the monastery under cover of darkness and at reduced distances, where a careful aim was more likely to result in a hit or a kill. The fact was that over the last several days, the warriors and the law had only been taking potshots at each other, considering the greater distances and available weapon calibers. Still dangerous, the exchanges continued this fourth day into the takeover. An assault plan by nearby checkpoints with Point 6 in the lead was in the making.

Brother Maurice met and had dinner with the FBI. In typical Bureau fashion, the discussion was a one-way street. Special agents were there to gather, not share information. The only things Neil Bennett and Brother Maurice left the meeting with were full stomachs. It was becoming more and more curious how much was known to the Bureau prior to all hell breaking loose in that village of Gresham.

Day 5—Sunday, January 5

Appleton Post Crescent—"Feed My Child," photo by Robert Beaten. "Indian woman holds out a loaf of bread toward state troopers manning roadblocks near the Alexian Brothers novitiate Saturday. Talks between a militant band of Indians that took over a monastery and the religious order which owns it, broke down Friday night after the Indians rejected an offer. No one has been allowed to enter since a Menominee Indian group seized the building New Year's Day."

Shortly after 3:00 a.m., the command post was moved from the Lamberies farmhouse to a motor home on the same property. Mr. and Mrs. Lamberies had likely grown weary of playing host and hostess to cowboys fighting Indians. Willis Lamberies and his son had already been pinned down under fire while attempting to access their farm to milk and feed cows, a task they had to perform daily. Perhaps it was decided it was just as safe for the family to remain in their home. That nice large barn between them and Indians with scoped rifles could take the sting out of random fire aggravated by vigilantes, at least.

6:20 a.m.: Roving car (four-man) assists Menominee County officers with arrest and search of four female Indians. They were attempting to go to the abbey. Contact made by Menominee County and our troopers provide backup. The girls were carrying ammunition and food.

9:00 a.m.: Menominee County deputies tell our car that about one hundred Indians from Keshena are en route. There are eight troopers, sixteen Brown County, and two Oconto men at Point 16. Sergeant Lampa calls by radio and asks Sheriff Montour to talk via radio to the Brown County officers as they started the pepper gas machine. Sergeant Lampa says he will pull our eight men out of the area if gas is used, as he felt it unnecessary. Sheriff Montour radios them and the machine is turned off.

This Sunday morning, electrical power was terminated in the wide rural area surrounding and including the monastery. It was no surprise. It did not take long for neighbors to realize this was an effort to starve—or freeze—the warriors out. This was not a terrible inconvenience to occupants of the abbey. They could still cook with gas. It, was certainly more than an inconvenience to locals and dairy farms. Feeding and milking cows is like running a factory needing significant electrical resources. This new maneuver by the sheriff angered the Indians. It was possible to keep the abbey in darkness and return power to most homes and farms, but not all without risking the lives of utility workers.

9:30 a.m.: A small gathering of news vehicles at Keshena. They are there to film a caravan of five Indian cars heading to Madison to see the governor. Very peaceful group and no problems encountered.

12:00 noon: Press conference held—Captain Walsingham attended. It is announced at 12:32 p.m. that a cease-fire is in force and that there is to be no movement of vehicles. We are advised by Captain Walsingham that an additional twenty-eight troopers are to be called to bring our strength to fifty. We are to man posts away from the abbey area and operate those twenty-four hours, therefore taking care of our own relief. Men are pleased with this as on previous days relief was erratic.

This afternoon, a single engine private aircraft made an appearance from the eastern sky. The plane, with red striping, made several low and slow steep turns over the monastery complex. Moderate gunfire was heard while the airplane, bearing no identifiable numbers, was overhead. It was assumed that on board was foolish cowboy news media violating the restricted airspace that had been declared by the FAA. The Shawano sheriff determined the aircraft had departed the Shawano airport earlier and eventually returned. In one of the lighter and more laughable moments, a deputy called and arrested the pilot by telephone after landing. A Green Bay television station suffered a hand spanking but got away with their valuable and exclusive aerial footage.

Perhaps spooked by the foolish aircraft, Mike Sturdevant contacted Brother Maurice and Neil Bennett. They used the hotline engineered by the telephone company when service and electrical was cut. All sorts of ingenuity came into play. The warriors found ways to utilize the low voltage that supported wired telephone service. In the basement, just below the chapel, the monastery contained a first-class workshop. Woodworking, electrical, and mechanical tools were available. Makeshift hot plates, dull lighting for reading, and pipe bomb construction kept Vietnam veterans creative. It seemed that all parties were amenable to meet again. A second face-to-face meeting was planned for later that afternoon.

Novice cell (room) on second floor overlooking the river
Photo WI Dept. of Justice

Homemade bombs, materials and wiring found in mansion library
Photo WI Dept. of Justice

Since the preceding Wednesday, Neal Hawpetoss, considered a Menominee Warrior, had become the external spokesman for the Indians inside the abbey. There was already a history of bad blood between Hawpetoss and Sheriff Sandy Montour. They just didn't like each other. Reluctantly, Hawpetoss had been allowed free reign to come and go as a messenger. In an effort to make the warriors uncomfortable, the sheriff now denied Hawpetoss access to the abbey. Hawpetoss was told that if he entered the monastery again, he would be arrested on his way out.

12:00 noon: Troopers start to arrive and all are in and briefed by 11:30 a.m.

The agreed-upon Sunday afternoon meeting never took place. It is unclear who canceled the negotiations but the excuse was the disagreement and role played by Hawpetoss. He desperately wanted the Alexians to circumvent all city, county, and state authority by coming to the former reservation and engaging in more direct conciliation. Brother Maurice was dubious. The warriors blamed distrust of the Shawano sheriff.

Disappointed, Neil Bennett and Brother Maurice Wilson flew out of Green Bay to Chicago that evening, empty-handed. If anything, the gulf between the Alexians and the Indians was greater this day than it had been that New Year's Day morning. The Alexian Brothers leadership needed to regroup with Brother Maurice. In some ways, the Alexians manage their business affairs in a democratic way. I say "in some ways," because when I was an Alexian, I knew very well the man really making the decisions, although from a distance.

Day—Monday, January 6

Daily Herald—"Lucey Urges Indians to Withdraw from Religious Estate."

"Gov. Patrick J. Lucey Sunday urged an armed band of Indians occupying a religious estate near Gresham in northeastern Wisconsin to withdraw from the site....He told them he was prevented by the state constitution from interfering with the sheriff's handling of the situation.... As for sending in food, he said "the more comfortable it is in there the more likely it is that the occupation will be prolonged."

Daily Herald—"Indians Exchange Gunfire with Police."

"Hopes of resuming negotiations with Menominee Indians occupying a north woods religious estate dimmed this morning as authorities exchanged the heaviest gunfire of the six-day siege....No injuries were reported and authorities said they were shooting in the general direction of the estate rather than at individual Indians."

5:00 a.m.: Troopers are on checkpoints around outer area of action zone. None are assigned now within gunshot range or sight of the abbey. More than fifty shots fired during early morning hours from both sides. None by patrol.

9:00 a.m.: Chief Deputy Chet Dahl tells Sergeant Mauel that the mutual aid people are leaving and that they will not have enough men to go more than three more shifts. This includes the key people from Winnebago and Outagamie Counties who will attack the building if that decision is made.

2:00 p.m.: Checkpoint 16 at Highway VV reports a busy afternoon. Several people, including Neal Hawpetoss, try to gain entry. All are turned back without incident. Six to ten news people take a lot of film in the area of Point 16.

The same man who had overseen my class of 1966 transition from postulants to novices was coming back online. More than likely, brother Florian Eberle was beginning to ignore his personal physician's medical orders.

It had not been that long since the leader of the Alexians in the United States had had his chest cracked open for cardiac surgery. Doing his best to shield Brother Florian, Brother Maurice, the United States secretary, gently folded his provincial leader in—ever so sparingly. Having known Florian briefly, nine years earlier, I can appreciate how difficult it may have been to hold him back. In 1968, he begged to be relieved of duty at the monastery. Then, a handful of my class members, behaving as young Turks, did battle with him at a time when the church was in transition. Now, Florian was, again, the man to be reckoned with, but carefully.

3:30 p.m.: Negotiations are broken off. The governor requests a conference call with Administrator James O. Peterson, Colonel Lew Versnik, Mike Spencer, and Skenandore. Two of the alternatives are to move back Point 6 or call out the National Guard.

4:30 p.m.: Allan Wilke confronts Sergeant Nickerson and crew at Point 16 that Neal Hawpetoss and some other young Indians have held a meeting and are going to start shooting some roadblock people in the back from the woods. Information is released to all officers.

That evening, the following statement was issued by Gov. Patrick A. Lucey. "Since the morning of January 1, Sheriff Robert A. Montour of Shawano County, with the assistance of mutual aid law enforcement agencies and state patrol, has carried out law enforcement functions in the vicinity of the Alexian Brothers novitiate in Gresham. We now believe that the continued protection of life and property requires the presence of the National Guard. For this reason and at his request, I have ordered the National Guard to the scene. The Guard shall take charge of the law enforcement responsibilities in the area and shall take charge of the negotiations with those who are occupying the novitiate. My actions will permit the many law enforcement officers assisting the Shawano County sheriff's department to return to the areas and the job of protecting life and property within their local communities. It will also ease the financial burden now faced by Shawano County, which must pay the substantial costs of law enforcement in this situation up until this time."

The governor went on to say, "Members of the First Battalion of the 127th Infantry of Green Bay, under the command of Col. Arthur Heinkle, had been called up and are expected to be in place and in command by 6:00 a.m. Tuesday. I have appealed to all involved that the cease-fire which has prevailed since early today remains in effect. Prior to making this decision, my staff and I have had extensive conversations with public officials and citizens concerned about this matter. As the commander in chief of the Guard, I intend to order that every responsible action be taken to negotiate the termination of the present occupation of the abbey and to avert the tragedy of loss of life and serious bodily harm."

5:30 p.m.: The Guard is to be called. The official time released 6:37 p.m., January 6, 1975. They will be in command by 6:00 a.m., January 7, 1975.

10:20 p.m.: Troopers McKinnon and Van Buren arrest three male Indians leaving the abbey. They are charged with unlawful assembly and taking of property by threat to injure. One of the subjects is also AWOL from service.

This hostile takeover was no overnight "rave" party, but some thought so, especially the very young among the warriors. Carl Maskewit, a native deputy sheriff found three youths on his front porch. They were lost. None of them could have been older than eighteen. The unlucky boys were trying to make their way to the abbey. Instead, they walked into the hands of the law. The Menominee deputy delivered the boys to Wisconsin troopers at Checkpoint 16. One of the boys was AWOL from the navy. Locked up for their own good, Arnold Chevalier, Christopher Chevalier, and John Haack, in retrospect, may have been kids blessed by providence.

11:00 p.m.: Word passes that it looks like troopers will be free to leave on January 7, 1975. The Guard will have peace officer authority per Governor Lucey.

Day 7—Tuesday, January 7

Daily Herald— "Lucey Calls Out Troops, Pleads for Halt to Gunfire." "The National Guard was told to take charge today of law enforcement and negotiations at an unused north woods religious estate seized last week by Indian demonstrators....Lucey said troops were requested by Shawano County authorities to relieve county deputies and municipal police who have maintained an armed ring around the estate and its sixty-four-room mansion....Weekend cease-fire pacts had been interrupted by gunshots, with law enforcement officials in snowy woods returning some of the fire."

At dawn, six National Guardsmen emerged from the well-traveled wooded area to the north. They announced that they were relieving all of the nearby law enforcement, particularly Checkpoint 6. The Guardsmen took command. Astonished, the "Broken Feather" contingent of mutual aid began to gather their gear and belongings to leave. As was his routine, Willis Lamberies was there that morning tending to his chores. Willis worked that morning with tears in his eyes. He did not view this changing of the guard as a promising indication of a near-term conclusion of the mayhem in his front yard.

During the process of turning over Checkpoint 6 to unarmed Guardsmen, all observed a rider-less white horse galloping northbound on Juniper Road, away from the abbey. The animal, with determined intent, turned into the Lamberies farm corral and made itself at home with a bite to eat. For better or worse, the horse's retreat was seen by Guardsmen, deputies, and the lone farmer as some portend to the local outcome. A new chapter was begun with the withdrawal of the borrowed and nearby local police agencies.

12:30 a.m.: Mike Spencer contacts Sergeant Lovas and tells him that the National Guard will need troopers for radio communications and security. Colonel Versnik calls.

It was not without consternation that the lawmen relinquished their post and a job they believed to be unfinished. Lt. Misch of the Winnebago County sheriff's department fully anticipated a debriefing with his men in Shawano with the Guard's Colonel Simonson. After their midmorning departure from Checkpoint 6, the infamous face-to-face checkpoint, they reported to the Shawano sheriff's office. Coincidentally, a contingent of Indian leadership was exiting the same building almost simultaneously.

The dismissed team of Checkpoint 6 walked into the government building with swagger and bravado. Colonel Simonson of the National Guard had told Misch and his men to enter using a different door to avoid a confrontation. Instead, the lieutenant reported, "After being shot at for four days, my staff and I wished to see who were shooting at us. We walked into the sheriff's department through the Indians. Colonel Simonson did not like what I did. Upon entering the sheriff's department, we were advised that we could go home. We were ready for debriefing. However, Colonel Simonson wasn't interested."

2:00 a.m.: Colonel Simonson requests at least forty-two men to man ten posts twenty-four hours. Colonel Versnik advises that the request be granted using the people we have on hand. All troopers are advised that they will be allowed relief soon.

6:00 a.m. to 9:00 a.m.: Men from the Wisconsin National Guard arrive and are placed on post. As of 9:00 a.m., all mutual aid and local officers are relieved. Colonel Simonson is now in command of the area, except for Post 11B—Winnebago and Outagamie County officers are still there.

Brother Maurice never did fully possess the carte blanche the warriors had hoped he brought with him from New Jersey. The Alexians had their weekend huddled in Chicago. It wasn't a lot, but Brother Maurice returned to the front line with a letter in his hand. Brother Florian Eberle, president of Alexian Brothers of America, Inc., wrote in his conciliatory letter on January 7, "I am willing to allow use of property for health care for the Menominee Indians and others as so desired as long as the compensation is just and health care is of high quality." Brother Maurice found it difficult to be enthusiastic that the letter would have a soothing effect. He had already been there and had seen the unyielding warrior faces across the table.

Seven years earlier, in 1968, Brother Florian had written another momentous letter regarding the novitiate. Only months after I voluntarily turned in my habit and jumped ship as a novice, Brother Florian was novice master, writing a letter to his superior in which he practically begged to be relieved of his Gresham, Wisconsin, duties. Florian was transferred to the hospital in San Jose, California.

Brother Florian, admittedly, had lost control of the dwindling number of novices and postulants willing to succumb to obedience and to give up money and sex. Reading between the lines, he confessed a more modern day had dawned at this and many other Catholic monasteries and in the communities. Many of my former classmates said this novice master was not fondly remembered. Florian was recalled to be rigid, uncompromising, and most conservative. In other words, this master possessed the very same management skills needed to keep young men in line.

9:31 a.m.: From Colonel Simonson—all persons leaving the abbey area will be granted free passage with one restriction. If the person is carrying a weapon, efforts should be made to confiscate it—say again— no hindrance to persons wanting to leave.

Convalescing after heart surgery, Brother Florian resurfaced at a time when Gresham was calling upon him again. But for health reasons, he had to fix what was broken from a distance. Twenty-five years earlier, he had fought with some of his own fellow brothers. The novitiate was in St. Louis when the Wisconsin mansion was given to the Alexians. Florian wanted formation and training in the isolated piney woods of Wisconsin. The other contingent of Alexians wished to retain this facility in the more local and convenient metropolis of St. Louis. It was decided to build in far-off Wisconsin in the late 1940s. However, the waning lure of a religious life to the young, and the Vatican Council II, sounded the beginning of a slow death knell for the "abbey."

Brother Maurice Wilson was dispatched back to Gresham with instructions that did not include giving up or walking away from such a fine place. His mission was to maintain the intent to make the facility an alcoholic rehabilitation center that had been agreed upon and was simply contingent upon funding. If folding in health care needs of the Menominee was practical, the Alexians were agreeable—within reason.

The Shawano sheriff provided an escorted VIP ride from Green Bay upon the return from Chicago by Brother Maurice and Neil Bennett. The deputy driving them explained that much had changed during their two-day absence. The Alexian team learned that, per the governor, the National Guard was wholly in charge. They were soon to find out if this was good or bad news.

Shivers ran up and down Brother Maurice's spine. Less than four years before, in what some call a massacre, the National Guard took charge and killed four, while injuring another nine, on the campus of Kent State University in Ohio. There was good reason for the Indians to be concerned. It was easy for Mike Sturdevant to envision another military debacle with dead warriors on both sides. Also, Brother Maurice feared bad decisions would lead to blood splattering marble walls and running down the cloistered halls.

7:00 p.m.: Seems this operation could last awhile and the record keeping is becoming a burden. The post is shared with the Guard and they approve all passage of people through Col. Simonson. Sheriff Wilmer Peters requests and has been granted that two cars patrol Menominee County all night; the arrangements are made per Colonel Versnik.

By the end of that night, twenty-two checkpoints had been reduced to ten. Electrical service was in the process of being reinstated and partial heat was to be restored within the novitiate. Food was making its way inside to the warriors. Checkpoint 6, no longer manned by forty sworn law enforcement officers, was now in the hands of just six National Guardsmen with virtually no ammunition.

Mike Sturdevant remained unconvinced of Simonson's sincerity. Throughout the day, Sturdevant had conversations on the hotline. Efforts to reach some protocol had been discussed all day long. All could not agree upon who should attend the next negotiating session. Mike Sturdevant went to sleep absolutely refusing to allow participation by the National Guard task force commander, Simonson.

8:00 p.m. to 11:00 p.m.: Meetings are held between Colonel Simonson and patrol personnel to coordinate efforts. Quite a bit of movement reported along roads and checkpoints. Could be people attempting to enter the abbey area.

Day 8—Wednesday, January 8

Daily Herald—"Indian Takeover Evokes Mixed Reaction from Residents," by Al Stamborski.
"These reactions range from fear to hope, disbelief to anger, racism to compassion....The *Daily Herald* learned that some people are fearful that the Indians will retaliate against the community if their demand that the novitiate be given to them for a hospital is not met....However, not all Menominees support the takeover."
Daily Herald—"Indians Open Talks, Agree to Cease-fire."
"A cease-fire continued in effect between those at the estate and the security forces surrounding the site....Also discussed Tuesday were steps necessary to restore electric and telephone service to the mansion, another step described by Simonson as an attempt to restore good will with the Indians....When talks broke down during the weekend,

the Alexian delegation said it wanted to outline to the demonstrators a lease offer which included a purchase provision for the estate, valued at $1 million."

Two days earlier, Joseph Butts came up from his home in Chicago. Butts was the community relations secretary for the Midwest Regional Headquarters of the American Friends Service Committee (AFAC), better known as the Quakers.

Butts was there as an early scout of a growing team of neutral observers. The Quakers were beginning to come to Gresham from all over. They preferred to be seen as mobile and nonaligned facilitators looking to defuse hot spots. They would propose twenty-four-hour ride-alongs with the Guard and law enforcement. They would discover that riding the middle of the road was perilously daunting.

2:35 a.m.: A band of about twenty to twenty-five Indians approaches Checkpoint 16 on Highway VV on foot. At least half the group is armed with rifles and some handguns. Due to short manpower on the post, they are able to push through. As they break the trooper's line, a male Indian sticks a .22 caliber rifle against Trooper Van Buren's stomach and tells him to get out of the way. After the group passes and heads for Checkpoint 5, the sergeant in charge of the Guard troops at 16 asks if he should give ammo to his men. Sergeant Lovas is advised by radio and he goes to Checkpoint 5 to take command.

2:44 a.m.: Radio message from Sergeant Lovas at Point 5 to the National Guard major at command post: "Advise may have to stop from going into abbey." Major advises, "Use what force is necessary."

3:04 a.m.: Sergeant Lovas lines up cruisers for roadblock and lights. Captain Conover from the National Guard is at the scene and is now in command of the force. Sergeant Lovas reports, "Pretty well set up here; men have orders not to fire unless fired upon." Status: eleven troopers and thirteen National Guard. From Conover, tear gas is to be used only as second to last resort.

3:31 a.m.: Point 4 requests an ambulance. No one injured, but a couple of the Guard people are having a nervous stomach reaction to the incident.

3:52 a.m.: Group arrives. Sergeant Lovas speaks to the leader, called Vernon. He tells the sergeant that he wants food to go to the abbey. Conversation carries on until Mr. Skenandore, Colonel Versnik, and Mike Spencer arrive. Weapons are finally turned over to police, and all subjects are given a ride back to Keshena. Weapons are returned to them there.

8:00 a.m.: National Guard commander makes arrangements for the electric company truck to go in and repair wires. Power is to be put back on.

Brother Maurice was looking for every opportunity to find a solution. It was clear the Alexians had friends both off and on the former reservation. Rick Stadelman, the new district attorney, advised the brother that it was probably useful to visit the drop-in center in Keshena. After all, most of the elderly and more mature Menominee had been encouraging a visit to get past obstacles fueling the takeover.

A morning telephone conversation with Bishop Wycislo of Green Bay would be the first of many in which Brother Maurice would discover that the Alexians were essentially on their own. "You're damned if you do, and you're damned if you don't," Brother would come to learn. The Alexians were looking for a little guidance from the bishop. Instead, the bishop was unmoved. The signal the Church was sending him was unclear. Were the Alexians supposed to simply throw up their hands, relinquish the deed, and make no effort toward a win-win situation?

9:24 a.m.: Power is restored to the abbey.

Two separate meetings took place that day. It was as if negotiations the previous week had been useless. There were many more new faces in town. Added to the mix was Dennis Banks of the American Indian Movement and local ministerial representatives. The number of players with new agendas grew, and with it the level of confusion.

Neil Bennett and Brother Maurice admitted they were "lost for a solution." Foremost, the Alexians sought a peaceful settlement and insisted the property be vacated. Neil reiterated the arrangement previously reached through Oneida Indian efforts and negotiations, which was soon to be consummated following funding. It was unknown how all were to get past the plan already in place with the Wisconsin Indian Task Force. The Alexians had already committed to an arrangement of lease-purchase to create an alcoholic treatment center.

7:00 p.m.: Lieutenant Artz and Sergeant Vande Zande make the rounds on Butternut and assure all the people that they will see to it that their property is patrolled.

External to the abbey, this was the first day that involved parties sat down to discuss the practical nuts and bolts necessary to reach a satisfactory disposition of the novitiate. This was a day of preparation without the

Menominee warriors. That was to follow the next day, and no one knew what to expect. What was certain—but unlikely to be discussed—was that some or all of the warrior negotiators would eventually be arrested.

10:00 p.m.: Trooper Branchfield reports that there is a lot of action at the youth center in Keshena. About forty cars are parked there, double what was there before.

10:00 p.m. to 12:00 midnight: A lot of movement about the abbey area. Lights seen in the woods and along the river could be people going in at night.

Day 9—Thursday, January 9

Daily Herald—"Policies of Guard in Siege Protested."
"Area whites mounted an angry protest over National Guard policies in the siege....About 30 area residents, all white, left for Madison early today to protest to Gov. Patrick J. Lucey....Adolph Krueger, a spokesman for the whites, said the group wants Lucey to order the Guard to provide more protection for area residents opposing the takeover."

2:35 a.m.: Trooper Zimdars catches five newsmen in the woods trying to get to the abbey. All are identified, warned, and released. Quiet early morning hours. Movement in abbey area all night.

Neil Bennett and Brother Maurice attended an early morning multi-denominational discussion held at St. John's Episcopal Church in Shawano. Even though Dennis Banks with AIM was a no-show, the growing potential for white backlash was addressed. The Alexians continued to reach out for community support.

8:45 a.m.: Roving car spots eight Indians near Point 5. Troopers Kueber and Peth find six rifles and shotguns wrapped in a blanket plus some food. The weapons are taken and the food given to Neal Hawpetoss. National Guard takes over and takes people and weapons back to Keshena. No arrests are made.

8:52 a.m.: Information about weapons as listed above are sent in for NCIC check.

It was becoming a whirlwind day. It was off to the sheriff's office to be brought up to speed and then on to the courthouse to meet with the fledgling, but learning quickly, District Attorney Rick Stadelman, who told Brother Maurice he was still deferring any formal charges. Martial law was in the hands of Colonel Simonson. More than likely, Brother Maurice and Neil Bennett were to expect prosecution of the warrior leadership only. It was awkward to plan successful negotiations when one side of the table held the cards yet had little to lose.

11:00 a.m.: Sheriff Montour comes into the command post and asks the Guard officer in charge for permission to get his blankets from Point 6. They were left there when the mutual aid pulled out. The arrangements are made with the Guard duty officer.

Brother Maurice and Neil Bennett made their way out to Checkpoint 6. The anticipation was palpable as the face-to-face meeting began. There was nervousness among the warriors. Trust was not on the side of any of the negotiators as opening remarks began on the meeting vehicle with a 360-degree visibility.

11:45a.m.: Negotiations start just outside the abbey.

That was the first day the neutral observers were to be officially in service. The Quaker-arranged civilian observers were there to keep a watchful eye on law enforcement. Consisting of church leaders from far and wide, they were to ride along with the Wisconsin troopers who provided roving patrols in and around Shawano and Menominee Counties.

Armed only with two-way communications by the state, the overseers were issued their own radio call sign. They could choose to be stationary at a particular checkpoint or ride the perimeter with a trooper in a squad car. The vehicle was to be clearly marked identifying that it contains an "Observer." The troopers had been instructed they had no responsibility except to allow an observer to shadow lawmen in uniform.

The arrangement was unsettling for these sworn officers. It was not that an observer might see or report misbehaving cops, it was the fear and potential that a squad car could be dispatched to a disturbance or an all-out gun battle. The only reasonable alternative was to stop and let the observer exit the car at a safe distance from harm's way.

12:00 noon: Sergeant Lampa and Captain Adler go to Point 8 to allow Captain Adler to walk into Point 6 to retrieve sheriff's blankets. The negotiators from the other side see the movement of the state car and end negotiations.

After all of the orchestration it had taken to get the parties together and seated, one of the most incredibly dumb things occurred. The state police began maneuvering around the Lamberies farm trying to gather up blankets and other miscellaneous county property left behind during mutual aid, and they inadvertently spooked the Indians. Mike Sturdevant and his men jumped up and fled the bus on foot back to the abbey.

12:35 p.m.: Colonel Simonson issues an order that no movement is allowed below Checkpoint 5.

1:00 p.m.: A request is made by U.S. treasury officers for a state patrol radio monitor. The request is denied per instructions of the National Guard commander.

3:00 p.m.: Neutral observer system is set up. They will be viewing checkpoints and may ride with our roving cars. They provide their own transportation, and we have no responsibility to them.

By some miracle it was agreed that the negotiations would resume a few hours later. The warriors were not comfortable until the guard bus had been relocated halfway between the farm and the monastery, south on Juniper Road. There it sat. The big bus, with the engine running, was pointed north between two treeless, windswept pastures. The negotiations then began in earnest.

There seemed to be unfolding, at last, "a trusting and constructive atmosphere," according to Brother Maurice Wilson. Remember, this was not one of those situations where there were only two sides seated at a table. It was as if the United Nations were meeting and everyone had something to lose or something to gain. Brother Maurice presented the letter from Brother Florian. Neil Bennett made it clear the Alexians were making the commitment commensurate with local efforts.

The negotiators kicked around the idea of some sort of conveyance of the property over to the Menominee. Proposals to convert the novitiate into a hospital to serve the nearby tribe fell under consideration. In a more urgent matter, a plumber was needed. With the power off, everyone was paying the price of frozen pipes. Backed up human waste was of immediate concern.

A daily journal kept by Brother Maurice noted, "The important thing of that meeting was that their position had moved from demanding an immediate signature of the deed to them to the point of ultimate conveyance via a reasonable business transaction." With a sense of accomplishment, the warriors trudged back to the abbey through accumulated snow. It remained to be seen if the dissident Menominee were moving toward achieving ownership of the monastery or just soon to have their disgusting toilets unclogged. Regardless, there was forward movement.

The engineering plumber arrived to make his house call later that evening. The giant boiler and other state of the art equipment that managed the utilities within the monastery were a challenge for the warriors. While there, I had come to learn the complexity and inherent danger of that boiler room. It took two senior brothers to manage the operation when demand was at its greatest, as in the winter when two parallel operating boilers were needed. That boiler room held some of the most sophisticated technology for miles around. There was the very real potential for explosion if they were not maintained properly.

5:45 p.m.: Point 16 advises that a Volkswagen van with Hawpetoss in it wants to take food to the abbey. Colonel Hinkle replies over radio that only Hawpetoss has clearance and the vehicle is to be searched. Trooper Jeschke searches it and finds marijuana, a pipe, and a gallon of wine. Entire matter with evidence turned over to the National Guard.

The community was anxious to learn of any progress that day. A late meeting was held that evening, Thursday. Notable at this assembly was

Ada Deer. Deer chaired the Menominee Tribe and also headed the Menominee Restoration Committee. Dennis Banks and Doug Durham represented the American Indian Movement. Ada's agenda was to get past, in her opinion, this embarrassing and unproductive takeover by political competitors.

Ada Deer chaired the Menominee Tribe & Restoration Committee.
Photo by Curt Knoke

In every direction she turned, this tough Indian woman came face to face with testosterone gone wild. However, Deer was encouraged by the day's takeover negotiations. It was also likely to be the last public encouragement she would offer this nuisance that derailed her principal focus, which was reversing federal tribal termination. Brother Maurice pulled Ada Deer aside. He was embarrassed that the bishop had reprimanded him for not engaging her earlier on. Efforts were made between the two to repair their contact graciously.

Even though this book is really about this place—this monastery-abbey-novitiate-mansion–real estate negotiation—it is also about a unique part of contemporary history partially played out there. A member of the American Indian Movement, Doug Durham played a supporting role in one of the "soap operas" on location in Gresham, Wisconsin. Much would be revealed about Indian-on-Indian politics at Gresham.

8:45 p.m. to 12:00 midnight: Mr. Peterson on Butternut Road advises of quite a bit of movement. Numerous reports of people going into and out of the abbey area. Occupants are ringing the abbey bells all the time.

Day 10—Friday, January 10

Daily Herald—"Whites Angered at Guard's Leniency," by Arthur L. SRB.
"A group of angry whites demanded Thursday that the state take prompt steps to end the occupation by armed Indians of a religious estate near Gresham, warning that failure to do so could result in bloodshed.... Delegation members said…move the Guardsmen closer to the abbey and prevent Indians from entering and leaving the institution, stop permitting food to be sent in to the Indians and shut off electricity to the facility, guarantee that as the Indians surrender, each will be prosecuted."
Daily Herald—"Special Prosecutor Asked for by Shawano County DA."

"Shawano County Dist. Atty. Richard Stadelman today asked that a special prosecutor be appointed to investigate the takeover of a north woods religious estate by armed Indians....Representatives of the Alexian Brothers, meanwhile, said they are hopeful a settlement can be reached and said they are checking into procedures to allow the Indians to establish a health facility at the estate, which has not been used since 1968."

Ada Deer planned a 1:00 p.m. press conference. Brother Maurice asked her for a late morning meeting. She agreed. Neil Bennett and Brother Maurice, wishing to be more forthcoming with Ada, explained the previous day's negotiations with the warriors. Coinciding with a gathering of the Menominee Restoration Committee, it was learned that a comprehensive healthcare facility, to be located on the reservation, was already in an advanced planning stage. This news made no sense to the Alexian team. It looked as if the abbey was not a practical location to provide medical care, as it was too far out from the patient base.

As an alternative, the Restoration Committee wished to propose the novitiate for a different use. Ada's committee envisioned a technical-vocational school as a better use for that location. It made more sense to have a medical facility where patients actually lived, on the reservation. Mike Sturdevant's arch-enemies saw this as a win-win opportunity for both sides. The proposal was to be sold in this manner: The abbey would be presented as a statewide Indian learning center, championed by Sturdevant and the warriors. In retrospect, it would have been good for these parties to have compared notes before the commitment letter was generated by Brother Florian.

As far as the lawful Indian leaders were concerned, it would have to work. Because the tribal chairman was adamant that she would reject outright accepting the novitiate and its land for health care. Collectively, they turned to AIM's Dennis Banks that afternoon to finesse the deal. The Menominee leadership and Brother Maurice agreed to conduct separate late afternoon press conferences.

12:01 a.m.: It is raining hard. Almost no movement except by Guard and patrol people. Trooper's morale quite high considering the weather and difficult low profile. Presence of Colonel Versnik in the field is having a good effect according to the feedback.

4:45 a.m.: Point 20 advises that there is a lot of dancing and ringing the bell at the abbey. Indians in the tower area are aiming a spotlight at Point 6.

12:50 p.m.: Trooper Kueber reports that a newsman, Harry Bloom from TV 6 in Milwaukee, has just come out of the abbey. Abbey calls Colonel Simonson to come in and get him and he walks in and is detained all night. His camera is still in there (value $10,000).

It was miserably wet outside. The cold rainy day placed a damper on the attitudes of cowboys, Indians, and all of those in between. People who wished to be involved continued to come out of the woodwork. Dr. Herbert Carr from the Dakota Sioux contacted Brother Maurice Wilson to inform him that he was on his way in from his home in McLaughlin, South Dakota. His automobile had frozen up and he expected to be later than anticipated. Dr. Carr practiced osteopathy, and he had a close professional medical relationship with the Indians in South Dakota and elsewhere. Carr's intent was to provide medical care for the warriors, evaluate the facility as a potential medical site, and attempt to mediate the takeover.

1:00 p.m. to 6:00 p.m.: Very quiet afternoon. Reports are that an hour-long religious rite will be conducted at the abbey this evening.

9:52 p.m.: The Gresham law-enforcement advises our Point 3 that there may be some action tonight. Seems there is a lot of talk in the local bars.

Day 11—Saturday, January 11

Daily Herald—"Indian Leaders Join Efforts to Reach Pact."
"Indian and white groups pooled their energies Friday in search of a settlement designed to persuade Menominee demonstrators to end a 10-day-old seizure of a north woods religious estate....The elected Menominee tribal committee, having 'rejected the philosophy of violence and anarchy,' said it is willing to bless the demonstrators' health-center goals."
Daily Herald—"Indians Hold Newsman for 12 Hours."
"Television newsman Harry Bloom, of WITI-TV, said Friday that he hiked more than three hours Thursday, then spent about 12 hours inside the Alexian Brothers novitiate being held by militant Menominee Indians at Gresham....Bloom said he spent the entire time in one room, guarded by armed Indians....Bloom said the Indians confiscated his camera equipment after he arrived and kept it Friday noon when they escorted him out to a National Guard checkpoint."

Warriors Meet the Press in the mansion library. Lew Boyd,
Apesanahkwat, John Waubanascum, Dennis Banks (AIM),
Mike Sturtevant, Neal Hawpetoss and Ken Fish

Photo by Al Bergstein

4:00 a.m.: FBI reports from Chicago that eighty to one hundred non-violent sympathizers from Chicago had a rally and are heading for Milwaukee. They are to join another group and go to Gresham. Three area residents report vandalism during the past twelve hours.

4:26 a.m.: Sergeant Lovas sees a suspicious male on Highway "A" trying to wave down traffic. Sergeant Lovas approaches the man and orders him to remove his hands from his pockets. Subject spins around, knocking sergeant down, and flees on foot. Trooper Jeschke catches him and subject is charged with obstruction, disorderly conduct, and resisting arrest. Subject had thrown something that looked like it could have been a gun, but metal detectors were unable to locate anything. Subject made a lot of threats to Sergeant Lovas and others around.

8:30 a.m.: Heavy wind and almost blizzard conditions. Rover 2 car finds people (Indians) who are lost and very cold. The National Guard is called. While waiting for a bus, troopers allow the eleven to warm up and try to thaw out. The Indians are from Chicago, Indiana, California, and Arizona. They had no idea what to expect here and had no warm clothing or overshoes. They are released to the Guard.

Doug Durham with AIM surfaced, raising hopes that a California group was considering putting together a fund of $700,000 to purchase the novitiate. Hollywood had reared its head and the name of Marlon Brando was being bandied about. Rumors of good and bad news were flying around. Brother Maurice Wilson continued to record the details in his diary.

9:30 a.m.: Four more people come out of the woods; this time one has frostbitten feet. Guard is called.

9:30 a.m.: Radio communications are terrible due to ice on the receiving part of antenna. Radio technician William Karner makes an emergency rig which will help until problem is cleared.

10:00 a.m.: Numerous problems with door locks and hoods because of the heavy rains yesterday and the subzero weather.

1:30 p.m.: Sergeant Lampa reports that Louis Hawpetoss at Point 16 has a station wagon loaded with food. The entire inside and roof packed full. While waiting for clearance, unit blew a tire.

5:00 p.m.: Due to a mix-up in relief from a district, the men at Point 11 stay on an extra five hours. Men make no complaint. Weather extremely cold; strong winds; chill factor close to 60 below.

5:05 p.m.: A new policy of apprehension and arrest is issued by Colonel Simonson. This order tightens security some and opens more avenues of arrest.

6:00 p.m. to 12:00 and midnight: Very quiet. Extremely cold. Guardsmen unable to keep tents up due to wind. They are sitting in patrol cars for warmth.

Day 12—Sunday, January 12

The Milwaukee Journal—"Here to Stay, Indians Say," by Sam Marino.
"The Indians said they planned to stay in the novitiate until they received assurance that the property would be given to the Indians for a hospital or school....During the one-half hour press conference, the room was ringed by armed members of the Menominee Warrior Society....
In another development Saturday, Shawano County Dist. Atty. Richard Stadelman announced that Daniel Aschenbrener, 33, of Shawano, had been named special prosecutor to consider charges against the dissidents."
The Milwaukee Journal—"Warriors Seeking Land."
"The Warriors were described as tough and militant by some nonofficials interviewed by reporters....Sheriff Gianoli said, 'We are not dealing with the good Menominees. These are renegades. These guys are revolutionaries looking for a cause.'....'We're taking back some land that was ripped off from us,' Wabanascum said."

2:20 a.m.: National Guard people are asking where their ammo is. Apparently there are mix-ups on relief and the clips are not being passed on. This leaves our troopers the only ones with live rounds on some posts.

Brother Maurice and Neil Bennett had made their way back to Chicago again. A conversation with Colonel Simonson revealed that Simonson had collectively met with hundreds of white citizens in Shawano. This crowd was angry, loud, and threatening. In the verbal confrontation, the whites expressed to Simonson exactly what they thought of him, and it was not good.

Simonson was taking a great deal of heat. Many people said that he brought the criticism upon himself. Citizens felt they were justified in their disapproval. During a private telephone conversation, Simonson told the brothers that the Alexians should express their concerns directly with the governor's office. Finger pointing was rampant. Colonel Simonson recommended that he be replaced—should there be a change in the governor's position.

10:15 a.m.: A marked state patrol roving vehicle goes past the abbey on Butternut Road. The driver and passenger apparently are confused. A short time later word comes from the abbey that they will shoot at the next vehicle that goes by. As a remedy, a snow fence has been set up on Butternut Road both east and west of the abbey. Sergeant Lampa, Sergeant Taylor, and Captain Walsingham interview the troopers who are later assigned a stationary post.

11:15 a.m.: National Guard officers are now assigned to ride with our field sergeants. This gives a much better control factor and keeps both sides better informed.

1:00 p.m.: National Guard is having a lot of trouble keeping their vehicles gassed up. Numerous reports and requests made for gas.

4:30 p.m.: UPI reporter at Point 2 requests interviews of troopers. Request denied and reporter Jone [sic] told to contact the public information office at the Fuller Motel.

6:07 p.m.: Neal Hawpetoss and his wife at Checkpoint 16 drive up in a U-Haul econoline van, 2JB225 Arizona, to wait for Colonel Simonson. Checkpoint 16 asks for permission to search the vehicle—denied by Colonel Simonson.

6:10 p.m.: At Point 16 Andre Le May takes off through Point 16 south on Box Elder Road. Investigation discloses that he had driven south out of sight of the checkpoint and dropped two people off then headed for the abbey. Mr. Le May arrested for obstructing and they are taken into Shawano sheriff. Trooper Holl is the arresting officer and the charge was made per instructions of Colonel Simonson.

Day 13—Monday, January 13

2:00 a.m.: Abbey reports to National Guard that a state patrol vehicle went by on Butternut. Sergeant Kuhn verifies that it was impossible that one of our cars did go past. It is later learned that it was a Guard vehicle going to Post 6.

2:00 a.m. to 5:00 a.m.: Numerous reports of movement and shots around the abbey and surrounding area. A report comes from Point 5 that they thought the abbey fired a shot at a snowmmobile in the area. Sergeant Kuhn advises that Indians are very close to the house at 11B and the feelings were running high. Request made for more National Guard support in that area.

5:40 a.m.: Abbey demands that the National Guard provide armed guards for Russell Means and Dennis Banks when they come or go at the Abbey. Colonel Simonson says he needs clarification.

6:03 a.m.: Armed guard furnished by the abbey to protect Mr. Banks from armed white people in the area. None noted by our troopers.

White backlash had been building since day one. That morning, Neil Bennett made an effort to speak by phone to all of the trusted individuals involved. Arrangements were made for the principal parties to meet in Green Bay on the following day.

12:05 p.m.: Trooper Daniels hears a report that the town of Richmond chairman was going to or attempting to deputize a number of people. The intent is not clear, but could be to storm the abbey. Even though the community is very upset, the chances of vigilante action are rather slim.

The monastery as a whole, straddle the village boundaries of Gresham to the West and Richmond to the east. It is likely the chairman of the township of Richmond was threatening to use some obscure law allowing him to deputize citizens and take aggressive action to remedy the takeover. It was appearing that Richmond was considering a legitimate solution by deputizing vigilantes.

Brother Maurice Wilson recorded in his diary: "About 2:00 p.m. the Provincial in Chicago was deluged by calls from local citizens of Shawano relating their fears and concerns and their advice as to how to terminate the hostile situation there."

2:00 p.m.: Several cars of network TV people hold up at Point 16 per instructions by Colonel Simonson. They are very upset with our troopers over this as they wanted Colonel Simonson to talk to them about delivering a supply of blankets to the abbey. Later NBC is allowed into Point 5 and the rest left.

After an afternoon telephone conversation, the Alexians were not comfortable with the governor or satisfied with his approach to ending the stalemate. In particular, the Alexians were losing confidence that Colonel Simonson had been making good choices. The "abbey" was beginning to seem like a comfortable place to eat and hang out. It was as if the governor had no understanding of what was taking place a few hours north of the capital in Madison. Citizens of Gresham and Shawano, and many on the reservation itself, had found the arrangement a little too cozy.

Two National Guardsmen manning a forward post seemed to sum things up. They had been freezing and watching for days while individuals were seen hauling in bags of groceries to the abbey. It was as if some mysterious Piggly Wiggly existed in the woods. The pair was heard saying, "They don't do Indian uprisings like they used to!"

4:00 p.m.: Neal Hawpetoss and Dennis Banks leave the abbey and are stopped. Sergeant Taylor finds two females and one male in the back of the van. Colonel Simonson tells Sergeant Taylor to have them return to the abbey as he approves all exits.

7:00 p.m.: Meeting in motel room at Fuller—Colonel Simonson, Major Couch, Colonel Versnik, and Sergeant Mauel. Colonel Simonson says he wants the perimeter pulled in some to provide more security and to try to keep people out. Points 16 and 17 are converted to roving patrols. Field sergeants are called in and posts changed right away. Five more state patrol radios are ordered from Districts 2 and 3.

Day 14—Tuesday, January 14

1:40 a.m.: Shawano sheriff calls us and asks for backup at a farm near the end of Birch Lane. This area is outside the National Guard control. Sergeant Hlavacka and two National Guard people respond. There are fresh tracks of about six people to the rear of the barn.

1:45 a.m.: Trooper Olson captures seven Indians on Box Elder Road. They say they are en route to the abbey. The Indians are searched and placed in a locked National Guard truck. After unloading the prisoners, a Guard officer found a 7.7 Japanese live round in the back of the truck. Troopers Du Playee and Dunford later find a sleeping bag in the area of the arrest. In it they find a 7.7 Japanese rifle and a .357 magnum revolver with a number of rounds for each. The Shawano district attorney questions the prisoners.

Three male and four female Indians aged sixteen to twenty-four had been found wandering around, trying to locate the abbey at nearly 2 o'clock in the morning. Although cooperative, there was something suspicious about their behavior. Only one lived nearby. They were arrested using the old reliable charge of "unlawful assembly." Locked in the back of a National Guard pickup truck with only a camper shell, the Indians were transported and booked into the Shawano jail.

The apprehension had taken place near a farmhouse. Backtracking footprints led to the discovery of a hollowed out area in the ground. Here was found the group's modest stash of weaponry. A trickle here and a trickle there, the abbey was amassing a sizable armory. Even counting weapons seized by law enforcement, the abbey occupants were outgunning the authorities. Before the National Guard took charge, it had not been unusual for law enforcement officers to bring along their personal deer rifles.

This incident had required cooperation among the National Guard, Wisconsin troopers, and the sheriff. Over and over again, these sorts of cat and mouse incidents were happening, regardless of the time of day. It was a mistake for Colonel Simonson to have allowed such permissiveness early on. The occupation made the most out of a liberal military man attempting to make everyone happy.

9:00 a.m.: A written neutral observer policy is submitted to the AIM group, National Guard, state patrol, and the Menominee Warrior Society.

To Neil Bennett and Brother Maurice, it was beginning to feel like a routine commute to work. Once again, they boarded a morning flight from Chicago to Green Bay. Their destination was the residence of Bishop Aloysius Wycislo.

That morning would prove how out on a limb and alone the Alexian Brothers were. Their meeting with the bishop was postponed because he had to be on a conference call. Bennett and Brother Maurice had no other choice but to wait and attempt to conduct business with Chicago by telephone.

The bishop's office told the Alexian team that local opinion was that that the Alexians couldn't care less about the outcome of the property dispute. It was being said that the brothers were only interested in retrieving their investment, regardless of who would eventually receive the monastery and property. The Alexian two-man morality play making the rounds in Green Bay was wearing thin.

2:00 p.m.: Members of the Shawano County Board pass a resolution drawn up by the law enforcement committee. This is sent onto the governor of Wisconsin.

2:55 p.m.: Sergeant Taylor checks out a report that armed Oklahoma Indians are attempting to get an old car started and haul arms and ammunition in it. The report comes from the owner of the house in question. Investigation indicates it was the legal owner of the car and it was clean. Both men involved are local.

Many meetings with diocesan Catholic authorities were not very helpful. Little was accomplished, with the exception of Bishop Wycislo committing to telephone the governor. In conversation with Governor Lucey, the bishop's job was to reinforce the severity of the local tension. The strain was proportional to the proximity to the abbey. On the agenda that Thursday was a meeting between Neil Bennett, Brother Maurice, and their attorneys in Green Bay. That meeting highlighted the need for some professional public relations skills. They then flew back home to Chicago.

4:00 p.m.: Numerous sightings of armed men in the abbey area. Much movement in the woods and some shots heard. Some shooting is the backfire of Guard vehicles and some hunting by Indians in abbey area.

Day 15—Wednesday, January 15

1:49 a.m.: Post 5 reports a driver under the influence at their post. Colonel Simonson is not concerned as it does not affect his operation. Clear to turn him over to Shawano sheriff. Shawano sheriff responds.

2:55 a.m.: Reports of four rifle shots from Point 5.

The neutral observers had been in place for a few days. Now, they wished to modify their functions at various locations. Law enforcement had to bite their tongues regarding a new proposal that increased observer involvement. These supposed neutral eyes and ears wished to be present each and every time there was a flashpoint or incident. It was impractical and an extra nuisance for authorities. The American Friends Service Committee (Quakers) was pushing for more autonomy. However, many felt their presence simply added more bodies and prevented frank dialogue.

The official observers wanted free rein to record and deliver their observations to any and all. They proposed one exception. They did not wish to be a source for the press or other news outlets. The use of neutral radios was suggested to provide running commentaries, not just urgent transmissions. Lastly, they wished to participate as arbiters during negotiations. This was viewed as a situation where giving an inch results in a mile. They also wanted more free access to hotspots, even at the cost of that individual being in the way.

This is how their proposal to modify their function was justified. They wrote in their document to broaden their scope, "Observation necessarily involves participation in some sense. However, it can minimize conflict, and therefore alter the situation; it does not otherwise involve participation in the conflict itself."

2:56 a.m.: Major Kerrigan reports he thinks he was fired upon. Sergeants Kuhn and Hlavacka respond to assist the major. No injury and no factual verification that shots were aimed at anyone.

3:44 a.m.: Trooper Randall reports he is very ill; he is taken to Shawano Hospital by the Guard ambulance. Found to be serious case of the flu. He will remain in the hospital one or two more days.

11:30 a.m.: James A. Vigue is stopped by Trooper Ebner. He finds two marijuana pipes and cigarette papers. Only residue is found. After placing the man under arrest, the Shawano district attorney later decides not to prosecute due to the small amount of residue and large workload created by Gresham incident.

The Alexian team remained in their Chicago offices that Wednesday. They spent the day fielding telephone calls from Wisconsin citizens wishing to know who, what, when and where they might expect some results. All concerned continued the daily grind of putting out political fires. The Alexians made plans to meet the following day in Green Bay with their attorneys.

12:05 p.m.: Captain Walsingham after meeting with Guard command advises that he feels too much time is being spent reporting, logging, and chasing down reports of armed people leaving and returning to the abbey. It is decided that too much time is spent chasing shadows and efforts should be made to cut down traffic on these matters.

Day 16—Thursday, January 16

The Milwaukee Journal— "Whites Fear More Takeovers," by Sam Marino.

"So far, the National Guard has refused to use force and has encouraged the Indians to negotiate with the owners of the abbey, the Alexian Brothers, for a peaceful solution....Another concern of the residents in the area is fear that the Indians will stage other takeovers of property, particularly in the Legend Lake area of Menominee County....'We want the Indians out promptly,' said Ollie Burmeister, a Shawano florist....Burmeister reflects the feelings of many residents in the area who want Lucey and the National Guard to take a harder line."

The Milwaukee Journal—"Alexians Want Plan for Use of Abbey."

"The Catholic order, however, demanded that the Indians come up with a sound plan for using the facility before negotiations are resumed.... The Alexian Brothers, in a statement issued from their Chicago office Wednesday, said that the brothers 'are still pledged to a peaceful settlement as well as a pledge to help the Indians and others of the area in a quality type and meaningful use of the facility.'...The Alexian statement also said the brothers had hired a Green Bay law firm to represent them because of the state laws involved."

Rather than take a commercial flight, Neil Bennett and Brother Maurice took Neil's car up to Green Bay. There they sat down with Bert Everson and Phil Brehm, attorneys. If the Alexians were to execute a sale of the monastery, the law firm would be needed and engaged to represent the Alexians.

10:00 a.m.: A woman reports to the Shawano sheriff's office that she was harassed by five Indians at the Shawano-Menominee County line while changing a flat tire. One of them pointed a rifle at her during the harassment.

12:35 p.m.: Point 14 calls and says three people were spotted heading north through the woods. Sergeant Taylor responds with Captain Rentmeester and his men capture two young male Indians. They are taken to Point 5 by our roving car and turned over to the Shawano sheriff.

Brother Maurice and Bennett were stopped by a state trooper on the highway near Bonduel, Wisconsin. The trooper escorted them to the sheriff's office in Shawano. It had become almost routine, but still unnerving, when law enforcement, as Brother Maurice recounts, "apprehended us." Breaking news and false alarms had become the norm.

3:56 p.m.: Car stops at Point 28 with dead pheasant inside. Troopers assume occupants armed because of that. Backup is requested. Sergeant Taylor searches car and finds nothing. Subjects are released. Pheasant is a car kill.

The sense of urgency today was vague. But on arrival at the sheriff's office and command post, all were introduced to John Levine, the publisher of the local newspaper, the *Shawano Evening Leader*. Lavine was a personal friend of Governor Lucey, vice president and a regent of the University of Wisconsin. In his notes, Brother Maurice wrote that he understood that Levine was clearly speaking on behalf of Governor Lucey that particular afternoon.

First, contact was established with Mike Sturdevant over the hotline established with the existing telephone lines. Not long after that, the external negotiators traveled out to the Lamberies farmhouse to eventually meet face-to-face with the warriors. Once there, the parties used more secure communications. The National Guard ran a hard military telephone line connecting the abbey and Checkpoint 6 over the snow-covered ground and across the road.

4:00 p.m. to midnight: Routine checkpoints to manned and constant circulation of the two field sergeants and Lieutenant Artz. Col. Simonson enters abbey with a plumber at Checkpoint 5. On return, left area with a white van following his car.

Col. Hugh Simonson negotiates while warriors hide faces from camera
Photo by Al Bergstein

Always cautious of logistics, Mike Sturdevant wished to be in agreement over the field telephone before stepping out the door en route to the farmhouse meeting. The session got underway in earnest around 5:30 p.m. and lasted about two hours. Colonel Simonson was winning the hearts of the Menominee Warriors Society, if not the neighbors. Simonson entered the abbey and participated in the negotiations.

With all present, a telephone call to the governor's office was overheard by the negotiating participants. Mike Sturdevant was heard telling Madison that he and the Alexians had reached unspecified agreements.

Enthusiastic but not exactly exuberant, Brother Maurice telephoned and briefed Brother Florian in the evening. Florian was in Signal Mountain, Tennessee, on other Alexian business. More interesting, however, was the pending meet-up with actor Marlon Brando in Atlanta.

Neil Bennett telephoned Bert Everson, the attorney they had met with earlier. The progress made that day accelerated their need for legal representation. Bennett requested that Phil Brehm come to Shawano right away. There was an immediate need to craft a sensitive statement to be delivered to the public by the Alexians in the next day or so.

Dave Zimmerman, a concerned neighbor, had gathered together several other citizens of the area that night. They invited Brother Maurice to join their covert gathering in the Zimmerman basement. In his notes, Brother Maurice observed that Zimmerman was pushing for a safe and useful community use for the novitiate. He was campaigning and pushing for it to become a junior college. Others were there to turn up the heat in order to defeat the warriors' progress.

Still others simply wished there to be no Indian enterprises in their backyard—ever. The group was especially dodging radio, television, and the printed press to keep the Indians from learning of their efforts. There had been both clandestine and public organizing in the county long before the takeover. The takeover raised the heat to a boiling point, and there were individuals that evening who were prepared to go toe-to-toe with the governor. Brother Maurice had simply accepted an invitation to speak with the monastery's neighbors.

The Alexian team retired to the Fuller Motel bar. It is unknown if they imbibed, but the two certainly deserved a liquid break that day of considerable progress. The Alexians, as I learned in my postulant days, considered beer a normal staple during evening meals, owing to their German heritage. I will forget the beer varieties made available to us each and every evening during our recreation time at the monastery. Neil and Brother Maurice relaxed, chatting with locals.

Two weeks had passed since the beginning of this adventure, and the warriors and their notable guests had spent days and hours of boredom punctuated by brief moments of stark terror. Residue found later showed that the Menominee warriors had elevated their leisure time to a higher level with a certain substance. The fine art of smuggling weed into the abbey, past deputies and Guardsmen, was as much fun as the cat-and-mouse game of exchanging bullets. Marijuana was preferred over cheap wine.

Menominee rifleman looks south toward the Red River from cloister walk
Photo by Al Bergstein

Day 17—Friday, January 17

The Milwaukee Journal—"Warrior Leader Criticizes Outsiders," by Pat Hensel.

"On Wednesday, the leader of the Warriors was reported to have said that outsiders were interfering with negotiations. 'He wants to get it over and get out this week,' the Guard official said of Sturdevant.... A National Guard official said Thursday that the 'time is at hand' for resumption of negotiations in the dispute over disposition of the Alexian Brothers abbey, seized by armed Indians on New Year's Day."

4:00 a.m.: Sergeant Kuhn reports four armed people within fifty feet of a cruiser. Colonel Simonson put out over the air to cool it and not provoke a fire fight.

5:04 a.m.: Reports of four armed people at Point 14. Troopers Branch-field and Borzymowski say they are within fifty feet of their position. Backup cars arrive and three females and one male are taken to the Shawano sheriff's office where they are turned over to Mr. Skenandore.

5:20 a.m.: Colonel Versnik advises that we are to abandon Checkpoint 5 and pull back roving patrols from the north. Post 14 is strictly an observer post.

6:37 a.m.: From Colonel Versnik—we don't want any state patrol cars in the area of Points 5 and 14, which may cause persons coming out (of the abbey) not to do so. Troopers are to patrol the outer areas only and allow anyone to freely leave.

That busy morning began with an internal senate meeting of the Alexian Brothers. Those who could gather at Signal Mountain, Tennessee. Brother Maurice and Neil Bennett joined via telephone conference call from Wisconsin. There were other senate issues on the agenda, but the future of the novitiate was priority number one. The Alexians needed to establish and vote on their position and decide upon a commitment to be presented to Mike Sturdevant.

Neil Bennett presented to the Brothers the prior day's progress with the warriors at the farmhouse and other developments germane to Menominee and Shawano politics. The Alexian senate especially wished to know about the potential and likelihood of "white backlash." Akin to a family meeting, the brothers continued to hear from Brother Maurice and Neil Bennett, the layperson.

The brothers really had a mess on their hands. There were no clear directions to turn. Based on feedback from the Alexian duo that had been there on the front lines, the senate voted to make the best out of the awful choices. Even though he was an extremely trusted employee of the Alexians, Neil Bennett excused himself from their internal community business, as was the norm.

During the private segment of the senate meeting, Brother Florian explained that it would be necessary for a few additional brothers to be dispatched to Gresham following the Indian withdrawal from the novitiate. He explained that sort of task would be voluntary. On that day, there was no Alexian Brother, including Maurice Wilson, who knew how miserable that hazard duty would prove to be.

11:15 a.m.: Sheriff Montour, District Attorney Rick Stadelman, and special prosecutor meet with Lieutenant Artz. They ask that we tighten security on the abbey as they feel that many people are going to leave. Lieutenant Artz explains that our people were removed from the critical areas earlier in the day and we are still under Colonel Simonson's orders. Colonel Versnik calls the district attorney and explains our position. He assures them that any arrest we make will be complete with pictures and all evidence.

The Alexian team made the rounds that late morning and afternoon. They drove up to Keshena to meet with the attorney representing the tribe in their process of completing Menominee Restoration. Brother Maurice and Neil Bennett also called on the Shawano courthouse to apprise George Grill, the chairman of the county board, and District Attorney Rick Stadelman on the Alexian position on conveying the property.

The newly contracted attorney, Phil Brehm, joined the Alexian team. Together, they made their way out to the Lamberies farmhouse to attend a previously scheduled negotiation meeting. Again, it was becoming the norm for chaos, confusion, or contrariness to rule. That afternoon was anticipated to be simply a continuation of the very satisfactory day before. However, the General, Mike Sturdevant, was not in an agreeable mood, forcing the cancellation of the afternoon meeting.

The balance of that afternoon and evening was spent crafting the Alexian position and statement. By telephone, Governor Lucey approved the wording and the Alexian decision. It was written to encompass the recent face-to-face meetings with Mike Sturdevant. John Lavine, publisher, and attorney Phil Brehm helped the Alexians perfect their statement.

Day 18—Saturday, January 18

6:33 a.m.: A National Guard bus is requested as soon as possible to Checkpoint 3. This order came from the National Guard colonel. Bus is to be empty.

7:19 a.m.: Sergeant Honish is requesting to telephone the command post and instruct to remove all roving patrols out of areas north and west of Points 3 and 4. Twenty-eight people, all females and children, are escorted out of the abbey by Colonel Simonson. They are taken to the drop-in center at Keshena and released. No identification or charges made. We feel there are about fifty people left in the abbey, mostly Indian males; however, reports have it that some white males and other women and children are still there.

Unknown to Neil Bennett and Brother Maurice, Colonel Simonson had made hasty overnight arrangements with Mike Sturdevant to remove the women and children from the monastery. It was either a ruse or the governor had been convinced to play hardball. One National Guard bus was sufficient to load and remove all but the warriors and others who wished to remain and record the inevitable. Photographers Owen Luck and Al Bergstein chose to remain.

One of the photographs taken by Al Bergstein inside the abbey is especially poignant. The boy-child, known as Monolito, was there with his mother, Oralann Caldwell. Eto, as he was nicknamed, had come to be known as the littlest warrior in the abbey. Undeniably innocent and a child not responsible for his circumstances, Bergstein captured Eto's facial expression. Not quite five years old when this picture was taken, he is seen at play and not sure he trusts the individual who just delivered his bottles of milk.

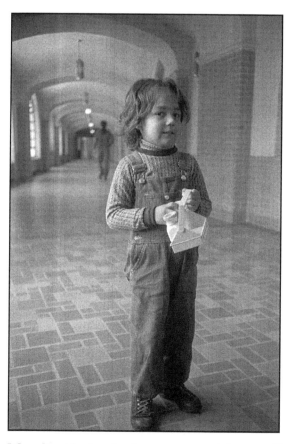

Monolito playing in the monastery cloister walk
Photo by Al Bergstein

Oralann evacuated the abbey with her son, Monolito, along with the other women and children as instructed. Then, after dark, Oralann would return with food supplies. Eto's mother tells the story finding her way back to the abbey. The National Guard was using night scopes after dark. Oralann described the eerie red scope-light exposed by the light falling snow. It, instead, was exposing the guard's location. So, the Indians use the light to navigate in the dark as long as it was snowing. Monolito was left behind with a family member rather than risk the child. Sixteen months later the littlest warrior, while riding a horse, was kicked and died.

Royal Warrington, a local Menominee and spokesman for Mike Sturdevant, made arrangements to deliver a joint press conference. Vernon Bellecourt, a spokesman for the American Indian Movement was to share the same stage. An ominous rumor made the rounds that morning that the National Guard was on the verge of penetrating the abbey walls to introduce noxious gas, then overrun and capture all remaining inside. Fatalities were anticipated. An overwhelming number of non-native local citizens anticipated the action they had been wishing for. It was very eerie

3:40 p.m.: "Mike" calls on the hotline and says a lot of people are moving around. He is mad and says they are going to shoot to kill.

Colonel Simonson, after personally directing the evacuation of the women and children, assembled the Alexian team and John Lavine. Simonson explained what had taken place overnight. The position paper created by the Alexian side of negotiations had been presented in person to Mike Sturdevant, by way of Simonson, the National Guard Commander, who also delivered the warrior response. The dramatic reply was the proposed agreement ripped into four pieces.

3:43 p.m.: Shooting has started from the abbey.

Everyone was testy and had short fuses. Having had the Alexian position paper and proposal thrown back in their faces overnight, the principal external negotiators huddled that morning and tried to pick up the pieces. Rev. William J. Merriman, executive director of the Wisconsin Council of Churches, was a man wearing many questionable hats. All along, he was one of the acting observer-coordinators organized by the American Friends Service Committee (Quakers).

Merriman verbally challenged the Alexian Brothers and suggested that the Alexians had acted irresponsibly. Merriman accused them of causing the lack of trust that had crept into the negotiations with the warriors. Resentful of Merriman's insinuation, Neil Bennett jumped down his throat. Out of character for Bennett, the encounter led to Rev. Merriman being asked to leave the meeting. Merriman was seen as counterproductive and was not wanted. The meeting was quickly adjourned to allow the built-up emotional smoke to clear the room.

4:30 p.m.: Colonel Versnik, Lieutenant Artz, and Sergeant Mauel hold a planning session for transfer of people from National Guard busses to the Shawano sheriff's office. It is decided to use three school buses from Shawano with a sergeant and troopers in each. One sergeant and remaining troopers will be used for abbey area security. Everyone seems optimistic that it may be the nineteenth that they come out.

Later on in the evening, the Alexian duo invited John Lavine to join them in their room at the Fuller Motel. Brother Maurice observed in his notes that Lavine had rethought the earlier confrontation with Merriman and seemed to side with the Alexian position. A friend of the governor, Lavine had earlier been in contacted with the governor's office. The Alexians, along with Lavine, believed Merriman had over-stepped his position as an observer. Further, it appeared that Merriman had acted in the capacity of a provocateur, rather than a peacekeeper.

9:00 p.m.: An extra arrest team kit is requested from District 1. Troopers Misener and Terlikowski are alerted, and Trooper Misener instructed to bring the bomb kit. The Guard has no one available to check out explosives.

Touching base with Chicago by telephone, Brother Maurice learned that the Chicago Branch of the Central Organization of U.S. Marxist-Leninists had targeted the Alexians. FBI involvement and other federal agencies investigating the abbey takeover must have made the brothers seem guilty by association. Always looking for a place, time, and a reason, the communist organization had marched and demonstrated against the Alexian Brothers at their North Kenmore offices earlier that day.

10:00 p.m.: Trooper Kujawa has a fleet accident. He loses control on a slippery bridge on Highway "A" and causes extensive damage to the cruiser. Sergeant Nickerson had asked the county to salt the area two hours prior to the accident.

Day 19—Sunday, January 19

"Novitiate Talks Halted as Indians Break Cease-fire," by Bill Knutson. "The breakdown in negotiations and the end of a long cease-fire came after the Warrior Society rejected what it termed a 'ridiculous' Alexian proposal for sale of the novitiate, and after the society tightened its demands, which now include total amnesty for all Indians who have occupied the religious estate for eighteen days, and clear title to the property...Wilson said the Alexians still have no intention of giving the novitiate outright to the Indians."

Neil Bennett and Brother Maurice Wilson encountered Colonel Hugh Simonson and John Lavine while the Alexian team was preparing for an early afternoon press conference. It was explained to the Alexian team that a delegation consisting of respected elders from inside the Menominee tribe, organized by Lavine and Simonson, were en route to the abbey.

This entourage intended to engage the General (Sturdevant), with kid gloves. Simonson wanted to try reasoning with the warriors, using a "father-son" approach. Simonson was attempting to soften all involved. In an "oh, by the way..." remark, Simonson informed Brother Maurice of the report that water pipes were leaking from the second floor of the beautiful mansion and a plumber was needed. Exasperated, the Alexian team reacted by saying, "It is not under our control."

12:06a.m.: National Guard units near the abbey say they have been fired upon by the abbey. Last shots were "real close." No patrol troopers in the area of shooting.

7:00 a.m.: Arrest team kits checked for proper inventory, etc. Spare batteries purchased. Video recorder sent for from District 5.

10:00 a.m.: Three school buses on standby as indications are that they may leave today. All equipment now ready for field arrests and building security.

The noon hour brought with it a press conference by Ada Deer at the Fuller Motel in Shawano. It was unclear if the young Menominee protesting with placards at the same location were in opposition or support of her comments.

1:00 p.m.: An Indian tribal meeting is held at the Legion Building in Keshena. New demands are made that all three female officers of the tribal leadership resign within twenty-four hours. There now seems no possibility of ending the occupation in the near future.

After some cooling off time from the previous day, Mike Sturdevant spoke with Brother Maurice and Neil Bennett. They used the hotline between the abbey and the sheriff's office. Using explicit language, Neil Bennett reminded Sturdevant that trust had been building after five separate negotiation sessions. He went on to say that if the proposal was not enough to establish good faith, nothing forward would.

With that said, Brother Maurice announced to Mike that he was leaving for Chicago this afternoon with Neil. The Alexians were approaching the end of their rope. They told Sturdevant they did not have the luxury of hanging around and waiting for the warriors' reply. Slamming down the phone, which had become one of his negotiation tools, Sturdevant lost his cool. Only a few minutes later, he called back to resume the conversation in a more civil manner.

Brother Maurice explained to Mike Sturdevant that misunderstandings and semantics were getting in the way of an agreement. Legal jargon was necessary as far as the brothers were concerned. Straight talk was preferred by the Menominee Warrior Society. Brother Maurice insisted the document that Mike tore up was a proper written representation of what had been verbally agreed to the past Thursday evening. He urged Sturdevant to reconsider and seek counsel.

With a 2:30 p.m. press conference behind them explaining their position, the Alexians took questions from the press and the citizenry. Brother Maurice reiterated that the Alexians were seeking a peaceful solution. Brother Maurice and Neil Bennett reviewed the hotline conversation with Sturdevant and stressed that the next move was to be of his choosing.

Before the Alexian team was out the door, Dennis Banks with the American Indian Movement telephoned. Neil Bennett reviewed the Alexian comments during the press conference with him. All were in hopes of a developing secret meeting, planned for the following week, at the Atlanta airport. This new twist would, perhaps, add needed positive momentum. At about 3:30 p.m. the Alexian team drove away to Chicago, optimistic they had done the right thing.

10:10 p.m.: Colonel Gerber, Gene Linehan, and Mr. Warrington enter Point 5. Attaché cases of the two lawyers are searched—O.K. Later in the shift, troopers are pulled from Checkpoint 5 per instructions of Colonel Simonson.

Day 20—Monday, January 20

The Milwaukee Journal—"Menominee Tribe's Split Widening," by Sam Marino.
"With armed Menominees still occupying the vacant Roman Catholic monastery near here Sunday, the split between the recognized leaders of the Menominee tribe and supporters of the militant group that seized the abbey New Year's Day seemed to widen appreciably....The warriors have accused Miss Deer and her associates of not giving them the opportunity to participate in the governing structure of the tribe....'We

Menominees and all other Indian tribes are engulfed by racism,' she said. 'This is one of the chief causes of the occupation, which has been conducted by frustrated Indian people with the best of motives.'"

9:45 a.m.: More food is brought into the abbey—sixty-five pounds of pork and venison plus thirty pounds of carrots and a chain saw. Also small bags of clothes.

2:45p.m.: Two plumbers are escorted to the abbey. Apparently one of them is a member of the National Guard. No official word on this to the patrol. However, one of the Guardsmen mentioned it in conversation.

All things considered, the natives and the cowboys were not restless, allowing the mood to seem promising and good. Not exactly missionaries, the Alexians were back in Chicago on their own turf enjoying a breather. A make-or-break meeting the next morning in Atlanta required they put their best foot carefully forward. They were to meet with Mr. Showmanship himself—Marlon Brando.

Before Brando and Atlanta, the Alexians were to experience a little more controlled "face time" before the camera. Collin Siedor, with Channel 11 television of Green Bay, traveled to Chicago to film the Catholic brothers in their natural habitat. So far, the world had only seen the man in black with a religious collar defending his position in an awkward venue. The Alexians probably should have been better prepared with a public relations specialist before being blindsided.

4:55 p.m.: Princi Transport comes to Checkpoint 5 with 7,001 gallons of fuel oil for the abbey (mv. #GE0240, dated 1-20-75). The fuel is purchased by the Wisconsin Council of Churches from Gustafson Oil of

Green Bay. The truck and the two plumbers come out together a short time later. A Mr. Harry Altergott states that there is extensive damage to the heating system. The upstairs rear portion is not being heated due to ruptured pipes. The plumber also states that there seems to be damage to the boilers; they are not functioning properly. They have heat in the main part of the abbey.

5:00 p.m.: Trooper McKinnon copies an out of state license plate number from a car at the drop-in center at Keshena. Got an NCIC hit—the vehicle was used in an armed robbery in Chicago on 1-15-75 by two Indians. Information is given to the FBI for follow-up.

Day 21—Tuesday, January 21

11:45 a.m.: The owner of the Pine Acres Motel tells Sergeant Zabel that two whites and one Indian checked into the motel. They tell her that they are from the American Indian Movement Institute and are here for training.

Brother Florian flew in from Signal Mountain, Tennessee; Brother Maurice and Neil Bennett came from Chicago; Phil Brehm, Dennis Banks, and Nick Dodge came from Green Bay to the Atlanta airport. All had arrived in time for a scheduled 2:00 p.m. meeting, with the exception of Marlon Brando. He did not arrive from Los Angeles until 7:30 in the evening. Surely someone broke the ice, reminding everyone that "If you're going to heaven or hell, you must go through Atlanta first."

4:40 p.m.: At Checkpoint 5 Lewis Hawpetoss and another male Indian stop at the point and consent to search. Everything is going along fine until a reporter starts taking pictures. This angers the Indians, who demand the film. The reporter is physically pulled away from the scene and threatened with arrest. Troopers report indicates National Guard did not assist or offer to help.

5:00 p.m.: Press conference held by National Guard in a bus at Point 5. Same demands. Clear title to the abbey and the three women resign from tribal affairs.

The Atlanta Delta Crown Room had seldom seen a more diverse group of men before that night. This was Brother Florian's first face-to-face encounter with some of the opposing players in this scene from a comedy of errors now playing out in Georgia. Cordial gestures aside, Brother Florian set the stage. He asked Marlon Brando to explain his reasons for involvement.

Brando already had a track record of sympathy for Native Americans. Alexian archival records record Brando's presentation. The actor asked that all "spend a few minutes in silent prayer asking for a divine assistance in the peaceful resolution of the crisis." Brando went on to describe some of his experiences in attempting to resolve Indian problems. He told his audience he would like to see the Alexian Brothers voluntarily give some of their holdings to the Menominee.

Marlon Brando contemplates harmonica music in the Abbey
Photo by Al Bergstein

In a memorable grand gesture, the actor took off his jacket and wrapped it around the shoulders of Brother Maurice Wilson. Due to exhaustion and the winter-chilled room, Brother Maurice had been seen shivering. This poignant act of sharing was seen as a bit theatrical by some. But this was the "Godfather" doing what he did best.

10:10 p.m.: About one thousand pounds of food is brought in. Vehicle searched by patrol. Eight to ten quarters of meat from the Inca Nation of South America. Local freight dealer Jim's Delivery says a total of about two thousand pounds came in.

From the Alexian perspective, not a lot was accomplished in the airport meeting, which lasted until around midnight. Skirting issues of substance and near-term solutions, Brando spoke in circles. He went to great lengths to stress how generous and satisfying it would be if the brothers were to do as he was believed to have done. Three weeks had already passed and, as was becoming the norm, everyone else was very generous when it came to giving away the Alexians' assets.

Once again, the World Council of Churches was suggested by Brando as an avenue to launder monies if necessary. He even went so far as to say that he would consider providing his own money to consummate the abbey transaction. With little accomplished, the participants returned to their individual corners. No future dates were agreed upon to meet again, and Brando certainly did not write a check upon leaving.

Day 22—Wednesday, January 22

1:55 a.m.: Rover 2 car and several others advised that they heard full automatic fire from the abbey. This is verified by Sergeant Spratz. Also quite a bit of movement in the woods is reported.

7:20 a.m.: Trooper Wrecke reports from Checkpoint 20 that he was fired upon. Says the bullet struck the snow near his cruiser. He noticed movement in the bell tower at that time.

Less than a week before, the Alexians had conducted provincial business relative to their personal lives as a Catholic community in addition to the business of administering their medical facilities in the United States. Subsequent to that, the European province of Alexian Brothers sent their delegates to Signal Mountain, Tennessee. The contingent of European Alexians arrived at a time that looked like cowboys, Indians, and missionaries from the Wild West.

Brother Maurice Wilson took some time off from the madness to recharge his batteries. He went to southern Illinois, where he had family. Brother Florian Eberle and Neil Bennett traveled to Signal Mountain to participate in the meeting that only took place every few years or so. Over the centuries and decades, there had been reasons why the brothers would have a need to forgo these major meetings—such as World War I and World War II. On this occasion, it had to be business as usual even with a monastery full of hostile American Indian warriors with guns.

With such a conservative and rigid outlook compared to the American Alexians, the visiting Germans must have been shaking their heads in disbelief. With the exception of jet air travel, it may have appeared that not much progress had been made since the first solo Alexian missionary arrived by boat in America in January of 1866. The current situation may have confirmed it for some of them first setting foot on our soil. It wasn't looking like civilization had yet been achieved on this side of the "pond."

4:00 p.m. to 12:00 midnight: Numerous reports come in about snowmobile and pedestrian movement in the woods around the abbey. No shooting recorded during this time period.

Day 23—Thursday, January 23

2:30 a.m.: About twelve people are sighted northeast of the abbey on foot. A camper vehicle is in the area, apparently there to pick the people up. Vehicle searched and driver released. Later in the morning this same group is seen in Keshena.

9:30 a.m. to 1:00 p.m.: Sergeant Vickerman and two troopers assist the National Guard contact and search area farms to be sure that they are secure and the people safe. Troopers wear flak jackets and carry shotguns on the detail. All is secure and the people are pleased.

Day 24—Friday, January 24

1:38 p.m.: Colonel Simonson advises that a snowmobile operator has threatened some National Guardsmen south of Checkpoint 5. The man is white and he carries a shotgun. Point 17 on Highway is activated for the rest of the day in an effort to capture the man.

9:25 p.m.: A fire is reported at Point 11. A garage in back of the Lamczyk farm is set on fire by unknown persons.

Day 25—Saturday, January 25

10:00 a.m.: A citizen group from Shawano to meet at the community hall and then march one block to the Fuller Motel. No serious trouble is expected. Six troopers standing by at police department with Sergeant Mauel.

On the Chicago front this morning, roughly a dozen individuals representing the Marxist- Leninists of Chicago demonstrated outside of the

Alexian province headquarters, then located on North Kenmore. They were there to amplify the revolutionary struggle of the working class. The Alexians let them have their say with no encounters or incidents. The wind and the cold limited the marchers' enthusiasm, sparing the brothers from battling communism in addition to everything else.

10:40 a.m.: Colonel Simonson is in the field and will not meet with the group. He says he will not meet with them at the Fuller but will do so somewhere else.

One of the Alexians in Chicago took a phone call from the office of the Shawano district attorney. The news was that the County Board, under the direction of the Executive Committee, had made a formal request of Governor Lucey to meet with them in Madison before February 1. This was sort of a veiled deadline for the governor to take some definitive action. The county was hoping for the Alexians to participate.

12:00 noon: Colonel Simonson meets with the concerned citizens group at the Community Hall. He answers numerous questions but does not commit himself beyond the point that his tactics soon would change. This seemed to satisfy most of the group.

Meanwhile, an estimated five hundred citizens of Gresham and Shawano marched on the Fuller Motel. This was another one of those situations where a mostly white crowd was there to challenge Colonel Hugh Simonson. The theme was generally anger and upset over the permissiveness allowed by the National Guard.

The Alexians in Chicago, particularly Brother Maurice, were kept apprised of the local pulse by telephone. Truth be known, the local "ears to the ground" who were calling the report to Brother Maurice were as much—if not more—interested in learning which direction the Alexians were leaning. The white citizens feared the brothers were about to capitulate, leaving them with a "there goes the neighborhood" scenario.

1:30 p.m.: The seven leaders of the group meet alone with Colonel Simonson at the courthouse. The same basic questions are asked with the same answers given.

Nervous that all sides were at a stalemate, the American Indian Movement reached out to the white citizenry. Local private individuals in leadership positions were invited to come up to Menominee territory. AIM wished to be prominent in any peaceful resolution. The problem was that the Menominee Warrior Society had always insisted that this campaign was their own, not the doings of the well-known national organization.

3:15 p.m.: A low flying aircraft is flying over the abbey. No identification is made. The plane is fired at three times from the abbey.

7:30 p.m.: Sergeant Vande Zande and Trooper Caramanidis assist Menominee County and capture a federal fugitive, Henry Welch. No injury or resistance.

11:00 p.m.: Between fifty and seventy cars are reported in Keshena at the drop-in center. Numerous sightings of movement in the abbey area.

Day 26—Sunday, January 26

12:00 midnight to 8:00 a.m.: During early morning hours a Guard helicopter arrives.

Sheriff Sandy Montour discouraged a white contingent from going up north to meet with the Indians. Montour had been quiet over the last several weeks since the National Guard had been present in his county. It was unknown why the sheriff advised that such a meeting should not take place. One possible reason was the sheriff's paranoia—or an attempt to exercise and reassert his bailiwick. The sheriff had become redundant.

12:43 p.m.: Mr. Larry Gehr goes with Alex Askinette to Keshena to talk to the AIM people.

1:25 p.m.: Troopers Sheldon and Began stop a car at Checkpoint 5. There are four males and three females inside. All are young American Indians. The driver refuses to identify herself and uses considerable profanity. Shortly after that, Trooper Began spots a shoulder holster being worn by one of the men. The action then starts and concludes with quite a battle and several felony charges including battery to a police officer and concealed weapons. Sergeant Vickerman is bitten on the finger, requiring medical attention.

Day 27—Monday, January 27

The Milwaukee Journal—"Shawano Deadline Dropped," by Sam Marino. "A white citizens' committee Sunday has abandoned its threats that it would take up arms against the Indians occupying the Alexian Brothers novitiate unless Gov. Lucey and the National Guard come up with a solution by Tuesday noon....He also said that the relaxation of the Tuesday demand was no sign of weakness on the part of the committee but just indicated an understanding that negotiations could not be conducted under an atmosphere of duress."

External to the Menominee Warrior Society was the Menominee People's Committee, which generally, yet cautiously, supported the warriors' takeover of the abbey. The committee was a more levelheaded body to negotiate with than the warriors. The Alexians agreed to meet with this contingent, who were political rivals of Ada Deer, chairing the tribal restoration efforts. It was becoming more and more clear that the Alexians were attempting to navigate through a circus of dangerous politics.

It was agreed such a meeting should take place at a substantial distance away from the novitiate. That afternoon, Brother Maurice and Neil Bennett flew in from Chicago to the Green Bay airport. There, they met with Ted Boyd, chairman of the Menominee People's Committee. Boyd brought with him a resolution unanimously supported by 148 of its members. Bennett and Brother Maurice viewed this document as substantial and carrying a great deal of weight.

Midnight to 11:00 a.m.: Routine slow time. Numerous calls for local to people to get permission to move within the perimeter.

11:25 a.m.: Troopers Ebner and Langley find a very small amount of suspected marijuana in a car. Due to the very small amount and present circumstances, they are ordered to confiscate the material and release the subjects.

Before returning to Chicago following the Green Bay airport meeting, Brother Maurice left behind a letter of intent that left very little room to turn back. Instructions were given for Colonel Simonson to hand carry that communication directly to Mike Sturdevant. Hopes were that a fundamental decision, reached by the brothers, would lay to rest these grueling January 1975 days.

4:30 p.m.: Checkpoint 6 advises that eleven shots were fired at the farm buildings. People in the abbey say they shot because they felt someone was in the barn with a scope. The Guard sends a team to search including a person to climb the silo—no one found.

Day 28—Tuesday, January 28

2:00 a.m.: A vehicle goes through Checkpoint 1 without stopping. It is stopped by Guard people at Point 13. They call for trooper assistance. Troopers Doxrude and Prusko respond. Some open cans and numerous full cans of beer are found in the car. No charges are made and the vehicle is escorted to Gresham.

Members of the Menominee People's Committee spent the night in the abbey following their meeting with the Alexian team at Green Bay. The committee worked on selling Mike Sturdevant on the idea of accepting and fine-tuning an agreement that was now very close to mutual agreement.

8:20 a.m.: Meeting conducted by Colonel Versnik regarding arrest teams and duties. Arrest teams from Districts 1, 3, and 4 are on alert subject to three-hour call.

From Chicago, Brother Maurice telephoned the National Guard command post in Shawano. He learned that an incident had taken place with the potential to upset and derail the precarious steps forward.

Details were sketchy, but one of the warriors had just been shot in or near the abbey. Dr. Herbert Carr was still an occupant at the abbey and was rendering medical aid. Blame was placed on unseen vigilantes having penetrated the National Guard perimeter.

3:38 p.m.: A low-flying aircraft is in the abbey area. After the aircraft lands, Troopers Reich and Olson proceed to the Shawano airport and warn pilot and passengers of the dangerous situation. Plane carries reporters and cameramen.

Colonel Simonson's staff informed the Alexians that Dr. Carr had removed a bullet from the upper leg of the warrior. It was also learned it was likely a superficial wound. The hysteria passed. What remained important was the letter of intent and the proposal presented to the warriors. Brother Maurice needed to know how he was to proceed.

Mentally, Brother Maurice had already moved on to the assumption that the worst was over. He asked what he should expect to transpire after the monastery was vacated. The National Guard told him to expect a few days of searching and securing the property and building. The Wisconsin Department of Justice Crime Laboratory Bureau would then have their investigators in. Responsibility would then pass on to the Shawano sheriff before the Alexians could reclaim the monastery.

10:00 p.m. to 11:00 p.m.: Reports of heavy fire from the abbey toward Point 20. Trooper Striegel reports that it sounded like full automatic. He also reports heavy caliber slow fire at Point 20. No return fire. Troopers say it sounded like three different weapons. Some of the shots sound as if they were coming from the rear of the buildings at Point 20. This is not confirmed.

Day 29—Wednesday, January 29

1:00 p.m.: A meeting is held to define responsibility in regard to the evacuation procedures. Special prosecutor Daniel Aschenbrener issues a written report.

Day 30—Thursday, January 30

The Milwaukee Journal—"Newsmen Question Lavine Privileges." "Newsmen are questioning the special access Shawano publisher John Lavine has to behind the scenes activities at the Menominee Warriors Society siege near here....He issued a report on all-night negotiations from information given him by Simonson....The 34-year old Lavine has accompanied Simonson on inspections of the novitiate area both by car and helicopter."

4:55 a.m.: Sergeant Hlavacka checks out a Guard truck at Point 26 that failed to respond to security check. Finds the three occupants.

9:10 p.m.: A deputy sheriff and state marshal from South Dakota stop at the command post looking for Dennis Banks. They had a summons for him.

Day 31—Friday, January 31

1:00 a.m.: The FAA has again imposed air restrictions within five nautical miles of the Alexian novitiate until further notice.

6:40 a.m.: Mr. John Tomasich called and inquired as to what information we had about three thousand AIM members coming into the county. Mr. Tomasich is the assistant superintendent of schools. He also heard that an attempt was to be made to kidnap Col. Simonson. Both seemed to be rumor only.

9:00 a.m.: Father Groppi and Marlon Brando are reported to be in Keshena.

It wasn't until this week that Marlon Brando resurfaced after his performance at the Atlanta airport. His sermon did not produce any funds to pay for Menominee Warrior intentions. The Alexians knew better than to expect anything except lip service. The brothers were clearly on their own. Marlon Brando did not arrive in Wisconsin with money from the World Council of Churches—or a single dollar from Hollywood.

Brando made his way into the novitiate through the back door, as had been well-practiced over the last three weeks. Most of the Menominee Warriors saw his visit as a stunt, delivering hollow promises. Deservingly, Brando was not well received. Native Americans, as a rule, are somewhat unimpressed with notoriety, including Brando.

While Brando wept dramatically, his tough audience questioned his real reason for being there. The warriors saw no value in Brando, with the exception of press coverage. One of the warriors challenged the tearful actor. Brando was wearing a Rolex. The warrior pointed this out, telling Brando he needed to give it up to the cause. So he did just that. The watch came off his wrist in a grand gesture of solidarity.

Marlon Brando was taken up to the roof of the mansion as part of the grand tour. He needed to enter the attic that we, as postulants, once called home. Crawling up a metal ladder leading to the metal hatch that opened to the outside, Brando was told to stay low. As if on the cue, "Ready, camera, action," a few of the warriors fired a short volley in the direction of their unknown target du jour. The burst of firepower from the mansion drew return fire from the woods. Brando nearly wet his pants. The Indians laughed aloud at brave Brando whimpering and begging to descend the ladder to safety. Fearful, Father Groppi declined and remained crouched below.

The next morning was the most memorable of the takeover. Before receiving large quantities of good food, the occupants of the abbey had been scrounging around for anything to eat. Evidence of that lay on the floor of the basement. Large quantities of blood, feathers, and other animal body parts decorated the tree trunk, ax, and hatchet nearby.

The abbey was not the Ritz Carlton, and even Marlon Brando did not rate anything better than a sleeping bag. Upon waking the next morning, Indian humor was still intact. The "Godfather" discovered he had shared his bedding with the nearby head of some poor pony that had been butchered many days before. Or at least, this was the story told.

11:15 a.m.: About fifty people including Father Groppi at Point 16. They pushed through, went about one hundred feet or so into the area, and then went back behind the roadblock outside the perimeter. Very peaceful.

All the ingredients for a calamity were in place. That last day of January was quiet—an eerie sort of quiet. So quiet that the silence was deafening. The National Guard had successfully camouflaged a military combat tank and hidden it less than a mile from the monastery. One way or the other, an end to the impasse was approaching. The brothers could not avoid the weight they felt upon their shoulders. Visions of Kent State casualties in greater numbers acted out in their monastery were frightening.

There was no turning back either for the General, Mike Sturdevant. Whatever the outcome was to be—and given enough time—it would be said that Sturdevant was a "standup" sort of man by admirers. At any time, Sturdevant could have bolted under the cover of darkness and made his way to safety as a fugitive rather than a martyr.

Mike was standing his ground to claim the empty monastery for his young followers. Although his methods were perhaps not the most sophisticated, Mike, so far, was proving somewhat successful in his maneuvers. Sturdevant and that momentum were nearing a suicidal brink.

Popular with some and clearly hated by others, Colonel Hugh Simonson was refereeing a dangerous game with multiple teams wandering off and on a changing field. Simonson was responsible for exercising the rule of law. Some would say he was managing a situation requiring the wisdom of Solomon.

Surely, visions of Kent State and young people face down in their own blood made sleep difficult for him, also. Simonson was swimming in a sea of freely volunteered advice from the public, which had no consideration for the eventual consequences. Governor Lucey was expecting his commander to make the right decisions.

12:15 p.m.: Another group combined with the first to total about one hundred. They built fires and stayed most of the afternoon. About ten troopers and numerous Guard people were there.

4:45 p.m.: Three young Indian girls were taken to Point 5 by Col. Gerber. A check with Col. Simonson indicated that the girls should be given the choice of being arrested and taken to Shawano or returning to the abbey. They chose to return.

8:00 p.m.: Checkpoint 11 reported someone was attempting to shoot the power line going into the abbey. Sgt. Holt and two troopers responded—no one located. The buildings in the area were searched. Mrs. Lamczyk appeared very haggard and tired. Father Sippel felt she was on the verge of a breakdown.

Day 32—Saturday, February 1

Brothers Maurice and Florian met for coffee at the home of Neil Bennett. The more relaxed atmosphere of the house in suburbia had become an invaluable oasis away from the incessant institutional ringing telephone. This arrangement created a needed filter for the three men who were making strategic critical decisions.

The Alexian team telephoned Robert Dunn from the governor's office. Dunn told the three Alexian men that the governor was to make a statement to the press that day in the midmorning. Dunn indicated that Lucey would make himself available within the next twenty-four hours. It was agreed that a telephone conversation would be an appropriate preliminary action before the face-to-face meeting.

Between the three that morning, the following collective decision was made: "After further discussion, we agreed that we should contact Gov. Lucey and to meet with him at his earliest convenience and explain to him that we had come to the conclusion that we felt we should convey the deed to the property to the Menominee Indian tribe in place of any further violence or in the face of imminent violence."

12:30 p.m.: A friendly crowd of whites, Indians, and reporters at Point 16. No attempts made to challenge Guard. The South Dakota officers serve papers on Dennis Banks.

That noon telephone call was placed to the governor, and Florian spoke with Patrick Lucey. He told the governor of the Alexian intent. All agreed the Alexian three would catch the 2:00 p.m. flight from O'Hare to Madison. The contingent was met by police and escorted to the capital. In the presence of the governor and his staff, Brother Florian repeated the Alexian decision expressed earlier that morning by phone.

4:00 p.m.: About one hundred sign-carrying Indians march on Point 16. Speeches made over loudspeakers. Crowd left forty minutes later.

Now that a decision had been made as to *what* was to happen, it was the *how* that needed fine tuning. Due to the volatility already demonstrated many times over at the abbey, all agreed on making an urgent call to Mike Sturdevant with the news. Governor Patrick Lucey used the special direct phone hookup to the abbey.

Mike Sturdevant's reaction was described as "jubilant and very pleased." He was told of the recommendation that a committee of six would be created. Mike assured the governor he would quickly respond with a recommendation of three good men to serve on that committee. This breaking news merited a special press release. Relieved but saddened, the men representing the Alexians returned home on a seven o'clock flight with heavy hearts. They had publicly committed to walking away from the monastery one of them had put so much into a quarter of a century earlier.

8:00 p.m.: A report comes in that a Mr. Stanford Peterson was shot in the head near his home on Highway A. The attacker is reportedly an Indian male. Sergeant Holt takes charge of the search for the individual, which is not successful. The footprints head directly toward the abbey.

Day 33—Sunday, February 2

"Gresham Snowmobiler Shot; Assailant Sought."
"Authorities said a snowmobile driver was shot and wounded Saturday night as tension mounted while the National Guard prepared to move armored vehicles into a tightened security ring around a religious estate occupied by a group of armed Indians....A spokesman for St. Vincent's Hospital said Peterson was shot at close range with a .22 caliber rifle.... There was no official confirmation, but a leader of the Concerned Citizens Committee of Shawano County claimed the shooting was carried out by an Indian on his way into the novitiate."

Neil Bennett called from Chicago to Shawano to test the political waters. More and more were becoming aware, by way of rumor, of the momentous decision made the day before in Madison. Joe Sensenbrenner, spokesman for the governor, felt it was best that the Alexians officially break the news locally rather than appearing to hide in Chicago.

Together, Brother Maurice Wilson and Neil Bennett made the oh-so-familiar forty-five-minute flight to Green Bay and the rent-a-car drive to the Gresham and Shawano area. Another Fuller Motel rendezvous, for the sake of strategy, preceded another westbound National Guard escort to the Lamberies farmhouse. Colonel Simonson had arranged for this meeting, if not the final meeting of the principals, perhaps one preliminary to the very end.

Sunday morning, Mike Sturdevant, a contemporary Menominee warrior, and Maurice Wilson, a modern Catholic monk sat face to face at 10:45 a.m. Not far away, Stanford Peterson had been shot in the head the night before while he and his wife were snowmobiling south of the river near the railroad tracks. The rear of the abbey had become a revolving door for vigilantes looking for trouble, and abbey occupant traffic was willing to oblige. Nothing was said at this meeting about Peterson fighting for his life in the Green Bay hospital.

Novitiate classroom blackboard depicts lethal human target locations
Photo by Al Bergstein

All at the meeting were walking on eggshells. It was now or never. Sturdevant volunteered the names he saw fit to serve on the interim committee to oversee the transfer of property. It was explained to Mike Sturdevant that the entire committee was not to be made up of his choosing alone. Governor Lucey had chosen two individuals willing to serve. The Alexians would also be making their recommendations. There seemed to be no further argument. With a little negotiation within the farmhouse, signatures on both sides inked the deal.

Early in the afternoon, Sturdevant returned to the abbey and the Alexian team left Checkpoint 6 to return to the hotel. There was much to do. Those who had facilitated the fragile agreement took the documents to the Shawano newspaper to make copies of the agreement, which had been written on Alexian stationary and executed in longhand. A courier, more than likely Colonel Simonson himself, delivered the originals to the exuberant warriors.

Brother Maurice and Neil Bennett spent the balance of the afternoon typing and recording their notes. A glut of calls were made and received. This was big news. To say the world was watching was not an exaggeration. The three U.S. television networks, printed press, and radio where there to learn the fate of the dissident American Indians and that handsome monastery next to the waterfall.

At 4:00 p.m., Brother Maurice delivered the news to approximately one hundred reporters. He was followed at the microphone by respected Menominee citizens, Sheriff Montour, District Attorney Stadelman, and others. Pleased an agreement had been reached, most were nervous the Alexian decision had the potential of sparking a commotion. Neil and Brother Maurice thought it best to fly home that very evening. The increased numbers of National Guardsmen were prepared.

7:25 p.m.: Meeting is held on final arrest and takeover operations. It is firmly decided that the turnover point will be Point 14 or 11B. No others considered.

The Guard began to use psychological operation techniques. Even Colonel Simonson was dropping veiled threats about what was soon to take place. The intent was to demonstrate to Sturdevant and others that force was building and fuses were growing short. The number of hotline conversations with Sturdevant were increasing in intensity. It was hard to tell how many occupants were inside at any given time. However there was visual evidence that their numbers were beginning to dwindle. The authorities allowed any and all who wished to leave to do so and denied, as best they could, access to the abbey.

10:55 p.m.: Fleet accident. Troopers Engel and Jeschke in the blackout area on Cherry Road run into each other going opposite ways.

11:59 p.m.: Removed all roving patrols on Highway "VV" per instructions from Colonel Simonson.

Day 34—Monday, February 3

The Milwaukee Journal—"Indians Expected to Pull Out of Novitiate Today," by Sam Marino.
"An agreement was reached Sunday apparently ending the 33-day occupation of the former Alexian Brothers novitiate near here by a group of armed Indians....The agreement calls for the deed of the estate to be turned over to the Menominees on the date the tribe will be restored to tribal status in February or March, and a good faith effort by the Indians to reimburse the Alexians for the property....Among the major provisions for the agreement were:...a promise by the Warriors to peacefully leave the novitiate building and grounds...the selection of a committee of seven for caretaking and managing the property during the interim period...."

LTC Ed Wulgaert had already served on miserably frigid days with his infantry troops outside, in the elements, coming down with the flu. Known as Red Arrow men, the 360 strong had been on abbey duty January 12–19. C.O. Wulgaert dismissed his battalion and they were replaced by others. However, Wulgaert remained semi-undercover in the vicinity.

In the event the warriors did not comply and remained holed up, the National Guard needed to activate an unpleasant alternative: the abbey was to be taken back using force. Colonel Simonson needed the right man with the right people, but not cowboys with itchy trigger fingers. The governor wished for Gresham to be bloodless. If not completely bloodless, he wanted results that certainly would not be seen as a massacre.

Chain of command agreed that a certain supervising principal of several public schools in his regular life was the right man to lead and follow orders in his occasional job as a National Guard weekend warrior. Ed Wulgaert was the man of choice. He had already come to know Simonson and what he wanted as well as what he did not want. He took on the risky assignment.

Ed Wulgaert and his 56 guardsmen were to storm and capture the abbey
Photo by Curt Knoke

Lieutenant Colonel Ed Wulgaert went shopping for a location. The assignment and preparations were kept under wraps. Ed Wulgaert needed volunteers, and the budget could afford sixty men, no more. It would be self-limiting anyway, because Wulgaert was picky and wanted only veterans. He wanted individuals who had already watched the world go by while manning the various checkpoints around the novitiate.

He found the perfect place. Clintonville is about sixteen beautiful and bucolic miles from the abbey. There, conveniently situated, was VFW Post 644, which could accommodate sixty men. The large hall and basement below provided enough elbow room. As typical for Wisconsin, the facility was built with beverages in mind. Suitable personal facilities were available for so many men living in such close quarters.

He was unable to recruit sixty, but fifty-six would have to do. So as not to draw attention, Wulgaert's volunteer personnel were trucked in and dropped off rather than using their own personal transportation. Few, if any, vehicle tracks in the snow and low-key activity allowed his special project some anonymity. From the outside, it did not appear there were five dozen men practicing an assault in pastoral Wisconsin. Now they needed to study maps, monastery floor plans, and strategy.

Arrangements were made to send in experts to train regular volunteer guardsmen from Wisconsin. They needed the skills to enter a stone fortress, then escort angry, armed, citizen Indians out the front door. As basic as a sledgehammer, an engineer's demolition gun (a tank on steroids), prepared for the worst.

Another weapon that had been useful in Vietnam to clear underground tunnels was planned for a unique use. When I lived in the novitiate, I had been given a duty that required another unpleasant claustrophobic challenge. Between the caretaker's residence and the mansion ran an underground conduit.

To allow maintenance, the tunnel was built to accommodate a bent-over grown man to walk the length. To many, it was a secret. I recall all manner of utilities coursing through the tunnel that allowed the caretaker's cottage to remain connected yet unseen.

A Mighty-Mite was to be used. Along with smoke, some tear gas or similar concoction would be employed to encourage choking and coughing warriors to give up for fresher air outside. Discovered by studying schematics, the underground tunnel appeared to be a great delivery system for something noxious from a distance. Although the warriors used the lower levels and believed they provided their best protection, they were in fact their most vulnerable point. Just as in Vietnam, there would be nowhere to hide from the ghastly blower powered by a simple lawn-mower engine pumping intolerable smoke.

4:00 a.m.: Assistance call from Menominee sheriff for help in Keshena. Subjects pull weapons on the local officers. Supposed to be about fifteen armed men with ski masks.

On the day before, the Guard reactivated 390 infantry men from the 2-127th Infantry. An additional 385 from the 1-128th Mechanized Infantry would play a backup role. On scene, 68 men staffed the Headquarters Company. And, of course, there were the 56 volunteers whose mission it was to breach stone walls.

5:00 a.m.: One of the cars with subject is sighted by our troopers. Road-block set up and arrests made by the Menominee officers.

By this time on the dark morning, two or so hours had passed with constant and impressive noises. Mechanized military vehicles crisscrossed the deep snow fields north of and adjacent to the abbey. It was partially theater. This show was designed to impress any takeover occupant that now might be a good time to leave. Each one of these thirty or so armored personnel carriers (APC) was capable of carrying eleven men.

8:00 a.m.: Seventy-two state patrol people on alert waiting for the evacuation. The day is spent waiting and preparing.

The official word was that the evacuation was to be during daylight hours. But, strategically allowing the maneuver to stretch into darkness would allow last-minute deserters time to slip out and into the woods is actually preferred. It appeared that it was working.

In more ways than one, the resistant warriors were beginning to see "daylight." Before them to the north and the east was an impressive array of power that had amassed in the early dark. Among the warriors, there were Vietnam combat experienced veterans. Surely, there were none who believed the occupants could survive a frontal attack.

To reinforce the statement made by so many APCs, Colonel Simonson allowed his men to reveal their scariest tool of all, which had been kept under wraps for several days. With the engines silenced on the APCs, National Guardsmen rolled out something that had not been seen or heard before. Different track noises were heard first, and then the big stick came into view, rolling west to east on Butternut Road. Finally, the warriors got their first peek at the abbey coup de grace.

To neighbors and warriors, it looked like a tank and sounded like a tank. After doing a double take, one could not help but notice the short stubby gun barrel that looked as if it were an unfortunate cat that lost its tail, or an overly aggressive circumcision. There was a reason for its perceived handicap. This was a combat engineer vehicle with a demolition gun. Its job at the abbey was to get up close and personal, while blowing giant holes in this beautiful building.

The APCs advanced on the abbey without incident. Resistance was not expected, but it was certainly planned for. Hardheaded to the very end, Sturdevant remained inside, still working the telephone for a better deal. The atmosphere relaxed a bit. The Guardsmen began to emerge from their protective vehicles. Armed dissident warriors were seen from their windows, and even on the rooftops. The Wisconsin National Guard was reminded of the potentially dangerous exposed electrical wiring. Homemade bombs were likely.

Ed Wulgaert examined the grounds and monastery. It appeared he would not have to take it with force. Standing outside, he saw how difficult it might be to penetrate the walls and drive an APC down the wide cloistered hallway. "Hey Dad!" He heard a voice shout at him. "Hey Dad, thanks for the birthday present." Whirling around, Ed came face to face with his son, Lee. It was Lee's nineteenth birthday. Ed had forgotten his son was a medic, assigned to one of the APCs. Ed Wulgaert was not expecting to see his boy or wish him happy birthday in the heat of battle. Birthday greetings given, the Wulgaert men returned to their responsibilities.

Throughout the daylight hours, less than forty appeared to remain inside. The occupants were looking increasingly unlikely to commit stupid suicide. Mike Sturdevant and his warriors were facing flak jackets, night sticks, face masks, M16s, .45-caliber pistols, M60 machine guns, M1 snipers with scopes, M203 grenade launchers, .30-06s, and shotguns. What a difference a day makes. Ironically, twenty-four hours earlier, Guardsmen had been sitting at their miserable posts with empty weapons. Collectively, the remaining Indians seemed to realize that they had pushed the envelope to its furthest limit.

Earlier, when some daylight had still remained Marlon Brando and Father Groppi made their way out. They were not arrested. They made their way to Shawano and Keshena to create a little spin on their adventure.

8:30 p.m.: All troops on duty. The buses are moved into Point 14. Arrest tables set up and area security is laid out.

The sun was no longer up, but loud helicopters were. Nearby farmer neighbors were treated to a nighttime display and aerial ballet of chopper spotlights, lighting up the sky and bouncing off the snow below. Sixteen male and fifteen female adults gave up and came out.

9:25 p.m.: A subject en route to the abbey walks almost up to one of the Guard vehicles. He is arrested at the scene, processed through the arrest team, and placed on a bus.

Among those arrested was Al Bergstein, the young photojournalist from Chicago. He hung in there until the very end. Owen Luck, Bergstein's buddy and mentor, was nowhere to be seen. He must have slipped out and away. I can only imagine he may have taken advantage of the very generous escape times and repeated warnings provided by the National Guard. He had rolls of film and prints to develop for sale. Al Bergstein probably believed that he would only be processed, released from jail, and not pursued by the district attorney.

9:45 p.m.: Three buses with prisoners leave the abbey and drive the short distance to Point 14. Captain Walsingham enters each bus and announces that all people from the abbey are under arrest for an unlawful assembly. The prisoners are taken off the bus one at a time, hand-cuffed, and then processed through an arrest team. The Guardsman who is with the prisoner stays with him until the arrest team is finished and he is photographed with the trooper and the prisoner. The trooper then stays with the prisoner until the person is turned over to the sheriff.

The arrest process seemed to be well orchestrated. With the warriors safely handcuffed, the most dangerous obstacle remained. Following the bus ride to Shawano and jail lay thrusting microphones, glaring lights and cameras, and questions shouted from ravenous members of the press.

10:32 p.m.: Checkpoint 14 clear, all buses en route to the sheriff's office.

It was tempting to enter and survey the abbey, but exploration was too risky after dark. Obvious dangerous devices suggested that more would be found. It was decided to begin the clearing process the next day. The "chilling vigil" would continue overnight until deemed all clear.

10:47 p.m.: Bus Two is instructed to remain on the highway until further notice. The bus is full of prisoners and guarded by two troopers, a sergeant, and one county deputy.

11:06 p.m.: About twenty-five Indians in cars descend upon the area where the bus is parked. An emergency call is made and about fifteen additional troopers arrive. The bus is moved in toward the edge of town and no further incidents take place.

Looking a bit dazed, Marlon Brando appeared to have had a reality check while inside the abbey. While exiting, his blank, expressionless face hinted relief from an ordeal. He appeared to be so flabbergasted that he was lost for words when approached by the press. The best he could do to describe his experience was to say, "It was, uh, a bit like Disneyland in the beginning. And then when we were up on the roof and the bullets started to fly all around us, then there was a certain kind of reality."

5

RED INK-WHITE ELEPHANT

If this whole episode were fiction, and with my sardonic tongue pressed squarely in my cheek, the previous chapter could have been presented differently. I could have written in such a way as to allow for a happy ending with clearly identifiable heroes and heroines.

Brave Indian warriors, having been cheated and mistreated for centuries by white men, would have been seen to peacefully rise up and successfully reclaim something belonging to them. I would have quoted U.S. Supreme Court opinions citing obscure federal law in favor of several dozen warriors dressed as pious altar boys. Apologetic white rednecks could be seen placing long-stemmed flowers into every upraised gun barrel. Governor Patrick Lucey would have hosted an all-you-can-eat picnic and named Ada Deer Mother of the Year. To maintain the festive and frivolous atmosphere, all would take turns playing Pin the Tail on the Donkey using the actual backside of Alexian Brothers as targets.

But reality wasn't so pleasant. The novitiate, caretaker's cottage, and mansion were trashed. There was not an area, room, or closet that escaped the ravages of the occupation. It could not have been much worse if the National Guard had actually used that frightening tank to blast holes through the stone walls for access. The interior was a nasty mess.

The National Guard removed crudely made bombs and bomb-making materials strewn about. The Wisconsin Department of Justice Crime Laboratory Bureau was among the next to enter and closely photograph and document the conditions inside. It was astonishing that such a magnificent property, so important to die for, could be so wantonly wasted by those claiming to be its champion of reclamation.

After authorities determined that the novitiate was safe to reenter, Brother Maurice, along with other Alexians, returned to pick up the pieces. They didn't know where to start. Almost immediately, the Brothers were startled by the arrival of a small convoy of private vehicles that looked very Indian-like.

Menominee people were unexpectedly returning, and the Alexians had no protection. But rather than threatening the Alexians, the Indians climbed out of their cars with brooms, buckets, plungers, and mops. This new wave was an apologetic and different generation than those behind bars under lock and key in Shawano. Middle-aged and the elderly insisted on efforts to clean up what the young people had left behind. The brothers were relieved and appreciative of those that pitched in.

Brother Warren Longo remembers those days of disgusting duty. He and some of the Menominee volunteers scooped month-old human waste from overflowing toilets into fifty-gallon drums. Even for a hospital-trained Alexian, this was bedpan duty at its nastiest extreme. The early-on decision to sever electrical power and telephone during the first week of occupation was catastrophic and proved to be ultimately irreparable.

During the duck-and-cover days of the 1950s and '60s, the monastery basement was assigned Nuclear Fallout Shelter status by the Feds. During my days as a novice, I remember seeing civil defense supplies stacked floor to ceiling throughout the subterranean level. Medical kits, radiation detection equipment, dry crackers with a long shelf life, and seventeen-gallon water storage canisters had been broken into and used.

The most popular item was the hard candy. Secondly, the sanitary supplies, which included a toilet seat, came in handy during the takeover.

The half-eaten, half-cooked food created its own special stench. The place might as well have been quarantined. In addition to trying to make a disaster look tidy, Menominee ladies cooked for other volunteering workers and the brothers. The sweat lodge, just outside Peters Hall, came back to life. With the return of nonthreatening warriors who avoided arrest, some more familiar native faces trickled back. In an effort to restore harmony, the traditional peace pipe worked overtime. Brothers Warren and Maurice choked and coughed their way through the pipe and smoke amid Indian silent laughter. Indians and Brothers were attempting, at great lengths, to avoid offending each other's religious standards.

The Alexians knew, sort of, what the sweat lodge outside was about. Timid Brother Warren Longo was invited to join some of the natives in that back-to-nature setting to purge, pray, and sweat. Comical to the untried, it could best be described as an ecumenical "Take a Naked Buddy to Confession" day.

Even without ever stepping foot into the sweat lodge, Brother Warren was already sweating, but in absentia. Although he committed to join some warriors, Brother Warren found a hideaway in the attic of the mansion. The Menominee men called out, searching for him everywhere in vain. Shy, retiring, and unwilling to strip in the snow, Brother Warren successfully hid like a mouse for hours until the potential embarrassment past.

Early on in this phase to reestablish order and recovery from the takeover, the Alexians elected not to discourage visitors and curiosity seekers. They believed that the more observers were around, the less likely hostilities would be rekindled. A trickling few grew into hundreds during the first few days. It was astonishing to see, regardless of their skin color or the side of the tracks from which they had traveled to gawk, all manner of mankind had lost all respect for ownership.

When I was growing up, my parents admonished we three Rick boys, "Look but don't touch." With one raised eyebrow, the rule was reinforced before we left the house and reminded again upon some special arrival. My idle hands spent most of my childhood safely parked away in my pockets. Surely, Marian and Leo Rick did not fear I would steal, they just wanted to reduce the possibility I would break something. On rare occasions, even while behaving, I would hear my father's throat clearing prompt my well-practiced reply, "I'm just looking!"

The Brothers were too exhausted to challenge smiling souvenir hunters. It was as if permission to steal had been granted due to the disheveled condition of the abbey. Visitors, somehow, had lost all good manners. The Alexians had cleared an area within the mansion where they could answer the phone, conduct small private meetings, and enjoy one of the few spots where the heat was functioning. With no permission or even a knock on the door, the public would walk right in as if they had paid to tour. Oblivious to the awkward circumstances, the curious kept coming. If the office was empty, those who were really nosy had no problem perusing documents that were none of their business.

The governor's office in Madison was now insisting that the Alexians arrange and pay for armed security and private guard duty. This request, of course, was following sworn law enforcement with the power of arrest from miles around exchanging gunfire, a National Guard battalion with artillery, and vigilante hell on snowmobiles. What Lucey expected of the Alexians was laughable. The ridiculous demand for security could not be bought. The Menominee Warriors Society repeatedly said openly that they could take it back at any time. A security guard service out of Milwaukee flatly told Brother Maurice they would not accept the job of securing the building because of the potential for litigation if they were to use firearms.

The next best thing was to turn to the Lamberies folks up the road. With hammer, nails, chains, and locks, Willis Lamberies, his brother Cubby, and his son Kim reduced the dozen or so entrances to only one accessible location. In the absence of the Alexians, the Lamberies family agreed to check in and periodically patrol the abbey property. This included checking the security of the doors and looking in on the boiler room. This minimal supervision would have to do.

During daylight hours, the Alexians continued to allow looky-loos. The numbers were so great that the Alexians and their trusted helpers made an effort to keep a count. Numbering into the hundreds, the curious continued. Keeping a tally of their egress and ingress, if nothing else, gave the inquiring the illusion of being watched. Quickly, it was discovered that a few religious men wearing their habit and singing a cappella in the chapel seemed to effectively soothe the angry. All were also reminded of the power of a large person at the door with a clipboard and a sharp pencil.

When the novitiate was originally built, a passenger elevator shaft had been incorporated to serve the administrative building at the east end. Probably in an effort to economize, no elevator doors, lifting mechanism, or a car were ever installed. Painted flimsy faux doors made it appear that all four floors had service. Those weak barriers had been kicked in, introducing the potential for a dreadful four-story free fall. Along with exposed electrical wiring, the shaft was just one of the many hazards that made the brothers hold their breaths while the public walked about.

Since so much had happened in the previous weeks, Joe Plonka, the caretaker, and his family and holiday friends had been partially forgotten. After the abbey had been vacated by the warriors, Joe Plonka decided it was safe to return and collect his family's personal property. His wife, Marlene, was discouraged from coming along to avoid the emotions of rage and fear. Instead, he brought along two burly friends.

Joe openly carried a firearm on his belt and it is safe to assume his buddies were not carrying some sad little Derringer this time. Brother Maurice arranged to meet Joe in the town of Gresham so that he could brace him on what to expect.

A loss by fire would have been, perhaps, a better reunion with their belongings. At least a fire would have been a more absolute loss. Instead, Joe Plonka wandered from room to room in the cottage, finding very little left unbroken, intact, or recoverable. Joe could not leave empty-handed, though. Important to Marlene would be the sort of memorabilia always cherished by mothers. Joe spent hours sifting through the disheveled cottage before moving on to search in the monastery itself. Much of the Plonka belongings had simply walked away.

Joe's timing could not have been any worse. He was working for the last five hours on recovering the family possessions. While Plonka was in the mansion, six to eight warriors happened by to reclaim one of their vehicles. It was left in the cottage garage. As the warriors were attempting to push that car off the abbey property, Plonka was inside, unaware.

To complicate matters, the warriors began pointing out multiple bullet holes in their vehicle. Somehow, they had learned Joe Plonka was back in town and nearby. The warriors insisted on blaming Plonka for the damage and were determined to confront him.

Gawkers, oblivious to the potential confrontation, numbered about one hundred in and around the abbey. Their cars crowded the narrow driveway out to the main road and beyond. Brother Maurice acted quickly to defuse the situation with Plonka inside while level-headed Menominee leadership cooled the angry warriors outside. It worked.

Upset and shaken all over again, Joe Plonka realized his return was premature. He chose to go back to Chicago and leave instructions for his friends to collect what was left. It wasn't much to return and claim, anyway. He would come back another day to gather furniture from his friends at a safer place to rendezvous. All of the peacekeepers, that afternoon, feared some sort of potential retaliation that evening.

Mr. and Mrs. Melvin Chevalier respected Menominee elders, left, then returned with food to share, staying until 2:00 a.m. The couple knew the routine. Since the taverns closed at 1:00 a.m., it was unlikely things would erupt after two o'clock. The night passed quietly.

During the active takeover, the Alexians had already gotten off on the wrong foot with Ada Deer, chairman of the Menominee Restoration Committee. Negotiating with the warriors while inadvertently excluding her political position and base, Brother Maurice needed to win back her favor. So on Wednesday, February 12, with hat in hand, Brother Maurice met briefly with Ada Deer in preparation for more future meetings.

Brother Maurice was frank in telling her he believed the Indian politics needed Indian solutions. She did not agree, firing back with her opinion. She saw it as a universal problem needing nontraditional solutions. She made it clear that she did not support the behavior of the Menominee Warriors Society.

If the Alexians had to do this all over again, Brother Maurice Wilson would have been face to face with Ada Deer far sooner. He wished the Green Bay Bishop Aloysius John Wycislo's advice to involve Ada Deer had been offered when it could have made a difference.

The brother recorded in his journal that she was a very strong-willed politician. Deer had been working on behalf of the Menominee for several years. She was the lawful chairwoman of the tribe's restoration efforts and believed the white man must play a role in righting past wrongs. Ada Deer did not believe taking over a monastery off the reservation land and holding it for ransom bought the Menominee anything except bad press. Truth be known, she viewed acquiring the abbey for $1.00, engineered by the warriors, as a setback to native progress.

This same week, pretrial hearings were heard locally. Of the forty or so arrested at the abbey, the accused had dwindled down to five defendants. The courthouse erupted into another circus. While Ada Deer hosted another civil meeting to resolve the abbey property issues, the five defendants, in defiance, took over the courtroom, locking and barricading themselves in the jury room. To make matters worse, law enforcement maced everything on two legs while trying to clear the courtroom. It was a bad day in Shawano, Gresham, and Keshena.

Larry Gehr and his wife Joan had invited the Alexians and other interested parties to their home for dinner. Larry was the current president of an organization called Concerned Citizens of America, Inc. (CCA), based in Shawano. These concerned citizens were primarily white and lived near the novitiate. During the takeover, this group had already attempted an unsuccessful caravan to Madison to try to force a meeting with Governor Lucey. Lucey refused to see them. This angered the CCA group into further action. Part of their strategy was to confront the Alexians and express their dismay over the Catholic brothers having agreed to hand over the abbey to the Menominee dissidents. The brothers were convenient scapegoats, caught up in an ever-tightening noose.

Now, the brothers had another faction to whom they were expected to answer. A written petition was beginning to take shape and make the rounds. Local money began to flow into the CCA treasury, to produce a document intended to awaken the "silent majority." Their motto was "Freedom through Law Enforcement." The deplorable photographed condition of the abbey was featured in the document. The petition was addressed to the various and appropriate state assemblymen throughout Wisconsin. Twenty undersigned citizens, believing the governor had violated his oath, sent the petitions to Madison in an effort to impeach Governor Lucey.

A subsequent meeting with the CCA took place at the home of Larry Gehr the evening of Thursday, February 20, 1975. Considering the late hour, nearly 10:00 p.m., Brothers Maurice Wilson and Warren Longo accepted the almost insistent phone call summoning them down the road. As expected, the brothers were verbally roughed up and challenged over the Alexian property decision by some present. The neighbors felt as if they had been betrayed by the Alexians. Followed by two hours of neighborly venting, the brothers left the gathering only to find their car with a flat tire. Larry and a few of the more angry and vocal came out in the cold to change the brothers' tire.

The next evening, the community of Shawano was shaken by two bomb blasts. The explosions were probably intended for the local newspaper, but they also damaged a medical clinic nearby. No one claimed responsibility, but suspicions seemed to point toward unhappy non-native neighbors. John Levine, publisher of the Shawano *Evening Leader*, had played a role in negotiating the abbey solution. Levine's close relationship with Governor Lucey may have made the publisher a possible target. A three-foot hole and blown-out windows for four blocks was amateurish but was nonetheless a statement.

Very little was making for a relaxed atmosphere at the abbey. It did not take much out of the ordinary to cause concern. The day after the bombing in Shawano, activity was seen at the water's edge on novitiate property. In the dead of winter, it was unlikely that local amateurs were having a leisurely SCUBA dive. Brother Maurice slogged down through the snow to inquire. The divers said they were from nearby Clintonville and offered not much more information. They were asked not to trespass, and they moved along with no further explanation.

The business of getting on with the inevitable transfer of ownership moved awkwardly forward. Everybody who was anybody was on somebody's committee—where nobody agreed. The Alexians and those assisting them at the abbey observed both passive and aggressive behavior from everyone who had some stake in the ultimate outcome.

For example, on the one hand, the Caretaker Committee received a proper letter from Ken A. Fish of the Menominee Warrior Society requesting to conduct a tour and prepare a meal for Menominee senior citizens. On the other hand, there were those occasions when greater numbers of warriors would gather unexpectedly, demonstrating hostility, possessiveness, and generally acting out.

The therapy purification from steaming hot rocks in the sweat lodge and a naked roll about in the snow seemed to soothe warriors. While writing this book, I have thought to myself, "Who among us has not benefited from a hot bath that did not experience some attitude adjustment?"

It is no surprise that warrior Ken A. Fish, decades later, would become an expert on treaties affecting his people and eventually serve on his tribal legislature. Ken was already showing skill in handling disagreements with calm. Ken invited the Alexian Brothers and supporters to come to the American Legion Hall in Keshena and attend a rather formal Menominee pipe ceremony.

As I read the description of the ceremony, recorded in detail by the Alexians, I thought the use of smoke was somewhat ironic. Brother Maurice understood the honor and importance of having been invited. Produced by tobacco, other popular herbs, or incense, as in Catholicism, smoke played a universal religious common role in things of earthly importance and those ethereal.

Already, the novitiate was coming to be seen as a white elephant. Brother Maurice had asked Ada Deer to cooperate in a feasibility study coordinated through the governor's office. Deer showed no interest in advancing a practical use of the novitiate. She was not about to pay respect to the methods of the Menominee Warrior Society sympathizers in attempting to acquire the novitiate or to the organization itself. The brothers and the warriors could expect no support from the members of the Menominee Restoration Committee as far as legitimizing the transfer of ownership to the Menominee was concerned.

Rumors were rampant throughout the countryside, and reconciliation among the many factions looked unachievable. One week earlier there had been a bombing. More were being promised. The brothers were nervous that the novitiate was a potential bombing target. It was becoming more and more important that the public be made aware that there was a peacekeeping human presence at the novitiate. Hopefully, that knowledge would discourage a terrorism campaign intent on killing people and destroying structures.

The Alexian Brothers continued their efforts to clean and fix up the place. Frozen pipes resulting from the weeks of occupation continued to be an expensive nightmare. It had proven to be a bad decision for authorities to turn off the electrical power, but the warriors were unable to manage the physical plant with or without electricity. The novitiate had been critically wounded, and any repairs would point toward future chronic and costly issues. Even if handed over in pristine condition, the novitiate would be financially impractical for ownership even with deep pockets.

Items of worth continued to "walk away" from the premises. With the easily two thousand or so visitors having toured after the takeover, there had been great opportunity for the facility to have been cased many times over. Beyond just the souvenir mentality, there were ample occasions for thieves to enter, take, look for more, and leave with items of great value. Since Brother Maurice and the others present in a caretaking capacity often had a need to leave the novitiate, anyone planning to steal would take advantage. The most popular items to plunder were large and small tools, printing and bookbinding equipment, and all one could imagine necessary to operate this striking facility.

Brother Maurice had come to be surprised at very little, until one early March day. Stepping outside, he discovered a sheriff's patrol car and several National Guard vehicles nearby, but no personnel seen. Investigating further, he found about a dozen men in a nearby field approaching the monastery. Uniformed Guardsmen were being led by Chester Dahl with the Shawano sheriff's department.

Brother Maurice was not pleased with the unannounced visit. He found it unsettling when approached again by military personnel. The Alexian Brothers certainly deserved the courtesy of a phone call or a knock on the door upon arrival. The flimsy excuse that the sheriff and the Guard did not know at which entrance to knock at least produced an apology from Dahl and the soldiers. Over the previous eight weeks, Brother Maurice and other Alexians had shown extraordinary restraint. This was one day Brother Maurice was entitled to exercise a rare short fuse.

Over coffee and Alexian hospitality, the National Guard explained that they were planning a return to the novitiate. Their mission would be to more thoroughly search the grounds for dangerous items left behind. One hundred twenty Guardsmen would return in a week on buses. With metal detectors, a more thorough search and combing of the grounds could be conducted than they were able to do one month before.

The Guardsmen explained that they would bring their own food service but were hoping to use the novitiate toilet facilities. They were anticipating Colonel Simonson's arrival by helicopter and hoped to prepare a landing site. During the briefing of the anticipated exercise, the novitiate telephone had already started to ring inquiring if there was a new hostile takeover. It was astonishing how quickly both news and rumor could travel in such a rural location.

Little was found that Saturday, March 8, by the National Guard and their metal detectors. Their fishing expedition only turned up a manhole cover and an electrical outlet. But there was one significant discovery that day. Ted Boyd, a respected senior Menominee, accompanied Tom Laughlin to the abbey. Tom Laughlin was hot property at the time. He had just released the movie he had produced, directed, and starred in, *The Trial of Billy Jack.*

Laughlin was interested in the recovery following the takeover. He was curious and hoped to foster support for whatever worthwhile outcome might blossom. His movie, released six months earlier, was reported to have cost $800,000 to produce, yet grossed $65 million. So he was feeling magnanimous. In contrast with Marlon Brando, Tom Laughlin was somewhat low-key in offering matching funds. During his day visit to the abbey, the movie star shared with the Alexian Brothers his disapproval of the warriors' methods in acquiring the property. Laughlin did not come across Brando-like. There was no entourage or press following him about.

There had been a few more sweat lodge ceremonies including Mike Sturtevant, who was out of jail on bail. A very possessive behavior was developing among the warriors. The caretaking team was concerned that the day visits were becoming overnight escapades attended by warriors and their female companions. It was feared that the novitiate was becoming an occasional destination for young runaway girls from foster homes.

The Alexians objected to the "hang out" atmosphere. Workers and those contributing some effort were welcome to stay, but the lack of participation among others and the reluctance to even give their names created an uneasiness. The Alexians even discovered that questionable substances were being smoked in the choir loft of the chapel. The nearby toilets that had been cleaned in anticipation of the spring thaw were being carelessly replenished.

The kitchen, which had been cleaned so well by Menominee mothers, was starting to look as it had during the last few days of the takeover. Beer and wine bottles were now simply tossed out of second-story windows instead of properly thrown away in a trash can. The Alexians approached and complained to Melvin Chevalier Sr. Not only did the juvenile behavior cease, some of the perpetrators returned and apologized, realizing they had been shitting in their own proverbial nest.

As April and spring arrived, there appeared to be a growing mistrust among all of the players. The Alexians and various supporting staff noted that the cooperation that existed near the end of the takeover was beginning to wear thin. All were beginning to question their personal safety. Candidly, those living within the novitiate were as concerned about white backlash as well as those acting out within the native community.

A naked female named Gypsy came to live with the brothers. This arrangement, allowing a bitch inside, was a first. It was tolerated because she was a six-month-old German Shepherd. Gypsy's duties included being alert and barking. She could cover a lot of territory with speed. Traversing the stairs and the once-cloistered hallways, she was capable of showing many teeth while encouraging troublemakers to think twice.

Lest there be any misunderstandings, Brother Maurice provided a press release to Sam Martino of the *Milwaukee Journal* and a copy to the *Shawano Evening Leader*. Since Brother Maurice was needed elsewhere and there was less of a need to baby-sit the property, he made a formal announcement naming the local members of the novitiate Caretaking Committee. They were Dave Zimmerman, Acting Chairman, Alex Askenette Sr., Ted Boyd, Mel Chevalier Sr., and Dr. Curtis Kurtz.

The Alexians felt the need to reestablish and be clear about the status of the property and former novitiate. The press release claimed that "a group of religious men and women will continue to remain at the novitiate for an indefinite period of time fulfilling a peacemaking and prayerful presence." It also reiterated the fact that the Alexians still held ownership and accepted the "responsibility for preserving the peace and protecting their property."

The new business at hand, agreed upon two months earlier with the Menominee Warriors Society, had not yet been consummated. The press release went on to say "The Alexian Brothers still hold official title and the property. The deed has yet to be transferred to the tribe."

During his extended absence, Brother Maurice was not surprised to learn the Gresham saga was not moving along well. The governor's office had dropped the ball in conducting a feasibility study. An effort to initiate any such study had gone nowhere. Joe Sensenbrenner in Madison tossed the hot potato in the direction of the Alexians. Also, Brother Maurice was told to reconnect with Ada Deer and her legal counsel to deal with the Menominee Restoration Committee. The Alexians sensed Ada Deer's lack of enthusiasm and her disinterest in the abbey.

Everywhere he turned, lip service was the only thing available to Brother Maurice Wilson. It was routine for sources with money to only talk about committing funds. Those veiled pledges would always be contingent upon some other entity performing. No one was willing ante up first. In other words, there was big talk and no action. The Catholic Church, disappointingly, was right in the middle of the collective insincerity.

Even with Mel Chevalier Sr. attempting to keep the young warriors at a distance, defiance was increasing. Those who were native and on the committee were increasingly tolerant of the possessive and challenging warriors. It was a test to be passive and live on the property.

The warriors could sense that they were losing to Ada Deer's restoration committee. This tug of war was being carried out with the Alexians' property as the unwitting sacrifice. Harassing stopovers at all hours, some of the warriors, like Neal Hawpetoss, were coming close to physical violence. Then there were those polite and professional encounters with warriors escorted by Ken Fish.

A group of nine clergymen asked to come out to the novitiate on April 14. It was an ecumenical gathering of Protestant, Jewish and

Catholic. This day turned out to be a significant wakeup call. Most were of the opinion that the Menominee would be unable to manage the financial commitment needed to operate any offsite program at the novitiate. The clergy voiced the irate intolerant tenor of their white congregations.

NIMBYism was alive and well in Shawano County. Things were not looking good in anybody's backyard. The next day was tax day, April 15. Late in the evening, the caretakers were aware of tremendous traffic and activity on Butternut Road. The destination was not the novitiate proper. A silent prank call was made to the novitiate, prompting a call to the sheriff's department to inquire. The novitiate staff was informed that the Alexians' east barn was on fire.

Brother Maurice was still away from Wisconsin, and Brother Rupert Trudel was in charge. Maurice learned by telephone that the east barn had burned to the ground. Other adjacent buildings had been scorched as well, including a building in which Willis Lamberies had been allowed to store his farming implements. That too, was a total loss.

Both the Shawano and Gresham fire departments responded, and the fire marshal from Wausau also lent his expertise. In his professional opinion, the cause of the fire was arson, not surprisingly. John Lavine from the Shawano newspaper photographed and wrote an article about the loss.

Unspoken assumptions pointed more toward white backlash terrorism as opposed to native intimidation. So much meanness was happening about. An electrical transformer serving the novitiate had been shot out of service. An anonymous telephone call to the electric company threatened that anyone seen trying to repair the transformer would be killed.

Under the cover of darkness, one of the beautiful lamp standards, a part of the monastery stone walls at the street, was demolished with some hit and run heavy equipment. The neighboring Lamberies family received new threats of additional structure torchings to follow. The barn burning, though, was one of the more spectacular and striking forewarnings close to home.

It was obvious those destructive messages were coming from nearby neighborly resistance opposed to the novitiate changing hands. Then there was the other problem that was getting worse by the day. Some known native warrior faces, such as John Perrote and Don Waukechon, showed up uninvited Monday, May 5, in the late afternoon.

The caretakers called the sheriff and reported a brief pushing and shoving scuffle erupting between those two and their women companions. The caretakers demanded they leave then hastily retreated, with Gypsy the dog, to the monastery, locking the doors behind them. Perrote and Waukechon were not alone in pushing the envelope and hoping to accelerate the transaction accomplished by the takeover. As far as they were concerned, the abbey was already theirs.

The frequency of unwelcome visits by inebriated as well as angry warriors and other natives had reached a boiling point. The caretakers feared personal harm if they were to remain on the property. By telephone, Brother Maurice authorized the only two remaining caretakers to temporarily abandon ship. They would monitor the situation while staying at a Shawano hotel.

One of the indicators of trouble was the increased purchase of ammunition. Both the white citizenry and native citizens were stocking up that mid-May. Farmers on tractors in their fields were openly carrying weapons. Tempers often flared at eating establishments when customers were mixed. Rednecks and renegades were behaving in equally uncivil manners.

Brother Maurice Wilson was working diligently to expedite the process of transferring the deed. But much had gotten out of control. There were too many cooks in the kitchen. So many individuals were now involved, it became bogged down and top-heavy with politics.

There had been a steady stream of sincere as well as insincere do-gooders wishing to be involved. In most cases, it would take weeks to sort out to whom it was best to say thanks but no thanks. Brother Maurice was nice…too nice.

Father Ralph Villwock was a Catholic priest who arrived in Gresham seemingly out of nowhere. He had a golden tongue and a credible story to tell. He claimed that some of his background included serving a native parish on a Sioux reservation in South Dakota. Now, he was on site in Wisconsin offering to pitch in and work miracles for the Menominee. Initially, he spent several days as a guest of the Alexians. Then he was seldom seen except for some of his possessions and his U-Haul trailer parked nearby.

Villwock spoke of some effort to create a program for alcoholics at the novitiate. It was reported he was making the rounds collecting funds for that effort. This was this very sort of free spirit and counterproductive behavior the Alexians wanted to avoid. He was receiving large amounts of mail. He was also beginning to receive dunning telephone calls—local merchants wanted to speak with him about money due them. Since Brother Maurice was away, he left instructions that Father Villwock call him and discuss the problems he was creating. Villwock was encouraged to move along. Already resolved to give away their monastery, the Alexians did not need that kind of help.

It had been over six months since the initial hostile takeover. The Novitiate Committee members were anxious to receive the feasibility study promised by the governor's office. All they could do was wait. When the feasibility study did arrive from Madison, it offered no encouragement to move forward with an off-reservation medical facility for the Menominee. This was the last straw. The brothers had had enough.

The Alexians began to explore how they could best recover their losses from months of thievery. It was one thing to pick up, sweep and mop the monastery. It was another to repair the unseen and yet unrepaired extensive damage to the plumbing behind the walls. The Alexians were advised to pursue Shawano County for the freeze damage. That catastrophe was a direct result of the sheriff's decision to terminate electrical service that first week in January. In retrospect, that very bad strategic decision would prove to be the original death knell for that proud edifice.

On July 8, 1975, Brother Maurice recorded in his journal, "Father Stan Maudlin, a Benedictine priest from Marvin, South Dakota, who is in charge of the American Indian Cultural Research Center at Marvin, South Dakota, contacted Mrs. Ada Deer at Keshena, Wisconsin, and related to her the plans of the brothers regarding the agreement of February 2, 1975, and our plans to dissolve the agreement based on the fact that we feel that we have fulfilled our moral commitment because the Menominee Indian tribe has been unresponsive in accepting our offer of the deed to the property of the novitiate,"

Father Maudlin reported back. He and Ada Deer met at 9:30 a.m. She appeared pleased with the Alexians' decision. Maudlin said her words were "Now we can start talking about health care services on the reservation."

Brother Maurice Wilson had just experienced an intense six-month on-the-job crash course in public relations. This time, the Alexians were to engage a professional public relations firm. Jim Frankowiak with Public Communications Inc. (PCI) of Milwaukee began to prepare the Alexians for the inevitable bad press. Frankowiak's first duty would be to prepare a statement for the Provincial, Brother Florian Eberle.

After Ada Deer, next in line to officially notify was the Novitiate Caretaking Committee. Brother Maurice took it upon himself to deliver that uncomfortable news. Written as succinctly as possible, the statement was read to the committee. The brothers defended their having lived up to their side of the bargain, finding no solution to multiple problems and no success in transferring the deed.

The Alexian bombshell news was received with shock and awe. Brother Maurice recorded the evening of July 9 the meeting was adjourned with committee members walking away disappointed, surprised yet without antagonism. It was more difficult for committee members who were aligned with and sympathetic to the Menominee Warriors Society. Brother Maurice returned to his hotel room in Shawano. Alone, out in the rural novitiate, was not the place to spend that particular night.

Over the next several days, the factions seemed to hover on the brink of war again. Brother Maurice was swamped with telephone calls. This time, he had the concise statement to read to the callers. Jim Frankowiak and his PR skills helped the brothers avoid being blindsided as they had been before. They controlled the story by strategically releasing information to the press this time.

The governor's office was not happy with the Alexian Brothers. Madison was placing demands on the brothers to arrange for private armed security at the novitiate. Colonel Simonson telephoned, upset. The Alexian Provincial in Chicago, Brother Florian, received a personal call from the disgruntled Governor Lucey. Television, radio, and the printed press all beat a path back to the Gresham monastery.

Brother Maurice did comply and made arrangements for expensive private security guards very late the same night the Alexians had gone public. Colonel Simonson had returned to the area as violence was erupting again, but more so in Menominee County. At two o'clock in the morning, Brother Maurice and Simonson met with Sheriff Montour. The sheriff was marshaling his forces to prepare for the worst. The state troopers were aware as well.

The Alexians could add the Shawano sheriff to the list of folks unhappy with their decision to bail out of the lose-lose circumstances. Sheriff Montour was reportedly acting very distant with the Alexians. In his mind, he had somehow forgotten the evolution of the novitiate saga that began New Year's Day. The Alexian Brothers, in fact, had recently invoiced the Shawano County for the freeze damage created when the sheriff cut the electrical power. The sheriff believed he had been stabbed in the back and the Alexians were suing him. He was mistaken.

The next day, Colonel Hugh Simonson unloaded on the Alexians. The *Milwaukee Sentinel* did report with balance. The paper published the Alexian decision but also criticism coming from Colonel Simonson. The colonel interpreted the Alexian decision as "Indian giving." To make matters worse, Ada Deer was claiming that she was unaware of the Alexian reversal. She went on to suggest the predicament was of the Alexians' own making. Somebody was lying.

The media were enjoying this reversal of fortune crisis back at the abbey. Visually, armed white guards three stories up were providing a great camera backdrop. It wasn't as if the Alexians had fought a battle with the warriors over the last six months and won back the monastery, fair and square. What the brothers still had was something no one really wanted anymore.

The warriors were not happy with the news and their loss. It was humiliating—another stab at their masculinity. Unintentionally, the Alexians were both the goat and the executioner. The warriors had, again, been emasculated by a perceived successful win and an effortless matriarchal challenge from Ada Deer. The restoration committee was successful by default. They had simply ignored Alexians correspondence to transfer the deed.

Brother Maurice wrote that he "felt just a little uncomfortable being so close to armed guard activity and being responsible for their employment." He and Chicago were in agreement that the private guard presence transmitted the wrong signal. After all, the warrior motto was "Deed or Death" and the brothers subscribed to "Life and Peace." Soon after, and in the face of the governor's request, the Alexians terminated the armed guards.

Chicago police intelligence contacted the Alexian's Provincial head-quarters on Kenmore Avenue. The police anticipated some sort of crowd reaction and wished to caution the Alexians in handling those potential circumstances. On July 15, at 1:00 p.m., Jim Frankowiak sat down with Brother Maurice at the Kenmore offices. They discussed upcoming television interviews in Green Bay and Milwaukee. In addition to preparing for print and media interviews, they discussed and reviewed talking points.

An individual reporter with the Associated Press came knocking. He had been led to believe that there was to be a demonstration at that location. Obviously, he was either tacky and too early or just fashionably late. He left thinking it was a false alarm. Something did materialize, however. A man with a few ladies and about half a dozen children showed up with cameramen from obscure and independent stations or agencies. It turns out the man was Catholic priest James Edmund Groppi of Milwaukee.

Since my high school days in the early 60s and Beaumont's fledgling efforts toward racial integration, I knew of this priest named Groppi. Depending on who was speaking of him, Father Groppi was painted as a renegade Catholic priest or regarded as a martyr for civil rights.

My school buddy, Frank Robichau, recalls our having learned of an upcoming nighttime Ku Klux Klan gathering in Beaumont. That day, as we drove through the streets accomplishing nothing worthwhile as teenagers do, another car chased us down, thrusting a Klan flyer in our open window with directions and details. Out of youthful curiosity and adventure, I attended from a distance with another friend whose name I cannot recall. I do remember seeing ample beer bellies under silly hooded white robes, masked faces, the FBI recording license plates, and a burning cross. The visual experience was enough to answer any questions I ever had.

On this particular day in Chicago, Groppi appeared wearing his Roman collar and his signature dark glasses. He was pursuing a role sympathetic to the Menominee Warriors Society. He wanted answers to the abandoned agreement between the occupants of the abbey and the Alexian Brothers. He also wanted an argument, which he usually did so well.

Recall that near the end of the occupation, Groppi was the priest who escorted Brando into the abbey. The attention, of course, was squarely on Brando. Father Groppi already had a decade of experience as a champion of human rights under his belt. He was known as an in-your-face sort of organizer. A different story was told about Groppi of those heated days in the abbey. The vigilantes had been pumping lots of lead from the forests into the abbey. The warriors mocked the priest as he was rolled up in a ball and whimpering from fear.

Now, a half year later, Father Groppi and his entourage were there in Chicago to verbally spank the Alexians. The small gathering was allowed to come into the office and vent. How could the Alexians back out of their deal with the Menominee warriors, they asked. Groppi was hostile and the ladies were loud and shrill in addition to hostile. Groppi was told that Ada Deer and the lawful leadership of the Menominee were offered the deed but refused to accept the paper and new owner-ship. These details took the wind out of Groppi's sail. He tucked his tail between his legs, returning to Milwaukee.

Less than a year later, Groppi married his secretary from one of his Catholic Church assignments in Milwaukee. His commitment to celi-bacy aside, he attended an Episcopal seminary, abandoned the idea of conversion, and fathered three children. As a Milwaukee County transit bus driver, James Edmund Groppi died of cancer in 1985.

Meanwhile, on July 17, 1975, adjacent to hot, sticky Lake Michi-gan, Brother Maurice and PR man Jim Frankowiak drove to Milwau-kee. Jim had made arrangements for Brother Maurice to hit as many news outlets as possible. Television was primary. Brother Maurice had learned well and developed a good camera presence. The printed press

wanted good "head shots" and the Alexian cooperated. Brother Maurice
continued on to Green Bay on his media whistle stop.

Concurrent with the brothers' visit to Green Bay, he had an opportunity to speak with the bishop. Ada Deer had complained to the bishop
that the Alexians needed to be reprimanded for saying she had been
aware the Alexians were terminating the February 2nd agreement. Several days later, Brother Maurice called Ada and reminded her of the
morning visit to her office by Father Stan Mauldin. He reiterated the
purpose of that courtesy visit: Father Mauldin had been speaking to her
on behalf of the Alexians.

Even in the face of the obvious, all the players seemed to dismiss
important details that were only six months old. Nothing was written or
recorded by many, but the Alexians, at least, kept a journal hour by hour
when necessary. The Alexians had seven hundred years of documented
history. The necessity and discipline of recording medical data was a way
of life for the registered nurse–brothers. Ada Deer could no longer hon-
estly continue to deny that the Benedictine Priest had met with her ten
days earlier to share the Alexians' intent. The brothers had grown weary
of providing the proverbial cake for those wishing to eat it too.

The Alexians approached the Knights of Columbus and asked if
they could use their counsel hall in Milwaukee for a press conference.
A date of August 15 was set to present a new method to determine the
novitiate's future use. The day came, and the Alexians announced they
were opening a thirty-day window during which they would accept proposals. The very next day, Ada Deer and the Menominee Restoration
Committee went public, announcing that the Menominee would not be
offering a proposal.

As far as the Alexians were concerned, several proposals presented
before the September 15 deadline were acceptable. The best was determined to be from Crossroads Academy, Inc. Crossroads, out of Milwaukee, was proposing a school for juvenile delinquents. The remoteness of

the academy would serve well as a farm-based science education extension. It was to be an alternative school for students on all levels.

On Sunday, October 12, Willis Lamberies telephoned the Alexians. He had bad news to share. It had been very foggy that morning when Mr. and Mrs. Lamberies drove to church. The smell of burning wood had not been alarming until they returned from church, at which point the fog had lifted just enough that they could see Peters Hall from the main road and discern fog from smoke. The mansion was on fire. Willis had to make the short drive to his farmhouse to call the fire department, and by the time the volunteers were deployed, the blaze was raging out of control. It was determined the mansion must have smoldered most of the night. Most believed it was arson—the fog would've provided a perfect opportunity and disguise. The fire door between the mansion and the newer building prevented the fire from spreading. The mansion, however, was gutted. The only thing left was the stone shell, concrete floors, and steel superstructure. How disheartening as well as heartbreaking it must've been for Brothers Warren and Maurice when they arrived from Chicago that late afternoon.

Later that month, the Alexians made the decision to award the property to Crossroads Academy. In addition, about fifty acres of land near the Red River had been set aside as a gift to the adjacent Township of Richmond to be enjoyed by the public. On November 13, 1975, all was legally transferred to both new owners.

6

ELECTIONS & ERECTIONS

Feeling I let myself down in leaving the Alexian Brothers, I returned home from the Gresham, Wisconsin, and tried to ease into hometown college life. The transition from my monastic experience was a challenge. However, I found a shortcut by pledging one of the most hell-raising fraternities on campus. I was "rushed" as the Pike's token monk of Pi Kappa Alpha. I was very compatible with the raucous, rude, and raunchy juvenile behavior that Greek college life had to offer.

I have come to learn this sort of behavior is not uncommon with individuals who were just released from religious life. I was definitely a little behind the curve in the romance department, but I discovered that my native sense of humor bought me a comfort level with the ladies. Relieved, I found I had not been permanently crippled by practicing silence and chastity. Poverty didn't seem to be an issue either. I always had just enough to acquire beer, booze, and books, in that order. Thank God for inexpensive Texas state college tuitions and tolerant parents who allowed me to come home and find myself. They were right; the cat came back!

Lamar University in Beaumont, Texas, was known best for basketball, the Mobil Oil refinery next door, and a highway with railroad tracks running down the middle. The petroleum processing visibly polluted the air on campus. It was a well-known fact that the air we breathed melted

pantyhose off the legs of coeds and competed successfully with cigarettes for our lungs.

There was—and still is, though it is dwindling—old money in my
hometown and Southeast Texas. Many magnificent homes in Beaumont
owe their existence to the boomtown days there in the very early twentieth century. On January 10, 1901, a certain drilling operation struck
black gold. Known as Spindletop, this rig and oilfield took center stage
in leading the U.S. production of crude oil.

It was clear that I was never going to be able to shake my attraction to and desire to be part of the medical and leading-edge adventures. I already spoke the technical language, and now I was learning the
discipline. A new modern psychiatric facility at home had opened and
became my next target. I needed a college job. I found myself an orderly
position in this fascinating world of people with mental health crises.

The staff experimented with wearing no distinguishing uniform.
Literally, it was often difficult to tell who was running the asylum.
Thinking back, it was scary as a skinny kid to help manage unbalanced
patients twice my size or greater. I learned that there was strength in
numbers and how to pile on when necessary. Participating in administering electroconvulsive therapy and witnessing visiting judges conducting legal competence hearings certainly catapulted me into another one
of the realities of the adult world.

Aside from my fraternity-arranged blind date with Janis Joplin's
younger sister, Laura, my college accomplishments were few. Then I met
Marlene Fallin. We married while I pursued various medical opportunities and professions in the Beaumont and Port Arthur area. Marlene
taught school. On-the-job training became my preferred path to success. Echocardiography won out, and I was recruited by the University
of Texas Health Science Center-Dallas. It was connected physically and
professionally with Parkland Hospital, Dallas. In February 1974, upon

moving there, the bottom fell out, resulting in a personal blow and an early adult low.

In the early afternoon of February 12, 1974, I heard my name paged to the hospital burn unit. Parkland Hospital requested I set up some medical monitoring devices normally used in the coronary care unit. I was not fond of seeing or hearing the misery and pain that goes along with burns. On the other hand, I thrived on participating in emergent situations as a participating team member. I also had no problem with dead people; they don't suffer. On occasion, my work included cardiac follow-up and data-gathering before, during, and after autopsies.

I did what I needed to do and got out of the burn unit. Already feeling ill and miserable with something flulike, I left work early for home rather than coughing and sneezing on the very susceptible burn patients. Worthless to staff and patients that afternoon, I dragged myself through the Parkland hallways and to my car. A decade before, these same corridors had witnessed the mayhem following the assassination of President John F. Kennedy.

Dallas police were seen crawling, literally, under our first floor apartment window that early afternoon. A knock on my door, and I found myself under arrest. Handcuffed, I was taken downtown, booked, and charged with aggravated rape. My pleadings of who, what, when, where, why went unanswered by detectives. I would learn much later that they desperately wanted me to be the man that had been terrorizing North Dallas women.

The mystery perpetrator had been eluding the law for months. He had been described as having bushy brown hair and a mustache. Well, who didn't in the 70s? Intimidation and threats of humiliating treatment if I did not confess made me one frightened twenty-six-year-old. There I sat in the jail of a new city with no support system beyond Marlene. It is true; they allow you one phone call. Mine went out to my childhood

Beaumont neighbor, the criminal district judge, George Taylor. He said, "Pat, you better get an attorney!"

Thankfully, today, details here are no longer important. The timing of my mistaken identity is important. To have gotten past 1974 was a struggle; it was my year of extreme anger. My family loaned me money to pay for legal help. That unnecessary encounter with the law included an expensive examining trial and grand jury proceedings. Emotionally, I was spent and useless. I lost respect for authority.

The good news was that, in addition to my innocence, a polygraph exam in my favor, and witnesses on my behalf, the Dallas grand jury handed down a "No Bill" decision dismissing the wrongful case against me. I would learn that it was said that a good prosecutor could indict a ham sandwich. It would prove to be a learning experience for me, and I would teach Dallas a few things. That lonely day before the grand jury, I proved I was neither guilty nor a ham sandwich.

My out-of-character encounter with the Dallas police certainly put a damper on my career in the big city. I had been recruited by James T. Willerson, M.D. Then, after only a few weeks of new employment with the medical school, I became a person of interest. I can only imagine what Willerson and the staff really thought of me from that point forward.

Subsequently, Guy Marble, the vice president of a Dallas advertising agency, would be arrested, tried, and convicted of serial rapes, including the one of which I had been accused and charged. Even after my grand jury proceedings, there would be three more years of bad and bothersome police behavior. It would not be until February 1977 that police would arrest the real "friendly rapist." Marble, the bad guy, went to prison for twenty years. Partly humiliated, I went away livid, yet determined. No one apologized and no one reimbursed me. I was left far from "friendly."

In a way, I was broken. On the other hand, I felt challenged and hardened. At that same time, the Menominee Indian warriors in Wisconsin were planning and executing their "deed or death" takeover of the Alexian Brothers monastery, the "abbey." Focused on getting beyond my personal hell in Dallas, I was oblivious to the Indian takeover back in Wisconsin. Although it was certainly reported around the world, the takeover of the novitiate could have been front-page news and I would have missed it for fear of seeing my own name in the newspaper police blotter. Things would change for me, however.

Before Marlene and I had made a family with Ian and Sarah, I was well into a lucrative career selling and marketing medical equipment. Diagnostic ultrasound equipment fell into my lap from clinical experience. MRI, CT, PET, and a host of other new imaging technologies followed that. I would learn there is a typical lifecycle of your average peddler; what goes up must come down.

I acquired a Piper Cherokee Six private aircraft. This particular one had a history of transporting human remains throughout the Southeast. I didn't care; I pretended any lingering ghosts helped keep the plane aloft. The aircraft, capable of seating five plus the pilot, had been used to recruit and lure me away by a competitor. It worked. I was sitting in the proverbial catbird seat. Marlene and I with our newborn, Ian, moved from the Dallas-Fort Worth area to Baton Rouge, Louisiana. I covered a multi-state sales territory of Texas and adjoining southeastern states. I thought it would last forever.

I developed a successful reputation for calling on those tiny hospitals and rural medical imaging professionals. I would remove four seats from the airplane to make room for mobile ultrasound equipment to demonstrate. Delighted they were not being ignored for the big cities and medical centers, backwoods radiologists and hospital administrators met me with their pickup trucks at dirt landing strips. We scanned every pregnant abdomen and gallbladder between Muleshoe, Texas, and Toad Suck, Arkansas.

While chasing the dollar, Marlene, two-year-old Ian, and I found ourselves back in Texas in the late 1970s. Austin was and still is probably the most sought after destination to live and raise a family in the state. With the exception of the arrival of our daughter, Sarah, our high points were becoming limited and declining. Looking back, that decade is very much a blur; there seems to be a human protective mechanism that blocks bad memories.

That move resulted in my growing apart from Marlene. I was not alone in facing the devastating Texas oil economy. We divorced, and in 1989 I was offered and accepted a sales management opportunity with a medical imaging company on the West Coast.

My new resident alien British girlfriend and new love from London, Jane Deak, and I moved from Austin to California, bringing her two children, James and Sarah. Yes, another Sarah! My two children looked up to Jane's children because of the differences in their ages. We blended reasonably well, and I asked Jane to marry me. Her career bloomed. Jane brought her know-how from employment at the University of Texas law school. She successfully parlayed that experience into becoming the firm administrator of a bank-law practice in Orange County. Then the bottom fell out for me.

It looked like I had been prematurely selected to play the role of Willy Loman, the main character in *Death of a Salesman*. I was fired! I was having trouble duplicating my Texas success in California. Amazingly, someone under forty with inherently different anatomy and working for the competition would replace me. It was becoming a classic corporate maneuver. I began to wake up and pulled the plug on traditional employer-employee relationships. After all, it was the only way an individual could fight back while no longer a Young Turk. I reinvented myself by marketing my skills and experiences from the past in both the clinical and commercial medical fields. Remodeling myself as an independent contractor, I became an authority, expert, specialist, consultant, advisor, and all the other titles qualifying one to be out of work and not having a real job.

"Has anybody ever said you look like Bill Clinton?" I would hear. The first few times I would ask, "Who?" Usually star struck and sympathetic, Democrats would respond, "You know, the governor from Arkansas running for president?" No, I didn't know, but I would shortly. I can truthfully say I did not see the resemblance. Initially, I may have even resented the likeness and suggestion that I had a semi-pudgy and liberal appearance. Unsolicited encouragement from family, friends, business associates, and strangers on the street caused me to explore further.

Living next door to Tinseltown, it should have come as no surprise that a supportive and active cottage industry thrived right here in my own backyard, Hollywood. I jumped on the fast track, landing on both feet ready to run. I thought it was unlikely Bill Clinton would win, but I rolled the dice anyway. I produced my 8 x 10 black and white head shots and hit the streets looking for agent representation with some modest success. I would learn that television and film credits were great for bragging rights, but they were not nearly as lucrative as corporate and private appearances.

A sardonic sense of humor has been a personal lifelong boon and occasional bane for me. But it was beginning to look as if I had discovered a way to harness a talent. It was perfect timing, coming at a time my thirty-year career in medicine was waning. Surprise, Bill Clinton did of course win the presidency, and then won a second term. This serendipitous adventure would have a limited lifespan. I differentiated myself from my look-alike/professional impersonator competition by writing and honing my act. For eight years, I felt people's pain and bit my lower lip so much, I'm surprised there's any lip left. Wisely, I took the classic Hollywood advice: "Don't quit your day job."

The Murphy Brown, Letterman, Leno and other appearances were valuable. The "B" movie casting helped me achieve some modest notoriety. It was easy to see how the entertainment industry has a reputation for chewing up newcomers and spitting them out. This was my serendipity—right time— right place. My Screen Actors Guild card and Internet Movie Database.com exposure would buy me 2 cups of coffee today.

Truth would prove stranger than fiction. During any given week, I could find myself one day in surgery wearing scrubs and a mask, then the next day behind a podium in Puerto Rico delivering a mock State of the Union address. One of my clients in my medical consulting business was a manufacturer of breast and penile implants. My diverse duties had successfully combined the dual careers. Good morning, doctor. What shall we do today? Is it to be saline or silicone? Elections or erections?

7

GOING BACK

One evening, in the very late 1990s, my flight had to skirt weather in the Chicago area for an approach and landing into Milwaukee. It is always impressive to see the "loop" from the air. It's especially beautiful at night when you are east of the city over the blackness of Lake Michigan and see the abrupt sodium street light display that starts with Navy Pier and stretches west to O'Hare and well beyond Elk Grove Village. Under the left wing was Meigs Field, the troubled downtown waterfront airport adjacent to the McCormick Place convention center. The Radiological Society of North America had brought me there approaching nearly two decades. That night I was going a little farther north.

The Sears and Hancock Towers stood tall, watching over the city. So many aspects of my life have taken me into and around Chicago over the last forty-five years. This was to be another brush with the city. Extensive air travel had honed my internal compass. Either at the controls or in the back with a beer, I fancied myself a human GPS, capable of making the mental calculations necessary to get a fix on a flight location at any given time. Had there been anyone in the seat next to me, I am sure that passenger would not have been impressed that I could identify Chicago, however—it was obvious.

We all fantasize. My fantasy is that of a flight attendant abruptly shaking and awakening me. She has found both the pilot and copilot unconscious. She is desperately looking for a pilot, any pilot, to come forward and take the cockpit controls. Fortunately, the autopilot is in the on position, so, of course, I successfully land an unfamiliar jet. Humbly, I refuse interviews, book offers, and rights to the movie. Then, I wake up.

The scene slid past the port side window and dimmed a little in the northern suburbs as we flew north, descending. The less spectacular landmarks of Kenosha and Racine were the last two jewels on the water's edge I could identify before landing in the city that "made beer famous." There was no stopping at baggage claim.

As usual, my wardrobe was on wheels behind me. It would have to be a week of business travel before you would see me pack anything needing to be checked as luggage or that would not fit in the overhead. My philosophy over the years became "different city and different people got the same man in the same clothes." Clean and neat were one thing, but I preferred efficiency.

The routine, regardless of the city, took me to the car rental express pickup. From there, instinct helped me navigate off airport property. On rare occasions, a taxicab was the answer instead. My destination this time was that Hilton Hotel along the interstate just north of downtown Milwaukee. Thirty years before, the train had taken me and a dozen or more other young men from downtown Chicago across the Illinois/Wisconsin border through Milwaukee and into Shawano.

Tonight I was not going that far. I had to get to my room and call the hospital in Janesville to confirm the surgery for the next morning. There is usually no staff in the operating room of smaller hospitals at of that hour of night. It was necessary to track down the nursing supervisor or speak with the admitting department, which has access to the next day's surgery schedule. I discovered that the case was canceled with no reason offered. Once again, plans were made to swing out of my way to cover a case, only to learn at the last minute that it was not going to happen.

For the last many years, my responsibilities as an independent contractor and consultant included representing medical companies as my primary source of income. Usually, my duties included being present in the operating room to advise the surgeon and staff on how to best use the company's products. I like what I do. I have always enjoyed the operating room environment. The work allows me to breeze in, be the expert, and leave. It was the attraction to a career in medicine that had brought me to Wisconsin in 1966: now, I was back.

Even though the case was canceled sometime that same day, the information, as usual, never reached me. I had planned this trip for several weeks in advance, and it involved a reasonable airfare with restrictions. Now, I did not need to be there at all. I had planned to be in Milwaukee for two nights due to the timing of the case. Flying out earlier would cost a lot more money.

Then it hit me. "I have the time and a car, why not drive up to Gresham and see what the old place looks like?" For twenty-three years, businesses had brought me near but not close enough to investigate. The opportunity was presenting itself: finally, I had a chance to return to the novitiate.

The lousy little map included with the rental car had a worthless detail of Milwaukee on one side and an even worse portrayal of Wisconsin on the other. It was good enough, however, to get me on my way north past the Harley-Davidson plant and headed the general direction of Oshkosh, Appleton, and Shawano, then Gresham.

I wanted to be there immediately. I wanted to be already walking around looking in its windows and standing by the river. I guess I had similar thoughts forty summers before, during the all-day train ride from Chicago, but this time I was alone and not with my classmates. This time I thought I knew what to expect, or did I? I had imagined going back there over and over again. During various stages of my life, I had even entertained the idea of "reenlisting."

As Milwaukee disappears in the rearview mirror, Fond du Lac marks the point the highway takes you around the west side of Lake Winnebago, then Oshkosh finally comes into view. I was not getting any familiar visual clues—no déjà vu happening yet. Three decades of change had made the highway look like they all do wherever you go. Wisconsin now had its share, too, of exit ramps to outlet malls.

Appleton was coming up quickly, and I had not decided to approach from Green Bay or take the back farm-to-market roads. Anticipation makes these "going home" journeys very long, it seems. You find yourself driving faster and faster to compensate. Should I take the major highways through Green Bay at faster speeds or jump off at Appleton and navigate through farmland? I had had enough of Highway 41. I desperately needed a dose of Dairy Land.

It was the right decision. Only a few miles from the turnoff I found some hope of seeing what I so fondly remembered. Farmhouses near the road began to appear. Many of them had an adjacent silo. As I was trying to get into a sentimental monastic mode, I thought to myself, "These tall silos are the everyday cathedral and bell towers." The faithful were cattle painted like the boxes in which Gateway ships their computers. I was anxious to arrive, and my head swam in vague glimpses of the past. I found myself driving in excess of eighty miles per hour on that two-lane stretch. I slowed down only to go around pickups and farm implements with the triangular reflectors on the back.

The further north I drove, the thicker the stands of trees became. This looked promising. The hills began to roll. The occasional bridge and stream I would cross helped the memories flow. To be honest, it was not a particularly pretty day—it was autumn and gray. But that was OK, because what I remembered was full of gray. Gray was what Wisconsin offered in the winner. An eighteen-year-old kid from Southeast Texas remembers Wisconsin winters the most.

It was reassuring to see the mile marker indicating Shawano was only eleven miles ahead. Now I could slow down. Shawano played a big part in my memories. That's where we got off the train. That's where I got my first pair of reading glasses. It was time to begin to savor the journey. Intersections and landmarks would surely look familiar. The two hours of driving like a bat out of hell had done little to refresh my memory. I guess I was expecting absolutely nothing to have changed since the mid-'60s.

Approaching from the east, you see a glimpse of Shawano Lake off to the right. Things looked prosperous on the outskirts of the city of Shawano before I got closer to what I would remember as downtown. There were snowmobile and ATV dealers to support the winter sport and a new movie theater on the left. On one occasion, we had been loaded onto the old baby blue school bus and taken into town to see a private screening of *The Gospel According to St. Matthew* at one of those classic downtown theaters with a sidewalk box office and a marquee.

The local newspaper the *Leader* had a new building. The previous one had been damaged by a bomb during the trouble here in the mid-'70s. Wal-Mart and Kmart had strategically placed themselves on the north and south side of the east-west route into town. The graveyard looked unchanged, though its population had to have increased in the years since 1967. The new residents, as in any other city, were still six feet under, in the back, and away from the main drag.

The closer you got to what used to be the heart of Shawano, you could see places of business that had worn many signs over the years. Some had been closed for a while. Some had survived, and many were on their last leg as gasoline stations converted into video rental stores, vacuum cleaner repair shops, or liquor stores.

Ahead, I could see railroad tracks crossing the street. On the left side was a characteristic looking depot. Weeds grew between the rails next to it. There was no sign this was a stop for trains from anywhere anymore. The building did not look run-down, it just looked unused. I know we were one of the last classes to arrive by train. Who knows how long after we arrived in 1966 the train continued to run from Chicago to Shawano? Hopeful young men no longer stepped from the train coaches to be driven twenty more minutes to the monastery.

"Still living" was the general appearance of the heart of the town. Shawano seemed to be more alive and thriving on the periphery. It looked used and worn within the central business district but clean at its major crossroads. I realized I wasn't clear on how to get to where I was going. At this point, I had not stopped to get out and smell the air. I remembered the crispness of the evergreens and how the cold punctuated their scent. I had not planned on getting out of the car until I was there, but that determination gave way to the reality that I needed directions.

Continuing across the Wolf River Bridge, I stopped at an auto repair garage, where I could see some activity. "Excuse me, can you give me directions to the Alexian Brothers novitiate?" "The what?" I could see the younger man with grubby fingers did not have a clue. I rephrased, "The abbey, the old novitiate out toward Gresham, can you tell me how to get there from here?" "Uh, I think so, just a minute." He walked away and huddled with an older man and they both came back to me. "You're looking for the Alexian Brothers' place? Well, it has been a while since I was out there, but..." and he proceeded to reel off some directions.

Back in the car, I felt the need to speed again. The only thing between the monastery and me now was a few miles and my ability to follow the directions I had not taken the time to write down. It was time to turn on the internal GPS. "I don't ever remember coming or going to town this way," I thought. Evidently a Highway 29 bypass had been built around the south side of town. Turning off the unfamiliar bypass, I was sure I was closing in as I traveled north on County Road U.

In only a few miles, the road forked. If I were to veer left, the sign suggested it would take me into Gresham, but it felt familiar to go right. I followed my instincts and took that way and made several more turns based on gut feeling alone. One of those decisions took me past a small dam with water releasing from it.

The dam held back the Red River upstream from the monastery. I expected to see a railroad crossing adjacent to the dam, but it wasn't there. I knew I was within walking distance at this point. This route had taken me south and southwest of the property. One more right turn would put me on Butternut Road and the novitiate would appear on the right.

I slowed again so this last stretch would give me the payoff I had looked forward to all day long. I was driving past neighboring farms that we had walked by many times for recreation. The taller stands of trees and acreage brought familiarity, not necessarily the individual farmhouses, barns, and silos. My car window was down, and it smelled rural and good. The intersection I could see ahead looked like the road that came from the north and dead ended at Butternut.

I could see and read the street sign before the wooded area stopped and the grounds began. Juniper Road came from the Menominee Reservation and Lamberies' dairy farm. Juniper Road stopped at the monastery and so did I, because it was there. I had found it.

It took some time for it all to sink in. Suddenly a significant part of my past life stood before me. I had driven so far and so fast, I now had to back off and take it in. It appeared that the pace of life had increased very little since I left so many years ago, something I was pleased to discover. Out there on rural Butternut Road, you could stop in the middle of the road and it would be many minutes before anyone drove toward you or approached you from behind. Even if they did find you in their way, they would slowly and politely drive around without rude gestures or sounding their horn.

That is exactly what I did, until it occurred to me to pull forward into the easternmost approach to the drive onto the monastery grounds. I remember there being two driveways that created a U-shaped loop in and out of the novitiate. The approach at the west side was missing. It was the one closest to the mansion and the caretaker's house. For security and privacy reasons, the owners must have eliminated that entrance to the property.

Now that I was off the rural road, I got out of the car and stood there looking. This was like returning to a childhood home after an adult lifetime of years. I believe it is a common experience for those places to look small, as if time had shrunk them. This was my observation. The mansion, the monastery, and the cottage looked overgrown by the vegetation. The foliage was dwarfing the complex. What used to look like a wide and proud structure from the farm road thirty years ago looked reduced and hidden by mature trees and neglected undergrowth.

A hinged iron gate stood guard over the drive with a "No Trespassing" sign attached. The makeshift entrance was a good place to hold onto as I leaned there between it and the car surveying what I could see from several hundred yards away. A large, black dog approached and barked at me from about the halfway to the cottage. It had a smaller but silent companion. They watched me as I watch them, and the black one barked less the longer I stayed. If anyone was home, my presence had certainly been made known.

I could not stand it any longer. There was no chain or lock to hold the gate in place. The dogs were not intimidating enough for me to honor the "No Trespassing" signs. I pushed one side of the gate inward to create enough room for me to drive the car in. Blowing the horn to give the residents some warning as I neared the cottage seemed the right thing to do. I drove slowly, as if I was coming home, and savored the approach. Straight up the drive toward the novitiate main entrance and a right turn, paralleling the classrooms and dining area, took me to a parking spot between the old boiler room and the cottage.

There was a stark difference between the wooden Cape Cod–style cottage and the adjacent stone monastery. It was obvious that someone cared for the cottage. I noted several external signs that someone lived inside, such as dog bowls, a broom, and a doormat. My noisemaking had not brought anyone outside or even to the door, however. I left my car in the drive that had once been well defined but was now overgrown with weeds and grass—it was hard to tell where the drive stopped and the lawn began.

The furry greeting party had continued to bark as I made my way up the drive, but the dogs now waited with wagging tails for me to exit the car. I took my time, giving anyone who happened to be inside the chance to come out and meet me rather than surprising them with a knock on the door. Finally, I made my way to the back entrance near the garages. The dogs escorted me past the various automotive projects and various all-terrain toys belonging to the current owner or tenant.

It was a minute or so before I received a response to my knocking. I was later to learn that the lady who came to the door was named Mirga. "Hello, my name is Pat Rick. I am a former Alexian Brother who used to live here. I was wondering if I could look around," I asked. "Just a moment," she said, disappearing into the cottage. A very tall fortyish man replaced her with a half annoyed and half stern look on his face. I repeated my rehearsed request, expecting to be turned away and reminded of my trespassing.

"Well, OK, but don't go inside. It is not safe in places there," he warned. I could not believe it. I had just gotten the green light to poke around outside. I had the feeling an exception had been made because of my connection to the Alexians. His face had turned slightly friendlier.

I thanked the owner, who I later learned was named Frank Matuzney, and promised him I would return to let him know when I would be leaving the property. My initial visit with Frank revealed that he was not the first owner following the Alexian Brothers. The Matuzney family would prove to be very frugal—the entire monastery, mansion, caretaker's home, and choice riverside lots were purchased for a mere $40,000 to satisfy back taxes.

Frank Matuzney, wife Mirga and son, Aaron, once owners
Photo by Curt Knoke

Both dogs were eager to take me on an escorted tour of the former novitiate and monastery. The dogs, by now, realized I was probably a good guy. The canines, however, were probably unaware of my reputation regarding surgery and dogs. One was older, and the other was a puppy. They were happy to come along with me for the walk, with the younger nipping the older in play. Since the cottage had been built to serve the mansion, my starting point was Peters Hall. The Alexian Brothers renamed the mansion after Jennie Peters gave it all to them.

Georgian in style, Peters Hall faced west and was buffered by a stand of trees that stretched the full depth of the property. The estate was built to take advantage of its seclusion, proximity to the Red River, and the Freeborn Falls that created its southern boundary. Very few steps away from the Matuzney' home brought you in front and in full view of the mansion. From the front steps, you could see and enjoy the falls. This entire long, sloping expanse down to the water's edge used to be a carpet of grass and a manicured show place. Fruit-bearing apple trees, willows at the water, and stone-bordered flower gardens had all once flourished on the lawn that was created from landfill on what was once a swampy marsh

It was all Frank could do now to keep the grass down in the spring and summer. It would require a significant staff and millions of dollars to restore and maintain it to its former glory. Originally, there had been a circular drive branching off of the main approach at the mansion front door. No evidence of the drive could be seen, much less the statue of the Virgin Mary who lost her head during the siege. The windows were boarded up, and a wooden plank barrier to keep the curious out had replaced the once-elegant entrance.

Stepping up on the semicircular porch gave me a better look at the falls. The elliptical stone landing provided a base for four bullet-scarred stone columns and they, in turn, supported an overhead canopy with the same geometry as the porch. Even in disrepair, grandeur from the past was not difficult to imagine. On these very steps, a variety of people over the years had been welcomed into the mansion. The wealthy, bishops, indigenous warriors, religious hopefuls, Indian chiefs, abbots, America's military heroes, poor farmers, poorer Native Americans, an A-list of movie stars, and orphans all had visited under a variety of circumstances.

Turning back to the water, I realized that the river and its formations had changed little since the glaciers that created it passed through, and almost not at all since we swam in the always-cold waters. However, the manmade structure I was having a reunion with that day had a history that was the substance of which novels are made. I just did not realize to what degree at the time. Time for me here stopped in 1967. In the mid-'70s, I was off and about my business of career and family when the novitiate was falling victim to difficult times. This visit was the beginning of a consuming passion to uncover the facts and tell the story of this place and past.

Peering into the boarded window frames of Peters Hall today reveals a gutted interior. Steel and concrete support beams hold up a concrete second floor, and the angle of the several staircases allows you to see a third floor of the same construction. The charred interior shell offers no hint of its former beauty. Interior walls separating once-lavish rooms were consumed by fire. Rich wood floors and paneling in the living and library area had once led to a sunroom with a terra cotta floor and a panoramic bay window that overlooked the falls. The view was through crank-out casement windows that once opened to catch breezes from the river.

The fireplaces that had warmed my family when they visited those two January days when I became an Alexian Brother were intact but missing their ornate mantels. I noted that they were still apparently keeping somebody warm, because they contained fresh ashes and a large amount of chainsaw-cut firewood neatly stacked in places and strewn about the gutted expanse. There was a bench in front of one of the hearths.

I strolled along the sidewalk between the water's edge and the mansion. Attached to Peters Hall, the cloister walk acted as an umbilical cord between the old and the new. This intentionally zigzagged corridor connected the back door of the mansion to the construction built by the brothers. Ms. Peters maintained an impressive greenhouse that provided herbs, vegetables, and year-round blooming flowers for entertaining and her pleasure. That hothouse had to be dismantled before the Alexians built on. The exterior sidewalk paralleled the indoor passageway that ran the length of the novitiate. The cloister, too, had lost all of its glass windows, which had been fit into beautiful arches and provided a river view and observatory for Wisconsin's four distinct seasons.

Since this was the side facing away from the road, unseen and malicious vandals over the years had left very little space for any additional vulgarity. The solid wall of the cloistered walk contained every manner of inscription from local youth making midnight visits and rendezvous. The walls were a bulletin board of real and imagined sexual conquests. Included in the mix of graffiti were the obligatory tributes to rock bands. Looking through the large vertical windows of the chapel, I could see into the choir loft. Written in giant letters above the pipe organ, with what must have taken a full can of spray paint, was the word *metallica*. I laughed to myself. Remembering the monastic standard of grand silence, I had no memory of that rock band ever performing in concert at the monastery while I was there!

Only the mansion suffered directly from fire late in 1975 and would present a challenge to uncover details. The rest was simply in advanced decay. The chapel, for example, was crumbling, with the ceiling falling in. The original wall colors and some of the woodwork remained. Except for discarded scraps, there was no sign of the beautiful green and pink marble, furnishings, altars, or any artifacts. This was once a spectacular place and the scene of many young men transitioning into the religious life. I was itching to get inside.

The chapel had a side door I could not resist trying. It failed to open. A level below the chapel had been a very large area that included a fully outfitted workshop with food processing facilities and other areas that supported the institution. Windows at ground level allowed me to see down and into the basement area. A motion detector had been placed there to warn of intruders that could easily get in this way.

It was more than a little spooky bending down and looking into that dark dungeon-like chamber. I wasn't sure who or what might be looking back at me from that subterranean level. All I could make out was disarray in the flooded abyss. It was down there with the fine wood-working tools that Brother Simeon had supervised my building of a redwood picnic table. I stained it an even darker red, lacquered it, and placed it out among the apple trees. I did not expect to see the table inside or out after forty years. No doubt, it was probably chopped up and used for firewood; perhaps it was used to keep the occupying warriors and their families warm.

The chapel was about equal distance between the original mansion and the novitiate residential portion of the complex. On either side of the chapel were two three-sided courtyards. These areas were open to the barrier of trees that stretched to the water's edge, connected by long and winding sidewalks.

Moving on to the second courtyard and looking up, I recognized my room on the second floor at a corner of the building. That double-hung window had not been spared either. Compared to others, it was clearly a choice location. As I stood there remembering, I wanted desperately to be on the second floor looking out my old window, taking in the view of the waterfall. The view was transient and dependent upon the fall foliage and winter. The trees in the summer allowed only the sound, not the view. Shards of glass poked out like stalagmites and stalactites in the broken panes.

I had promised Frank I would not enter the building. The motion detector seen earlier indicated he meant it. I already had a sense that this was not going to be my last brush with this place. As I turned the corner to walk the last leg of the exterior tour, I knew I would be back, and well before several more decades passed.

The entire property sloped toward the river and Freeborn Falls. Walking back toward the main road required climbing steps or walking up an earthen incline. Reaching the top and on level ground again, I could see where the soccer and baseball fields once were. The goals were missing. That area was now overgrown with underbrush and small trees. I could see that some structure had been built there after I left but had also been torn down. Between the playing field and the river downstream was the old cesspool. I will never forget learning to ice skate on the frozen wastewater. I referred to it then as "holy shit."

I was losing the afternoon's light and needed to say goodbye to the monastery. While standing on the street side looking into the old classroom windows, I noticed a few slate roof tiles leaning against one of the exterior doors. In the better days of the monastery, the building was crowned with these sturdy, blue-gray and random earth-tone tiles, which were surrounded by shiny copper gutters, fixtures, and downspouts.

Most of the valuable copper had walked off over the years. The resulting moisture penetration due to the yearly freezing and thawing underneath the tiles caused them to individually give way and fall three stories to the ground. Given the right time and right place, decapitation crossed my mind. After saying goodbye to Frank and his wife, I thanked them and they allowed me to take two of the souvenir slates. I found it difficult to drive away.

I drove slowly, glancing frequently over my shoulder as the novitiate disappeared behind the trees again. Many questions were answered that day, but they were replaced with new and many more unanswered ones.

Months went by; then I returned. This time, I had a handful of copies from the yellowing dog-eared newspaper clippings from my first visit to the Shawano Public Library. The name Melvin Chevalier kept surfacing in my sparse but growing research file. It seems there were other siblings: Arnold, Christopher, and Robert. However, it was Melvin I heard and read of more often. More digging and phone calls revealed that Melvin Chevalier had taken the name Apesanahkwat. There had to be some mistake. Apesanahkwat was the name of the current Chairman of the Menominee Tribe. He was a responsible elected leader in Keshena. I was looking for the guy who was a member of the Menominee Warriors Society and had participated in the hostile takeover of the novitiate. Several attempts by phone and a letter to his office failed to move him to reply until one unexpected June day in 1999 my phone rang. "Pat, this is Apesanahkwat, what do you want with me?" His voice was slow and measured, and there was a frugal economy in his words. I thought for a while I was speaking to an old man, not someone who was only three or so years my senior. The crackle in his voice did not match the person I ultimately met face-to-face months later.

I am certain he thought he knew exactly what I wanted. He had been asked so many times before about his participation in the occupation. He perceived me to be another reporter wanting him to pose for photos in front of the "abbey," and I detected it had become boring for him to tell that years-revised version of the winter of '75. I very much wanted to hear his story, that was true, but I was not a reporter. I was, instead, a former member of the Alexian Brothers. Depending on point of view, I represented a group that had been his opposition or, at least, an unwitting player during his warrior days.

The results of our conversation were no surprise. Apesanahkwat was very dismissive about the whole thing. He suggested that if I wanted details, I should speak with Ken Fish because Ken had kept "detailed notes" and had written a book about the novitiate. He said I would do better by interviewing Fish rather than wasting my time with him, the Chief. Our conversation was friendly, and I detected a dry sense of humor behind that native-like voice. After we established some rapport, he shared with me that he had a modest acting career and found himself working in California from time to time. "Perhaps we could meet then," he said. This was a character I wanted to meet.

I followed up that first contact with a letter thanking him for his time and tried to keep the door open for a face-to-face encounter. He never acknowledged the letter. I learned that "AP," as he likes to be called, is not a correspondent. In all contact with him, I have never received anything on paper. His style is an oral policy only. Perhaps his heritage gives him a predisposition to discount things in writing. A long track record of broken treaties can make you that way. This has not deterred me from trying to learn more about a dissident of the '70s maturing into a leader of a sovereign nation. I had found someone who was colorful and articulate and had a fresh perspective on and a connection to a part of my past: the monastery. I would try again. The Chief had been found!

For the next several months, Apesanahkwat alternately avoided and took some of my phone calls. It was important for me to sit down and interview him on camera. Always, he played down his importance and insisted that I speak with Ken Fish, the tribe's expert on treaty rights. Ken seemed to be expecting my call. His friendly and easygoing voice and demeanor over the phone had elements of suspicion regarding my intentions. Fish told me he had made copious notes during the siege and possessed a self-written manuscript. He referred to it as a book and further conversation indicated that it had not been published.

My developing interest at the time was to produce a documentary about the property and the Indian takeover. If Ken had what he said he had, it would be a great resource on the warrior perspective from inside the walls. My conversations with Fish were friendly but unproductive; we made no progress toward collaboration. We did not know each other well enough for there to be enough trust to result in sharing information. We agreed to talk again and I promised to make an effort to travel to the Keshena area and visit him in person.

The opportunity presented itself sooner than expected. Only a few months later, business took me back to Chicago, and I added on another side trip to the Menominee Reservation. Ken Fish met me at the tribe's casino restaurant. He had rolled in like small thunder on his Harley-Davidson dressed in his leathers and sporting a long salt-and-pepper ponytail. Grinning ear-to-ear, he apologized for being late, sharing that he been out late the night before hunting deer and had returned later than expected. We went through the buffet line, taking generous portions, and then Ken made a second pass. He was short, fit, and stocky, needing the extra portions. Word had it his build had garnered respect on the high school football field.

We had lunch together to the sound of white people pumping change into the Indian slot machines. During our meal, Ken agreed to ride with me out to the Alexian Brothers monastery. I was surprised he accepted the invitation. I didn't feel like we had connected at the casino. I held out hope he would see that I was interested in uncovering the facts, not just scratching the surface of a stale story. During lunch, he reiterated that he had a manuscript and the only thing holding him back from publishing it was that elder family and friends were still living and hard feelings could result. We took my car to avoid the silly sight of a paleface hugging a warrior on the back of a Hog, wind-slapped by his ponytail.

It was a comfortable autumn day, and I had already gotten permission to revisit the property. Ken and I drove right up to the original mansion and parked. We got out of the car and immediately went to the front of Peters Hall. Fish walked over and peered into one of the boarded-up windows. I took pictures as he reflected back on those January and February days in 1975. He pointed out the room on the second floor that he had occupied with his girlfriend during the siege. He turned around to the west and pointed out where they had set up their sweat lodge, just inside the wooded area beyond the mansion front door. Ken silently put his finger in some of the bullet holes that pockmarked the columns at the entry.

We were retracing the counterclockwise exterior route around the novitiate I had taken several months before. This time, though, I had a warrior with me, and he was sharing very little. Standing between the river and the building, Fish remembered the various angles from which they took fire and fired upon the authorities and vigilantes. I regretted that we could still not go inside. Perhaps in there and looking out he would have felt the urge to open up and talk to me about details. It did not happen.

Our tour was cordial but sterile. It was clear that Ken wanted some assurance that he, too, would be rewarded for telling the story. I understood his reticence and recognized his need for some professional relationship with me before he would reveal stories from within the walls during the occupation. For all he knew I was just another apologist looking to rewrite history and selectively shed favorable light on anyone except the Menominee Warriors Society. He did not offer to show me his writings, nor did I ask to see them. I took him back to the tribal casino and his motorcycle, where we agreed to speak again.

Later, Ken did remind me during our walk around that there were friends and family relationships that would suffer if he were to make public his journal and writings. He told me that, on February 4, 1976, his uncle, also named Ken Fish, participated in shooting and killing two men in the line of duty. The incident occurred exactly one year following the abbey climax. His uncle, known as "Paddo" Fish was the chief of police and later to become the sheriff on the reservation.

Those two men were Arlin J. Pamanet and John Waubanascum Jr.. Waubanascum would be remembered as the menacing heavy-handed Menominee warrior that threatened the captives that 1975 New Year's morning. That killing in Neopit was described by authorities as an attempt to arrest the pair with warrants. There are plenty of credible beliefs that Paddo Fish operated outside of the law. Existence of a "goon squad" wearing badges was feared according to many on and off the reservation.

Wisconsin State Trooper, Elroy Stroming, was also a paramedic when not on duty enforcing the law. The night Pamanet and Waubanascum were killed, Elroy Stroming responded on duty as a paramedic. Both young men did not survive the encounter. A decision was made to conduct autopsies at the state capital. To maintain proper custody of the evidence, Trooper/EMT Stroming was the right man to accompany the two bodies to Madison. The autopsy findings did not exactly coincide with the report written by the reservation chief of police.

Elroy Stroming recalls his Wisconsin Trooper days from Freeborn Falls
Photo by Curt Knoke

The Ken Fish I had spent the afternoon with was an unapologetic member of the Warriors Society who, at the hands of his uncle, had lost a friend and fellow warrior. It was not difficult to understand why Ken preferred to hold the story close to his vest.

The reservation is a tight little world, and Ken held a respectable position with great visibility. Managing the treaty rights department of the Menominee government required diplomacy. He also intended to run for public office. At best, it would be difficult for Ken to reopen that can of worms and jeopardize his livelihood and relationship with those who were still living and still polarized. Even today, there are very strong opinions regarding the actions of the youths who took part in the takeover of the Alexian Brothers Novitiate.

Aside from another visit to the Shawano library and rummaging through their dog-eared file on the abbey siege, it was not a terribly productive trip in search of warriors. It was a bit of a disappointment not to move any closer on some collaboration with Ken Fish. I thought working with Fish could be symbiotic. I was lacking in political savvy and believed it might be possible for a former Alexian Brother to put his head together with a Menominee warrior and tell the story about that January/February 1975 event that got the world's attention. Middle-aged Menominee men and women were not tearing down my door to tell their story. Besides Apesanahkwat and Ken Fish, the only other individual willing to speak with me was Royal Warrington, who was also involved in tribal government and was in charge of the legislative department in Keshena.

Warrington was confined to a wheelchair and was the most hesitant to speak with me. He was very defensive about the actions he and the other warriors had taken. One of the explanations for their actions offered by Royal was the tribe's dire need for a hospital at the time. He said the former novitiate was ideal for a medical facility. In 1975, the tribal hospital was inadequate and no longer met the basic state standards of care for that type of institution. He and many others believed that the off-reservation monastery could serve the health-care needs of the tribe and/or serve as a rehabilitation center for substance abuse. Steadfast in their convictions at the time of the siege, these warriors provided little or no anecdotal material. They stuck to their story of civil disobedience for the greater good. Tyrannical treatment by the then-matriarchal government, they claim, drove them to their extreme actions.

There was plenty of evidence that under the right circumstances, the trio of Apesanahkwat, Fish, and Warrington would be willing to speak. My research had turned up several newspaper articles in which the three had both individually and collectively retold the story, usually around the anniversary of the siege. It became clear to me that perhaps I had to work a little harder than the average investigator.

I had always introduced myself as a former Catholic Alexian Brother who had lived in the monastery. I thought it was important to be up front with anyone I approached on the subject. The Menominee men and women I contacted by phone and in person seemed to appreciate that sort of introduction. However, it always seemed to set the standard for their degree of disclosure.

I had made other telephone calls to Apesanahkwat and felt that he was beginning to soften. Each time we spoke, I continually drove the point home that I was interested in the facts. While it was true that I had a connection with the Alexians, I told him that he should not interpret that as an inability on my part to tell both sides. On one occasion, AP said that he was planning a possible trip to Palm Springs, California. I marked my calendar and called his office to coincide with the dates he had given me. I was told, "No, the chairman is not here right now. He is in Palm Springs at a meeting." Apesanahkwat returned my call on his cell phone and agreed to meet with me if I would drive out to the desert.

The little modest motel resort had a lobby full of very colorful indigenous Americans. Most of them seemed to have made some effort to represent themselves in native clothing. I had no idea what the chairman looked like. All of the articles I had read that had a picture were either in terrible condition or printed many years ago. I looked around the restaurant and the lobby and saw no one who appeared to be as I would have imagined him.

The front desk placed a call to his room, and there was no answer. He had given me his cell phone number so I called it. I was getting a sense that times, places, and punctuality were not terribly important to him. AP answered, saying he was in a meeting and would come to meet me in the motel lobby. I sat back and eavesdropped on the various private conversations and impromptu business meetings conducted by the attendees to this unknown Indian conference.

Strolling toward me was a very dark, lanky man. He dressed his skinny hairless legs in yellow silk Bermuda shorts and wore a very loud surfer type print shirt. He wore no socks and sported a fine pair of casual loafers. He had several gold rings on the fingers of both hands and held a big fat and wet extinguished cigar. At least one wrist had a sizable yellow gold-linked bracelet. The man's face had a pencil-thin graying mustache and a single diamond stud earring balanced by several gold chain necklaces occupying the space on his chest where his shirt would have been if it had been buttoned.

He resembled a laid-back American Indian version of Clark Gable. This was Apesanahkwat. The voice I had come to know on the telephone at first syllable now fit the man. I could tell at first glance that AP had survived harder knocks in life than most. To me, he looked weathered, worn, and frail, yet handsome. We sat down outside on the patio while I ate and he drank iced tea and had conversation after conversation on his cell phone. Apparently I had driven a long way just to hear him conduct Menominee business on the phone. Although we accomplished very little that day, our face-to-face meeting ultimately broke the ice and led to a formal on-camera interview a year or so later.

I was getting the picture. These warrior men had long ago put their past behind them. I was the one on the sentimental journey who wanted to reopen old and potentially dangerous wounds. They, on the other hand, did not want to miss the opportunities their unique stories might hold. Ken Fish and I would speak by phone on several more occasions.

I suggested to him that we jointly write the story. However, with the two of us having completely different perspectives on the events, circumstances, and the property, we couldn't find the common ground necessary to reach an agreement and launch the effort. I guess he was afraid I wouldn't respect his reasons for the occupation and I was afraid he wouldn't appreciate my point of view.

Ken Fish made it clear that he never has been in any hurry to pen his story and that he may very well die unpublished. By contrast, I was anxious to reopen the can of worms, dredge up the past, and revisit the story. It was naive on my part, but I decided to move on and do it myself with or without Menominee Warrior help. I had enough facts and interviews lined up to move on. I was confident that other warriors would come out of the woodwork and help me reconstruct their story from inside those monastery walls.

During a follow-up telephone conversation with Apesanahkwat, he unexpectedly agreed to a sit-down interview on camera. It seems that AP made a little money traveling the national powwow circuit. He was driving from Wisconsin to the southwest to dance at Indian gatherings and would then drive on to California to spend some time with his brother. He said we could sit down in Burbank and I could ask him anything I wished, and in return he asked that I help him with some of his cross-country driving expenses, gas money. That seemed reasonable to me, and I looked forward to the breakthrough.

Apesanahkwat was late for our Burbank appointment. I had forgotten to plan for "Indian time" and the disregard for punctuality. The chief's brother's girlfriend invited us in to their apartment. Since I was unfamiliar with my new digital video equipment, it was Lisa Cole joining me that day for technical assistance. Lisa had been recommended to me by an individual that would ultimately direct my project. I just wasn't sure, in the long run, what the project would be.

Lisa and I moved a recliner in front of the Navajo rug made in Korea hanging on the wall alongside the macramé dream catcher imported from China. We rounded up several potted cactus plants that probably had never seen the desert and arranged them near the chair. Then we waited for Apesanahkwat, chairman and tribal chief of the Menominee Nation from the land of deep rich forests and streams. We set the stage for him to sit while being interviewed. The best we could do was this contrived, stereotypical, impromptu, generic, and arid southwestern Native American setting. After all, this was Hollywood.

The silver-tongued chief arrived, late as usual. He had just met with his theatrical agent and auditioned for a television series. This French-American Indian was considering the role of a Mexican-American to add to his credits, including appearances on the television show *Northern Exposure,* a principal role in the film *Bagdad Café,* and playing the role of master of ceremonies at the Native Americans in the Arts awards in Hollywood. AP kept his name on the "B" list when casting was looking for a middle-aged male Native American. Seated there in his white linen pants and Hawaiian shirt, AP began his story, his wet cigar wedged between two fingers as a prop to punctuate with hand gestures.

"A group of young men and women got together and said we need to do something to focus national attention on our plight," he began. Not there to judge, I had no idea if the talented chameleon was revealing an accurate narrative. He verbally took us back to Wisconsin during a time of hardship and anger. He kept his promise by slowly and deliberately delivering a story of how the monastery had become international headline news on New Year's Day, 1975.

The tribal chairman explained that six months prior to the takeover in 1975, the warriors had assembled out near Legend Lake to strategize. They had hoped to initiate their actions that summer. Thanksgiving Day of 1974, the unrelated murder of Father Marcellus Cabo, a Franciscan Catholic priest, caused alarm both off and on the reservation. FBI surveillance activity and the suspicion of informants within the Warriors Society forced them to call off their plan and wait until winter.

In the late '90s, I enrolled in a UCLA course in writing a one-man show taught by the actress Beverly Sanders. Beverly is one of those career actresses who possess a very long and respectable resume in the entertainment industry, especially television throughout the 1970s. Beverly whet my appetite with her experience in supporting Valerie Harper and Mary Tyler Moore and their memorable contributions to comedy.

I knew that my brief brush with fame posing as Bill Clinton would eventually end after eight years, but I had been bitten by the comedy bug and was graduating from Class Clown 101. In an attempt to squeeze a little bit more out of the serendipity, a handful of us took additional lessons from Beverly Sanders to produce our own one-man personal shows. Mine went nowhere, but the class was a valuable exercise in writing and telling a story that coincided with my rediscovery of the novitiate.

One of my Hollywood classmates was Chris Sheridan. He had already earned, to his credit, a Student Academy Award. He, too, was exercising his creative side. Chris had cut his teeth in the '80s as a member of the rock band Sweet Savage. Chris and I shared aircraft piloting credentials. An adventurous airplane crash that broke his back had forced him to use that misfortune to his advantage. Chris had written, acted in, and filmed the personal documentary *Walk This Way*.

We, two unlikely characters, befriended each other. I approached Chris and asked him if he would collaborate with me in producing a short video piece I could use as a teaser. I planned to use it to generate interest in a potential feature film production. I had, and still do, find the Menominee Warriors Society takeover of the Alexian Brothers monastery to be unique but generally forgotten. Chris was curious and became enthusiastic for the project. A documentary began to grow legs.

Chris and I made plans for Chicago and Wisconsin. With limited resources, I made arrangements for us to interview as many real characters as possible on camera. Sheridan stocked up on videotape for his expensive state-of-the-art digital camera while I was busy creating an itinerary that would take us to several Chicago locations and to Wisconsin. Our appointments were set in the late fall. We left sunny Southern California. It was cold on arrival at O'Hare.

I had rented a pickup truck, believing it would best suit our purposes. A partial paraplegic, Chris lived in and out but mostly in a wheelchair as a result of his spinal injury. Otherwise, he could be difficult to keep up with. When necessary, he could strap on leg braces and go where wheels couldn't.

Like Felix and Oscar, we set out as an "odd couple." One of us was a former monk, presidential impersonator, and penile-breast implant representative; the other was a partial paraplegic, Academy Award winner, and former "kick-ass nonstop hard-rocking professional band member" accustomed to wearing spandex with groupies in pursuit. Who could ever make up that sort of joint venture?

The timing of our visit was fortunate. Donna Dahl, the Alexian archivist in Chicago, arranged for us to interview Brother Maurice. He was in Chicago on business from the Philippine mission. In a very matter-of-fact manner, Brother Maurice sat down wearing his black habit, seldom seen these days, and told his story. Brother pointed no fingers and showed no anger, but he did express disappointment in the overall outcome in 1975.

Beyond the obvious thirty-three-day turmoil and occupation, the most divisive issues lingered long after. Some convents with Catholic nuns had become hostile and challenged the Alexians. Dissident clergy in the '70s made an already difficult situation impossible. The brothers were faced with circumstances resulting in "damned if you do and damned if you don't" consequences.

Catholics turned against Catholics. Menominee warriors were not in accord within their own tribe, either. Politics had been turned upside down, and that monastery had been the flashpoint. Brother Maurice felt it was impossible to make *anyone* happy. Even the Alexians were not in harmony amongst themselves over issues needed to resolve the Gresham debacle. The brothers were desperate for assistance and support, and even Rome looked the other way. It was a lose-lose situation.

Our interview with Brother Maurice Wilson set the stage for our engagements scheduled for the rest of the week. Donna made the archives available to us as we attempted to document the story. Yes, many people had asked questions and shown interest in this seemingly last gasp of the American Indian Movement. But I could find no published books or film precisely telling the story. This was the beginning of a real opportunity. We set our sights on Madison, Wisconsin, where the saga partially played out.

Ada Deer was our next stop. She lived out and away from Madison in a nice warm country home. To my surprise, she asked if Chris and I would stay for dinner. We accepted, and she promised to treat us to wild rice, a signature dish of the Menominee. But first, she told us her version of the abbey, warriors, Alexians, and politics at the time. Our reason for being there truly paled in comparison to her later career accomplishments. But she was cordial while responding to our questions.

Chris was proving to be talented in helping me come up to speed while documenting the story of a person of importance. On occasion, Chris would inject a question that demonstrated his sincere interest in this project and story beyond just pointing a camera at someone's face. From 1993 until 1997, Ada Deer had served as head of the United States' Bureau of Indian Affairs where she had been appointed by Bill Clinton. Her credentials were many both before and after that accomplishment.

She was amused by Chris's background and curious about my faux-presidential escapades. Chris and I went away that evening with one significant finding. When asked to sum up the abbey takeover and the actions taken by the warriors, she said the Menominee Warriors Society were "boys behaving badly." Then we cleared the dining room table and sat down for some Native American hospitality and wild rice.

I didn't know until we began the trip that Chris Sheridan had a connection to Wisconsin too. Growing up, he had lived in Stevens Point and had some early jobs about town. The opportunity for him to reach back in time presented itself. We drove north toward Wausau. Everybody has heard of Wausau. However, we stopped in Stevens Point and Chris, unannounced, shook the hands of old friends. They all wanted to know about his journey and why he was in a wheelchair, and he told them. Then we drove to Shawano, but I could not resist a monastic drive-by.

After only two or three interviews under our belt, we were feeling like a team. In the Gresham, Shawano, and Keshena vicinity, we conducted more than a half-dozen on-camera interviews. Very few of those were with natives who were willing to speak on the record. That was nothing new. I had already grown used to the reluctance of the Menominees to speak out. Chris and I spent many hours filming and talking about the monastery, the mansion, the takeover, and the history. Even with all of the debris, hazards, and traversing the stairs, Chris kept up with me. Except for common sense, very little stopped Chris. We moved on to Milwaukee.

I was excited about the final interview. Frankly, I was surprised he had agreed. In an attractive neighborhood in a far north section of Milwaukee, Chris and I arrived in our rented pickup truck. We were greeted by Jean, the wife of the former governor, Patrick Lucey. She showed us to their study, where Lucey joined us.

Governor Lucey was quiet and volunteered very little. My questions were longer than his sparing answers. On occasion, he would ask me astonishing questions. It appeared his memory was not serving him well. I gathered that either I was being taken for a ride or dementia had taken control. I gained nothing from that very sterile encounter.

Once, Jean popped in and offered us something to drink. Chris and I thanked her but declined. With nowhere to turn, we were as cordially dismissed as we had been received. Leaving Milwaukee, I could not decide whether I had been handled well by a crafty yet aging politician or 1975 had been removed from his memory. I have chosen to err on the side of compassion.

I made telephone arrangements with Shawano Flying Service and Clarence Schampers, an owner and instructor. This was my opportunity to be privately airborne once again after many years. My mission was to fly the short distance out to and over the location I had become reconnected and infatuated with. My pilot's license was not current, so Clarence himself took me round and round, making multiple low slow steeply banked left turns. I recorded several minutes of video from the left seat. This was my chance to reenact the incident where an unauthorized aircraft had penetrated the official no-fly zone during the 1975 takeover.

From only several hundred feet above, it could be seen why Jenny Peters had originally included the construction of the carriage house, which had a multi-car garages and accommodations for a chauffeur and staff. The single-story wood-frame structure sat in stark contrast to the Georgian style mansion and matching monastic addition. It is hard to understand why this support building was constructed in such a modest and different style.

This aerial view offered a perspective unavailable on the ground or afloat on the Red River. The cottage sat between the property's north border, Butternut Road, and the original mansion. Renamed Peters Hall by the Alexians after the gift from Mrs. Peters, the mansion was always the draw. Its southern border, with a spectacular view, was the Red River at Freeborn Falls.

The mansion was not built to face the road. For Mrs. Peters, the attraction was clearly the River and the falls, not the mansion itself. She built her home facing the west so that as people approached the home on the private drive, they would encounter the architecture and the waterfall at the same time. This was made clear from the air.

The weather was not bad. I was treated to broken clouds, intermittent sunshine breaking through, and some brief snow flurries. It was as if the weather service had followed a script on demand to simulate the way things had been the winter of 1975.

We pointed the plane a little more northwesterly toward Mission Lake, only two or so minutes away by plane. Walking distance from there, I located below Curt and Martha Knoke's converted barn. We continued on to Neopit. I wanted to get a better understanding of the layout of the Menominee Lumber Mill. My budget aloft had reached its limit. We had been up about three quarters of an hour and I figured a flyover the tribes' casino and Keshena had provided me with a different perspective.

Anyone who has ever enjoyed being at the control of a plane must give out signals like pheromones to fellow pilots. I had said nothing about being a pilot to Clarence. I knew I was there to record the sights, not navigate. Clarence sensed that I was quietly chomping at the bit, and we only had ten or fifteen minutes left before we returned. "Do you want to take the controls?" He read my mind. How did he know? Clarence had said the magic words to me. Flight instructors are usually calm, considerate, and a special breed of people. I blurted out Yes.

We've all heard the saying about riding a bike. Even after decades, most of us can get back on a bicycle and ride again with little trouble. I was flying again, but it was a little less forgiving than a Schwinn with training wheels. The airport had no tower or involved communication precisely directing traffic in our out. It was one of those places where you are expected to play your part and follow the rules. In past years I had not logged many severe winter hours. Even if I had forgotten, Clarence the instructor would have reminded me to turn on the all-important carburetor heat. I had always been told it was a good landing if it resulted in the rubber side down and you were able to walk away.

Clarence invited me inside to have a cup of coffee after tying down his plane. Our aeronautical bonding had bought me the opportunity to pick his brain further. I had been told that during the occupation, a Green Bay television station had used a private aircraft to fly danger-ously close to the monastery, angering the warriors, National Guard, and law enforcement. The warriors threatened to fire on aircraft the next time. They feared surveillance or other aerial action. They had no way of knowing if authorities were breaking promises or if the plane was just aggressive cowboy news media wanting good film for their story.

The long arm of the law was comically exercised that day. Just about the same time the news crew had landed after invading closed airspace, law enforcement telephoned them at the airport. They asked the pilot to identify himself and informed him he was under arrest. This is how it had evolved into a Keystone Cops comedy of errors. Between the sheriff, the guard, and the state patrol, the best law enforcement could do was arrest, in absentia, and hope they would comply. Their hands were slapped and they were told to stay away from the potential powder keg building within the monastery.

The little airport was busy in Shawano while the world watched during the 1975 occupation in nearby Gresham. Still a mystery today, to Clarence, is the plane that dropped in unannounced, remained many days, and disappeared while no one was looking. The occupant or occupants must have been in quite a hurry to deplane. They didn't even perform the basics of parking and tying down to brace against winter winds. I found the story particularly interesting. I am no expert on the American Indian Movement. But at the time AIM was still riding a high following the 1973 standoff at Wounded Knee, South Dakota, on the Pine Ridge Indian Reservation. Federal agents and Indian activists were at each other's throats.

I have a theory about the mysterious aircraft, and I simply place it among the long list of possibilities. Douglas Durham was reported to be in the Gresham area early during the warriors' takeover. Durham, over the years, had become an admitted informer, penetrating the American Indian Movement. Dennis Banks, in his book, *Ojibwa Warrior*, claims he and Durham had been invited to come and help negotiate the novitiate standoff. All indications are that Banks and

Durham arrived by driving to the new hotspot and probably the last of any significance.

Durham was a pilot. At the same time, he was appearing on AIM political radar as an insider not to be trusted. Doug Durham had a knack for dropping in unannounced then disappearing with stealth only to show up great distances away. It is suspected he had frequent access to small private aircraft. This seems to be what may have happened since things were heating up for a man suspected as an FBI operative. Could Durham have used that plane as his ticket out of town when things were closing in on him? The Douglas Durham story was only one of many concentric plots that played themselves out with the novitiate/abbey/monastery as the stage.

Several years into researching this over all story, I came to meet two of the Czech brothers, Bradley and Scott. To clarify, I mean they are simply natural brothers, not members of a religious organization. The Czechs had driven down to Chicago to learn more about the history of the novitiate.

At the Alexian archives, we compared notes and learned of our similar thirst for historic detail. I was happy to discover there were other people around that were equally as enthralled. It was good to find younger people having taken dissimilar circuitous routes to the same destination, the banks of a river and a waterfall.

The Czech siblings explained to me their intense childhood connection with the novitiate. Scott and his younger brother Bradley were just kids the summer of 1976. The boys, apparently like many others, felt drawn to it but dared not trespass. There were posted warnings all around. They would have to settle for standing at the chained locked gate looking at the novitiate some distance away. Law-abiding parents and family members would not breach the perimeter without permission.

It was well known the Shawano County sheriff's deputies kept an eye on the vacant place and frequently patrolled, especially at night. This still remained the hot spot authorities wished to keep extinguished. The potential to erupt with the same ferocity lay just below the surface. The events here had caused people to lose friendships, family members, business associates, and political connections. It had caused some Indians to dislike other Indians. It had caused white men to dislike other whites. This nearly no man's land, of course, reinforced the racial divide that had always existed.

Before the Czech family boys were to grow into young men, there had been many a family camping trip in the vicinity of the Red River and Freeborn Falls. The lure of the burnt-out mansion and the attached novitiate became almost irresistible. They wanted to see for themselves. A female member of their family was a local deputy sheriff, and she secured permission to enter. The Czech youngsters got their chance to see behind closed doors.

Along for this particular and special Sunday drive in the country was another family member who had attended the original dedication of this once beautiful facility. She brought along, a cherished dog-eared publication that had been given to the guests attending the October 30 monastery dedication in 1955. This time, the family was to see far more than ever allowed two decades earlier.

The Czech family wandered from room to room and floor to floor comparing it with what it had been twenty years before. The keepsake document printed for the occasion contained a reprint of the official letter from Amleto Giovanni Cicognani, Archbishop of Laodicea and the Appointed Apostolic Delegate to the United States in Washington, D.C. On behalf of Pope Pius XII, Cicognani and Rome wished the Alexians a bright future in Gresham.

In stark contrast to what the boys were seeing in real time, Scott and Bradley took it all in slack-jawed and with eyes wide open. The booklet contained photographs and descriptions of what used to be. From the choir loft, the Czechs overviewed where all three of the altars made of

Verde Issorie marble imported from Italy once stood. They would learn that Alexian Brother Valentino Bianco came to Gresham soon after the takeover to supervise the rescue of Alexian property and valuable religious artifacts. Known as Brother Val, a talented artist in his own right, he gathered and crated up what he could. What had not been desecrated by a few takeover occupants was pilfered by local white neighbors.

Monastic protocol did not allow either men or women to tour the restricted cloistered areas in 1955. However, this was now 1976, and Scott and Bradley were no longer inside a consecrated structure. This was now an orphan, unwanted, a white elephant. The average man on the Gresham streets was unaware that this secluded place of mystery no longer contained larger than life statuary. Brother Val had made arrangements for the figures of Mary, Joseph, and Jesus Christ nailed to the stained walnut carvings to be salvaged and whisked off to Chicago.

A small fortune in stained glass depicting Alexian works of charity could not and would not be practical to move. That costly glass art was already well on its way to destruction by external vandals who didn't even need good aim. It would prove to be impossible to remove the massive wall of Brignoles Rose marble from France that stood behind the main altar. This was also true of another Florentine Rose Italian marble skirting the rest of the chapel. Brother Valentino Bianco did not know whether to curse or cry leaving such beauty behind. Rather than tossed by some thug to watch it shatter, one could only hope lonesome pieces of marble would find their way onto shelves or mantels of memory.

The boys listened to details, real and imagined. It was as if they were visiting a recent battleground. The novitiate had all of the internal scars created by cold, hungry, and angry occupants. It was difficult to separate the damage caused by the Menominee Warriors Society from that contributed by post-occupation souvenir seekers or neighboring thieves. The setting and the facility became irreversibly imprinted on that family's mind, especially the two boys.

Months turned into years as the abbey incubated its own urban legend reputation. The monastery had become a destination with no access for many. People drove out of their way to find the abbey—it became an adventure for the curious. A simple metal gate that an adult could crawl through and a short stone wall did not deter the determined. By canoe, through the woods, and using other more creative methods, the adventuresome came almost daily. The no trespassing signs were ignored and treated more like an inviting dare rather than warnings. This author is among the guilty trespassers.

The Red River and Freeborn Falls today is a sporting destination for water lovers. Wise paddlers take care to portage their canoes around the falls. The crumbling mansion-monastery seems to force the curious to linger and take it in. It's not unusual for visitors to beach their canoe and trespass this haunting place, leaving with so many questions unanswered.

In the early 1990s, Frank and Mirga Matuzney saw an opportunity to capitalize on this untapped need that people had to see and understand. Frank believed the abbey could make it as an entertainment destination. After buying the place for "taxes due," he made the caretaker cottage into a very livable home. Then he cleaned up the monastery and made it into a historic tourist attraction.

Only a few paying customers showed up early on. Matuzney had built a parking lot, souvenir shop, and area for ticket collection on the area the Alexian Brothers had used as a soccer field. When the business started to fail, a fire of mysterious origin burnt that to the ground. Truth be told, most of the locals had already trespassed for free over the previous several decades. Frank's "pay to see" venture had not counted on the greater thrill of breaking and entering. Well before that, my ticket had been "pray to see."

Scott and Bradley matured but remained fascinated with the property, buildings, natural setting, and history. By 2005, I had met them both and learned of their interest in following the disposition of the novitiate. Scott, in particular, would contact me by phone to ask about the progress of my book. Embarrassed, I would respond, "Soon." Bradley fell in love and wanted his wedding to take place at the banks of the pool created by the Freeborn Falls. He and his fiancée, Jessica Shanks, received permission to conduct their wedding there.

Sunday, August 19, 2007, was set as the date. They contacted me to provide some historic accuracy. The bride and groom wanted a printed handout they planned to include with the wedding program. I agreed to help compose the piece and accepted their invitation to come from California and attend the ceremony. As for me, it was heartening to see such an upbeat event come together at this site. Curt Knoke, my publication photographer, saw this as a camera-friendly event. Knoke wanted to experiment and shoot the scene from the other side of the river beyond the waterfalls. I did my job as a packhorse for the photo-artist and his equipment.

Marty, Curt, and I planned and successfully executed a dry run on Saturday, the day before the wedding. "Dry" is a poor word choice. Rain was forecast for Sunday, the next day. That did not deter Bradley, family, and friends. They mowed and policed the enormous lawn that sloped to the water. Chairs were set up along with carpet, a portable electrical generator, an electric organ for music, and a white canopy.

I didn't say so, but the little portable plastic electric water fountain looked a bit sad next to nature's more spectacular waterfall. It must've meant something special to someone. Scott and I had a chance to compare notes about recent events and the rumored plans at this location. We nervously joked, on the eve of the ceremony, about the long list of aborted and failed adventures there.

The next day, guests arrived and parked precisely where the novitiate building used to stand. I felt as if we were parking on the grave of something special and forgotten. Sprinkles were starting to be felt.

Oddly enough, a local television meteorologist was one of the attendees. She was asked about the forecast and she ominously rolled her eyes. What had been a beautiful week had turned into a soggy Sunday.

This was to be a new start for two young people. Instead, it started to resemble mourners gathering to pay graveside last respects at a soggy day funeral made for television. They were unable to crank the electrical generator, which had been working flawlessly the day before. The heavens opened up and serious rain fell. The downpour easily dwarfed the impotent portable fountain that had been reduced to a sad little birdbath.

Curt squatted in mud on the other side of the river protecting his expensive photographic gear. The walkie-talkies we brought along to coordinate failed due to batteries. The waterfall drowned out any attempt to verbally communicate. I flashed him the cutthroat sign from a distance. Curt put two and two together and gave up like a warrior escaping and going home through the woods.

Marty Knoke and I stood huddled and sheltered together with all the rest under the only roof available. The owner of the property had given Bradley and Scott explicit instructions that no one was to enter the burnt out mansion. This was a typical wedding party full of very young children running around and the elderly unsure of their footing. Every last guest migrated to the first floor of the interior of the off-limits mansion. We all wished to be warmer while we stood, waited, and hoped. The sturdy concrete floor was cratered with holes large enough to swallow a small child into the basement never to be seen again or break an adult's leg.

Destroyed by fire-weather, mansion stairs lead to nowhere 2011
Photo by Curt Knoke

The groom officially pulled the plug on this fiasco. The bride had yet to be seen. I can only assume she was lurking nearby with the engine running in some dry vehicle. It was announced the wedding was being moved elsewhere. Wet and bewildered guests scattered for another confusing destination in Green Bay. Some just went home wet and cold. I stood back and mentally wrote an unexpected chapter for the book. I had just observed one of the site's more recent failures run its course at that devilishly beguiling location.

It has been a privilege to be Curt Knoke's packhorse. A professional photographer does not travel lightly; I can testify to that. He seems always ready to go. From day one, I felt in sync with Curt, and we connected before he had made the transition from analog film to digital media. Coincidentally, I was making a living in the grayscale world of medical imaging. His productions are considered art, deservedly so. A challenging image of a frightening carcinoma takes skill but is hardly considered art. We set out for the nearby novitiate. As usual, I would be his apprentice. This was to be an historic day with an unexpected bonus.

During the 1975 takeover, there were many encounters by various factions at police roadblocks. Most were native neighbors gathering and offering symbolic support for the warriors holed up in the monastery. For the most part, they were peaceful. By the time the "abbey" had become a notable and dangerous episode, protesting for a cause had become a skill. Two years earlier, much had been learned from Wounded Knee. Everyone seemed to have their own playbook directing the next appropriate offense or defensive maneuver.

Everyone I interviewed recalls the weather contributing a miserable backdrop. The news media made the most of snow and ice. It looked and felt bleak. One of those defining and classic photographs captured indigenous solidarity and was flashed around the world. Rose Skinador was snapped with her full body wrapped in an upside-down American flag. Found and a little reluctant, Rose agreed to meet and reenact that pose. With the "abbey" as unfocused background, Rose again stood proudly for one of those "Where are they now?" pictures. Curt chose a location just off the novitiate property near the road. Staging this picture gave the vision of support from outside the captured monastery. There was a subtle twist, however. Knoke, the artist, took the liberty of righting Old Glory with no one noticing or even caring. Rose stood looking matriarchal and the soft side of this effort.

Rose Skinador draped in the flag recalls more defiant 1975 days
Photo by Curt Knoke

Mike Sturdevant paid a personal price to takeover the abbey
Photo by Al Bergstein

While last-minute adjustments and Polaroid test shots were made, Rose shouted out "Oh my God, look who's here!" Her reaction was alarming. A very beat-up car was slowly approaching us. Curt and I exchanged glances as the car continued past us, executing a slow drive-by. Rose spoke up again. "That's Mike Sturdevant, the General." I was concerned and curious as his car stopped several yards away. Then he reversed, backing up alongside us. How did he know what we were up to?

It was one of those "What the hell?" moments. I stepped up to his car and leaned in from the passenger side. I voluntarily introduced myself. He responded, "I know who you are. So what do you want with me?" "I have wanted to speak with you for the last several years." I told him. "Get in," the General ordered me, and we slowly drove easterly. Mike told me we would go down the road a bit and talk. Mike determined a safe visual range, made a U-turn, and pulled to the side. We were still within sight of Curt, Rose, and her teenage son. They watched us while pretending to rehearse photography. I hoped this was turning into an opportunity.

The car was cluttered. Basically, it was an ashtray with an engine on wheels. Mike wanted to tell me the rules of the game. He told me he was ill and had renal (kidney) cancer. I had already observed he was not the picture of good health. He went on to say he was dying and needed money. He believed that the only chance remaining for him would be a journey to see a special medicine man living out West. I listened.

I did not have the resources to say yes. I gently explained that I was not paying anyone to tell their story. I had to hold back the urge to feel guilty or responsible for his circumstances. Mike showed no disappointment during our brief meeting. There was nothing more either one of us could say. The broken down man started his broken down car and returned me to the driveway of the broken down monastery. Rose did not ask, nor did I volunteer, the results of our meeting. Later on that evening I shared my disappointment with Curt and his wife, Marty.

Months later it hit me like a ton of bricks. I was rethinking the long-awaited Mike Sturdevant encounter. It was ironic that I had unsuccessfully negotiated on neutral ground with a Menominee warrior with a dire health-care need. I could have kicked myself for not contacting the Alexian brothers in Chicago moments after speaking with Mike that day. My idea, now too late, would have been to urge the brothers to take Mike in for treatment or at least provide him with a comfortable death. I will always wonder if that would have been an acceptable healing gesture for that Menominee Warrior and the Alexians. That, I do regret.

Not long after our disappointing encounter, the *Los Angeles Times* reported early in 2005, "Michael Sturdevant, 60, the leader of the 1975 Menominee Indian takeover of a monastery near Gresham, Wisconsin, died of cancer Jan. 10 in Madison, Wisconsin."

Brother Maurice Wilson was among a half-dozen younger brothers from the Philippine mission. They were attending their provincial chapter meeting. Coincidentally, my surgical consulting business brought me to the Chicago area at the same time. I was pleased Brother Maurice had time to have coffee with me at the flagship hospital in Elk Grove Village, Illinois. I expected no more than that brief chance encounter before he was to board Korean Air and return to the island of Mindanao.

Four hours flew by, and we had barely scratched the surface of reminiscence. With a sigh, Brother Maurice regretted aloud how wonderful it would have been to go back to Gresham, but he brushed the idea aside. He dismissed the likelihood of launching a sentimental journey and traveling back to ground zero. Wilson moved on to another subject but I could not. I would not. I interrupted him and said, "Let's go."

We were instantly in accord. He began to wear the grin of a kid who had devised a plan to ditch school. So did I. We threw caution to the wind as juveniles on a poorly planned road trip. We drove north with Chicago in the rearview mirror. Brother Maurice Wilson was again, returning to a career-defining destination. This time, he was a tourist. This time, he was not a sacrificial lamb drawing the short straw.

I gave him a choice. "Brother, shall we drive through Shawano or use the newer bypass to the monastery?" His selection was as predictable as mine had been a decade ago. We took the route through Gresham and the "back door." We would save the maudlin tour through Gresham and Shawano for later, time-permitting.

I tried to refresh his memory and add some anticipation to his return. I must have overachieved. Because out of nowhere, preceded by a long silent pause, he presented me with an unexpected question: did I believe the property and buildings were hexed, haunted, or ghostly? In my decade of research, I had never allowed myself to seriously entertain the possibility of evil connected with our destination. We were only five minutes away. All I had learned about the unfortunate and troubled property history and the brothers' experience with demonic possession suddenly rewound then played fast-forward in my head.

His was a timely question. Because, coincidentally, I had stumbled upon a new and unexpected character, Greg Hollewinske. At the time, Greg lived in San Antonio, Texas. He was a retired army nurse, and he was also a former Alexian brother, like me. More importantly, this man was a rare find. As far as I know, there are only two living individuals with direct personal knowledge of the demonic possession and exorcism case that took place in St. Louis in 1949. They are Alexian Brother John Grider and Greg Hollewinske. Ironically, they both now live in an Alexian retirement community in Milwaukee, Wisconsin. Their recollections and descriptions are in sync.

On several occasions, I have had the opportunity to sit and discuss the 1949 exorcism in St. Louis with Hollewinske. Each time, I found Greg lucid, consistent, and matter-of-fact in recounting his experience with the Jesuits, the twelve-year-old boy, and a frightening experience.

Interviewing Grider and Hollewinske created an awakening within myself to look further. I contacted a Catholic priest. Within one of the major metropolitan archdioceses here in the United States, I located a foremost authority by e-mail, then telephone. He required my commitment to the following when he said, "I would be happy to visit with you on the topic of exorcism, under a couple of conditions: (1) that nothing I say be attributed to me or quoted as from me, and (2) that we speak on background only and not on the record. If these conditions are acceptable to you, then I would be available to chat about the case at hand."

I made it a point to accept his conditions and travel to meet with the priest. I brought with me a long laundry list, dating from the 1930s to this very day. Viewed in sequence, there is an impressive record of death, disappointment and failed ventures connected with the Alexian Brothers monastery. It is only now as I bring this story full circle that I step back and entertain the possibilities.

It was so out of character for me to even ask the questions. I wanted to know if it was possible for an inanimate object to be considered possessed. "No," he said and explained. The priest was an authority on the subject. He said that what I was revealing to him fell into the category of demonic infestation. The exorcist went on to explain the difference. I was so uncomfortable entertaining such an over-the-top departure from the main story, I chose to set it aside for another day—another book.

Yes, I did answer that question put to me by Brother Maurice. I told him the thought crossed my mind now and then. I shared with him that my frequent visits to the site were disconcerting on occasions. Usually, I had been alone shooting photographs, video, writing or just investigating and thinking. It was not unusual for a bird or a bat to startle me increasing my heart rate. Or, did I startle them first? Not to the point of paranoia, I did feel at times somebody or unseen, thing, was aware of my presence. Regardless, I felt protected and there for a purpose.

As Brother Maurice and I approached the monastery, the sky was weepy as if on cue. A new padlocked iron gate and chains forced us to park just off Butternut and walk in. He was not fully dependent upon his walking cane, but I suggested this would be a good time to bring it along. I was concerned about the slippery rain and treacherous traps ahead. I was feeling an overwhelming need to protect Brother Maurice Wilson, C.F.A.

We stopped on several occasions during our approach. I would point some to vacant space where a magnificent facility once stood. I gestured over here and over there for a man who had once known this spot very well. Time, distance, and responsibilities halfway around the world had dulled his memory of 1975. "What did they do with the destroyed buildings," he inquired? His quizzical gray bushy eyebrows wanted to know.

I had to mentally take him back a few years. After the property again changed hands December 2002, I located the new owners and principals of Whitewater Gresham Estates, LLC. Russell Obermier and Dan DeCaster were asked to consider preserving and donating to the

Alexians, architecturally significant parts of the former institution. After several phone conversations, it was agreed that the metal dome and cross topping the administration building and the stone lintel below would be ideal gifts to the Alexians.

DeCaster and Obermier graciously agreed. The partners gingerly removed the artifacts and stored them away. Dan made arrangements to transport the large stone to the Milwaukee Alexian property. I rented a U-Haul truck and drove the dome to the elk Grove village, Illinois hospital. We all felt as if we had done something good and right. The alternative would have been seeing those two keepers destroyed when the rest was razed.

Satisfied, Brother Maurice let me remind him that the building, dedicated October 30, 1955, and costing nearly $2 million, met its fate with dynamite several years ago. He wanted to know more, to put all into perspective. I explained that, unseen from the street, a mammoth hole behind the doomed building was dug to serve as its grave. Explosive charges strategically placed were inadequate to bring the novitiate down without it fighting back. Little, if anything exists today— existed in Shawano County anyway—that was built so sturdily.

To drive the point home, I reminded the brother that even after a clean morning shave, you still have a beard—inside. So, I explained, the fatally wounded novitiate took a final bullet, died, and was buried right where it fell. Except for a few choice pieces, memorabilia, and architectural relics, the novitiate lies in repose in the shadow of the mansion. It is poignant. The elderly and nearly dead mansion was like a parent outliving a child. This was not the first time this location watched the young die first.

When the monastery was destroyed and buried, the physical connection with the original mansion had been severed where it had been connected on the ground floor and basement. This left two gaping holes on the east side of the mansion. Notable is the view and access to the mansion basement. During the takeover, this subterranean area had been chosen as the area the Indians would make their last stand. Mud and debris has crept inside over the years. Frankly, it is frightening and ominous to peer into the darkness below Peters Hall. There, a visible earthen mound penetrates the concrete and steel foundation. Below, it appears as if a miniature volcanic uplift or something from hell is pushing its way out. Perhaps "it" has already escaped.

Brother Maurice and I were already past due as nearby overnight guests. Curt and Marty, at the last minute, had extended their hospitality the day before when we cooked up the road trip. They greeted us with the enthusiasm that has kept me returning over and over. The Knokes were charmed to meet this Alexian of the hour in 1975. After dinner and a tour of their barn converted into a home, we sat below their loft and enjoyed our dessert.

Site Map of Alexian Brothers Novitiate (abbey) and Surroundings.
Photo provided by Jake Hendzel

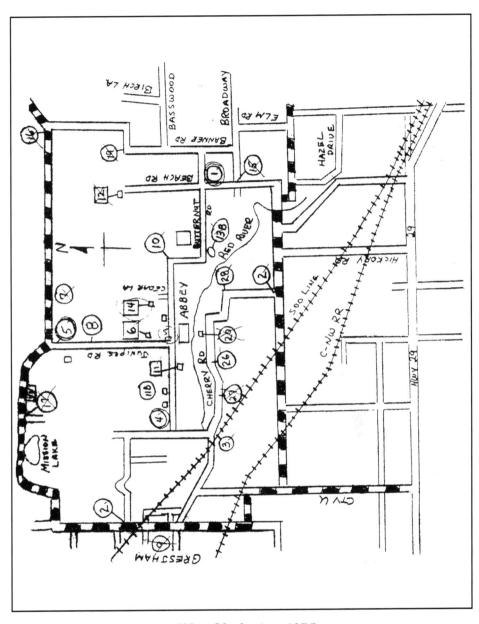

Abbey Checkpoints 1975
Alexian Brothers Provincial Archives, Arlington Heights, Illinois.

ABOUT THE PHOTOGRAPHER

Born in 1940 in Appleton, Wisconsin, Curt Knoke attended the University of Wisconsin at Oshkosh and graduated in 1964 from Rochester Institute of Technology (RIT) in Rochester, New York, with a degree in photography.

After graduation from RIT, Curt and a partner formed Image Studios, a commercial/advertising photo studio, and in 1993 Image I.T., a prepress facility, began operation. During his years at Image, Curt traveled throughout the United States and Europe on various photo assignments.

This itinerant photographer's bond with Gresham and the area surrounding the monastery developed when he retired in 1996 and moved to a farm property in the Town of Red Springs. A book grew out of a desire to give back to the community he loves. Curt Knoke's photo essay, **_Shawano County at the Dawn of The Twenty-First Century_**, marked him as the man to photo document **_The Novitiate_** and its eclectic cast of characters.

In addition to the Shawano County book and **_The Novitiate_**, Knoke photographed **_The Art of Labor_**, an inspiring book paying tribute to the tradesmen whose skill and dedication fashioned Wisconsin's Fox Cities Performing Arts Center. In this outstanding book, over 200 pages of his striking photography are blended with poignant words from Wisconsin's poet laureate.

More recently Knoke photographed the Green Bay Packers fans for the Green Bay Packers organization for **Green, Gold and Proud,** a book commemorating the Packers Fans.